THE STORY OF MILTON MALZOR

BY THE
REV. B.E. EVANS, M.A.
RECTOR

LONDON – 1924
WELLS GARDNER, DARTON & CO., LTD
3 & 4 PATERNOSTER BUILDINGS, LONDON E.C. 4

BRADFORD – 1997
MCB UNIVERSITY PRESS, LTD
60/62 TOLLER LANE, BRADFORD, WEST YORKSHIRE BD8 9BY

DEDICATION

To those, through whose sacrifice of the best years of their life, or even of life itself, during the Great War (1914–1918), our national freedom was preserved and our priceless heritage in the monuments of our historic past remained unscathed, and more particularly

TO MY BROTHER,

THE REV. JAMES EVANS,
Lieutenant in the Welch Regiment,

to the Memory of

my former pupil and old friend

CHARLES TREVERBYN GILL, B.A.,
Exeter College, Oxford,
and Lieutenant in the Manchester Regiment,

who fell gloriously at the Battle of the Somme, July 1st, 1916,

and to

THE MEN AND LADS OF MILTON,

who responded gallantly to their country's call, this book is dedicated in all gratitude.

CONTENTS

		PAGE
DEDICATION		2
LIST OF ILLUSTRATIONS		5
A PREFACE TO THE 1997 REPRINT		7
1924 PREFACE		11
BIBLIOTHECA		16

CHAPTER		
I.	THE SANDS OF A BURIED RIVER-BED	17
II.	THE STORY OF THE MANOR	27
III.	THE NAME OF MILTON	48
IV.	OUR CHURCH: ITS DEDICATION, ALTARS, SCREENS, ETC.	54
V.	OUR CHURCH'S STORY: TO THE REFORMATION	71
VI.	OUR CHURCH'S STORY: FROM THE REFORMATION TO THE PRESENT TIME	91
VII.	THE RECTORS OF MILTON	120
VIII.	THE BELLS	130
IX.	SANCTUARY SEEKERS	139
X.	MILTON PAROCHIAL SCHOOL	151
XI.	THE PARISH	157
XII.	PLACE-NAMES	205
XIII.	VANISHED INDUSTRIES	213
XIV.	MISCELLANEA: OLD CUSTOMS, QUAINT SAYINGS, THE REGISTERS, CHURCHWARDENS' ACCOUNTS, ETC.	225
XV.	THE CHARITIES OF MILTON	244
XVI.	WILLS AND OTHER DOCUMENTS	276
XVI.	LIST OF THOSE WHO SERVED IN THE WAR	304
	INDEX	315

LIST OF ILLUSTRATIONS

Milton Church	outside front cover	
Map of Ancient River-Bed	outside rear cover	
Milton Manor	facing page	32
The Manor, Milton	„ „	49
Ground Plan of Milton Church	„ „	65
Diagram of Capitals and Bases of Pillars	page	72
Milton Church, North Door and Diagram of Jamb	„ „	75
Mortimers	facing page	81
Milton Church, Interior	„ „	97
Portrait of James Harrington	„ „	113
"Collingtree Rectory" Milton.	page	123
Milton Rectory	facing page	129
Milton Church prior to 1856	„ „	145
Milton House	„ „	161
Milton Church at the Present Time	„ „	177
St. Catherine's Chapel	„ „	225
Plan of Wheel Window	„ „	225
Milton Church, Priest's Door	„ „	257
War Memorial, Milton	„ „	304

A PREFACE TO THE 1997 REPRINT
BY THE RECTOR
Richard Ormston

To have a thoroughly researched and well-documented village history is rare indeed. However, this book by Edward Evans does not merely record Milton's past. Many references to the village, the land, and surrounding villages are as topical as they were nearly 80 years ago when Mr Evans was Rector of Milton. The map on the rear cover shows the ancient river bed: Today we continue to experience the extraction of sand from the alluvial deposits around Milton, as we have for several decades. The links with Collingtree through the churches and the communities are just as strong, and at the heart of Milton is the village school, as it was so many years ago. Some things though have changed. What would Mr Evans have thought of Hunsbury on the horizon, or the constant roar of motorway traffic? Milton must have been so much more intimate and rural in his day.

Edward Evans put his pen down long before Europe was plunged into the Second World War. He had proudly listed the Milton men who served in the Great War (1914-18), noting those who made the ultimate sacrifice.

A PREFACE TO THE 1997 REPRINT

Accordingly it is fitting that we now record the names of those Miltonians who gave their lives in the 1939-45 War: Jack Digby, Harvey Folwell, Ronald Mallard, George Newcomb, William Oxley, George Pell, Leonard Proctor, Wyvil Raynsford and Bernard Rose.

Over the centuries Milton Church has been lovingly cared for by generations of parishioners. The ancient stones bear witness to the many structural changes that have been made as each generation has adapted the building for the use of our community. We must remember that our beautiful Church is not a museum but a house of prayer: a place to worship the living God. It is the focus of delight and anticipation at baptisms, of joyful celebration at weddings and of sadness at funerals. Down the centuries tens of thousands of Miltonians have come together to share the key moments of their lives within the walls of our Parish Church. I am pleased to say that, due to the work of the Churchwardens and Parochial Church Council over the centuries, the building is in an excellent state of repair. Recently we were encouraged to receive a letter from the Lord Bishop of Peterborough congratulating everyone who helps maintain Milton Church to such a high standard. However, there are always projects and regular repairs to undertake, so all proceeds from sales of this book will go towards the upkeep of the Parish Church of Holy Cross, Milton Malzor. We appreciate everyone's help in keeping the Church as a place of welcome to parishioners and visitors today and for generations to come.

The idea for the reprint of this book came from Alistair Muir, and my thanks go to him for taking the project through to the final publication. The second debt of gratitude is to Gordon Wills who lives in The Manor House today with Avril Wills. He undertook with his colleagues at MCB University Press in Bradford to arrange the printing of this magnificent volume. Without that generous assistance we would not have this continuing record of one Northamptonshire village, now available once again.

Alistair Muir and Thomas Jones,
Churchwardens

Colin Neal,
Deputy Churchwarden

1924 PREFACE

THIS work was begun soon after a short but nearly fatal illness that laid me by the heels in the autumn of 1920. Forbidden much bodily exertion during the long period of convalescence that followed, I amused myself with compiling what was intended to be merely a little pamphlet on the history of our beautiful church at Milton for the benefit of my parishioners. I little dreamt, however, when I first put pen to paper for this purpose, that I had embarked on a task the absorbing interest of which would cause it to assume proportions beyond what I ever intended or even expected.

The book has been written, as it was at first undertaken, especially for the villagers of Milton, that they should know something of the history of their own church and parish, of the people who lived here long ago in some of the houses still standing, the conditions of their life and their varied occupations. As its title implies, I have tried to present this chronicle in a simple form, without taking too much for granted, my chief aim being to let it be understood by all.

A few words of explanation are required as to the contractions and other things unusual in modern print.

1. The inverted comma in, or at the end of, a word. This signifies the omission of a letter or

letters by contraction, such as "p'rill" for peril, "p'rish" for parish, "com'ons" for commons. I have adopted this form of denoting a contraction, but sometimes I have used the usual horizontal stroke.

2. The "j" in Roman numerals. When the letter "i" came at the end, it was written "j," as "ij" for ii, "xvj" for xvi, "vij*d*." for vii*d*. This method is still used by members of the medical profession in the writing of prescriptions.

3. In the money accounts, the letters "li" or "lb" stand for £. They, as well as our £, are shortened forms of the Latin *libra*, a pound.

4. Most people know that "ye" in old documents stands for "the," the "y" being really a contracted "th." In the same way, when "yt" is thus found in this book, in extracts from old writings, it stands for "that," i.e. "th't."

Though it chiefly concerns Milton and Milton people, there is much in this book that may prove of more than local interest. I have been at some pains to verify every statement of fact by examining documents at the Record Office in Chancery Lane, the British Museum, the Lambeth Palace Library, the Bodleian Library at Oxford, and by correspondence with the sub-Librarian of the Vatican Library at Rome. Other documents consulted were: the Episcopal Registers of Lincoln and Peterborough, mediæval Wills, Deeds, etc., the local Enclosure Award and Map, the Milton Parish Registers and Vestry Minute Books.

Everyone from whom I sought help or advice has been most kind and sympathetic. I wish to record my thanks to Major C. A. Markham, F.S.A., for his valuable advice and the use of his published works elsewhere acknowledged ; to Beeby Thompson, Esq., F.G.S., F.C.S., of Northampton, for providing me with copious notes on the geology of Milton ; to the Very Reverend the Dean of Peterborough for the loan of the *Valor Ecclesiasticus ;* to my old fellow-student, H. S. Kingsford, Esq., M.A., F.S.A., Assistant Secretary of the Society of Antiquaries ; to my neighbours, the Rev. H. Isham Longden, M.A., and the Rev. H. Liveing, M.A. ; to J. W. Hall, Esq., of Peterborough ; to Christopher Smythe, Esq., J.P., for permission to examine the old Deeds belonging to St. John's Hospital, Northampton, and to E. M. Alexander, Esq., of Mortimers, Milton, for allowing me to inspect Deeds and Wills of the Montgomery family. The late James Asplin, of the Manor, Milton, who had shown a great interest in the progress of this work, provided several valuable hints and very kindly allowed me to consult the Title Deeds of his manor. I also wish to thank the assistants at the Northampton Probate Registry for their unfailing courtesy and the patience with which they bore my frequent invasions of the Office. My task, too, was rendered all the easier through the help afforded me by my dear wife, whose skilful fingers tapped off on the typewriter page after page of my manuscript which, sometimes written very quickly and with numerous corrections, was in many places no easy matter to read. Her aid and sympathy I acknowledge with deep gratitude.

For photographs of the church and St. Catherine's Chapel my thanks are due to my brother-in-law John L. Hopkins, Esq., and my nephew Harold Walter Manser, Esq. Of the other illustrations, Miss H. M. Asplin drew the delightful sketch of The Manor. Mr. E. M. Alexander contributed an old sketch of Milton House made before the road was lowered, and Major C. A. Markham, F.S.A., Editor of *Northamptonshire Notes and Queries,* very kindly allowed the use of the block for the illustration. Mr. J. C. Emery, of Milton, willingly lent for reproduction an old sketch, in his possession, of Milton Church as it was prior to 1856, and Mr. John A. Townsend, of Milton, drew for me his beautifully executed plan of our Wheel Window. I am grateful to them all for the help thus willingly afforded.

Without the aid of friends it would be impossible for me to publish a work of this description and I sincerely thank those who have helped me with generous subscriptions towards part of the very heavy expense.

The Preface, though appearing at the beginning of a book, is the last to be written, and I feel I cannot conclude better than with these words of thanks. Collecting and arranging the material for this chronicle has proved a source of delight and a labour of love spread over the greater part of the last three years, done at intervals because there were long periods when I was unable to give it the necessary time and attention. I trust it may prove to be at least of some pleasure and interest to those who in these modern days live here and love their village. The work has grown by degrees, " line upon line, line upon line, here a little, there a little," with corrections and additions as fresh discoveries were made. Now at last it is done, and I look back in review on the incidents of the past and all those people, long since dead, of the Milton of other days who have somehow become so well known to me, and with a sigh of regret that for the present the time of interesting and exciting discoveries is over, I lay down my pen.

B. E. EVANS.

MILTON RECTORY, NORTHAMPTON, 1924.

BIBLIOTHECA

THE following are some of the many books consulted :

The History of Northamptonshire. Dr. Bridges.
The History of Northamptonshire. Dr. Baker.
The History of Northamptonshire. The Victoria County History.
The *Valor Ecclesiasticus*, Vol. IV.
A History of the Hospital of St. John in Northampton. The Rev. R. M. Serjeantson, M.A., F.S.A.
Sanctuaries in Northamptonshire. The Rev. R. M. Serjeantson, M.A., F.S.A.
Sanctuaries and Sanctuary Seekers. The Rev. Dr. C. J. Cox, F.S.A.
The Church Plate of Northamptonshire. Major C. A. Markham, F.S.A.
The Iron Roads of Northamptonshire. Major C. A. Markham, F.S.A.
The Archæological Journal, Vol. LXX, No. 279 (Second Series, Vol. XX, No. 3), September, 1913, containing a paper on " The Parish Churches and Religious Houses of Northamptonshire." The Rev. R. M. Serjeantson, M.A., F.S.A., and the Rev. H. Isham Longden, M.A.
Northamptonshire Bells. Thomas North, F.S.A.
Numerous Books on Law, History and Architecture.

For many hints I am indebted to Dr. Cox's " How to Write the History of a Parish."

The Story of Milton Malzor

CHAPTER I

THE SANDS OF A BURIED RIVER-BED

NEAR the third milestone that marks the journey south from Northampton to Towcester, and within the proverbial stone's throw of the highway, but so tucked away as to be almost hidden from the casual glance of the passer-by, stands the little village of Milton. Officially, and in ecclesiastical documents especially, the name is expanded to the old-time form of " Milton *alias* Middleton Malzor," but in modern parlance it is modestly content with " Milton, Northampton."

A stroll along its mazy, winding ways reveals many a subject worthy of the artist's brush or the camera, since it abounds in picturesque thatched cottages grouped in artistic disorder. The architect of an antiquarian turn of mind will find much to interest him here, while those who love to delve deep into the hidden past can retell Time's ancient story from the clay or sand-pits with the darker gravel beneath, and give full rein to their imagination.

It may not be out of place here to say a little about the rocks on which the village stands, and the conformation of the district in prehistoric times, for the great sand deposits in and around, providing as they do one of the staple industries of the village, seem to demand some explanation.

I am indebted to that eminent geologist, Beeby Thompson, Esq., F.G.S., F.C.S., of Northampton, for information on which this chapter is based and for copious geological notes referring particularly to Milton, with which he most willingly supplied me. There is no better authority on the geology of Northamptonshire and the neighbouring counties, and those who desire further knowledge on this subject are referred to his masterly contribution to the Victoria History of Northamptonshire.

In the first place, it should be known that within the area occupied by Milton, three different geological formations may constitute the subsoil. Two of these are decidedly old, their age running into millions of years. The third formation is comparatively recent, perhaps less than a hundred thousand years old.

The oldest of these formations found at Milton is called the Middle Lias and it may be upwards of a hundred feet thick. It consists mainly of sandy clays, with beds of hard stone at intervals. Lying deep down as it does here, it is only the top beds of this formation that are ever seen at Milton, and then but rarely unless a well is being made, for these top beds of the Middle Lias yield water. The topmost bed is about four feet thick and is known as the Marlstone Rock-bed.

SANDS OF A BURIED RIVER-BED

Several springs in Milton rise from this, for instance, those in the meadow near the allotments, and the well at the " Greyhound."

Resting on the top of the Middle Lias are found here and there thin remnants of the lower beds of what is known as the Upper Lias. This formation which, if fully present, would probably be upwards of 180 feet thick, consists of clay. Parts of this thick clay-bed may be seen in the neighbouring brickyard and towards Gayton. Here are many fossils, those most frequently found being different kinds of ammonites, like curled snakes, the bullet-shaped belemnites, the pretty shells *Lucina bellona* and *Arca elegans*, and the dainty *Leda ovum*.

The most peculiar and interesting geological phenomenon, however, is that certain thick, moderately wide, sand-beds cut deeply into the geological formations which are referred to above. They take the form of an elongated, curved valley mainly on the east and south of Milton village. These sand-beds, which are from twenty to forty feet deep, with a width varying up to half a mile, can be traced for about eight miles on the south of the Nene Valley through the parishes of Heyford, Bugbrooke, Rothersthorpe, Milton, Collingtree, Courteenhall and beyond to Preston Deanery ; north-westward they can be traced as far as Hillmorton near Rugby. All the evidence goes to show that these sand-beds occupy an old river valley, as old as, possibly even older than, the present great valley of the Nene. The probable history of this deposit is sketched below :

The last great events in the geological history of this country occurred during what is known as the Glacial Period. Through some cause or other the climate grew colder until at last great ice sheets, in the form of glaciers, gradually crept down from the north over Scotland, the north of England and almost to the present Thames Valley. The ice itself, and the great floods which preceded and followed it, very greatly changed the surface of the country, ploughing it up in some places and elsewhere piling up heaps of material on it, especially filling up old valleys with boulder clays. On the melting of the ice, the subsequent great floods were largely responsible for the size of the present river valleys and for their gravelly contents, but it is quite possible that these valleys do not in all cases coincide with earlier ones.

This great series of events occurred very many thousands of years ago, and lasted for some thousands of years. However, there is adequate reason for believing that so far as a succession of hills and valleys and stream courses is concerned, the country was much the same before that time as it is now. Quite a number of these old-time valleys are known that have been filled up with glacial material and never cut out again, so that they remain to this day as " buried valleys."

It is one of these buried river courses of old that we have in Milton, and we think we know when it was filled in with sand and why it was not reopened again by the river after the Glacial

Period. Long before that time, how long, of course, we do not know, this prehistoric river ran by Milton along a course now marked by the sand-beds. Then came the period when the great ice sheet crept down from the north and stopped in its advance just before reaching Northamptonshire. The summer floods were greater and more prolonged than any person has ever seen in this country, and by these the river-bed was first deepened and widened, and afterwards filled in with sand. But how do we know these things? Well, only strong currents of water could have carried away all the finer clayey matter of a turbulent stream and have left a clean-washed, current-bedded sand and gravel such as we find. We know that the currents were strongest at first because of the steepness and even cliff-like character of the clay borders in some places, and the coarser material near the base. We know that the real glacier of the Glacial Period had not then reached Milton or Northamptonshire, because there are no " erratics " or distantly derived stones in the sand-bed, such as a glacier would inevitably bring, and demonstrably did bring later.

For the reasons above given, the sand deposit is sometimes spoken of as Pre-Glacial, but Pre-liminary-Glacial would appear to be a more appropriate term.

This Pre-Glacial valley and its stream evidently debouched into the Ouse Valley towards Olney. Then, after the sand had been deposited early in the Glacial Period, the ice sheet, in its advance, penetrated into Northamptonshire. The river at Milton became changed into a river of ice that slowly but irresistibly forced and rent its way along. Frozen in the ice were great lumps of clay with erratics in the form of carboniferous limestone and other material, and these were carried onwards by the sluggish current.

So far the Glacial Period has been spoken of as one, but actually there were milder intervals in it which caused a retreat of the glaciers through the melting of the ice. Thus it is that we find great deposits of boulder clay and other material from the glacier, about Salcey Forest and Yardley Chase, forming athwart the direction of our river and preventing it from continuing its way to the Ouse Valley. Naturally, the ice as it passed over the beds of sand deposited in the river at Milton must have carried off a good portion of the upper layers of sand. Though some few of the erratics that were deposited on the surface of the sand were left, to be found here and there at the present day, the rest of the boulder clay and stones was swept down stream by the great floods that followed on the melting of the ice during the milder intervals.

One such interval in particular was a very long one, probably lasting for some thousands of years, after which the great ice sheet crept down again from the north, and once more passed over Milton, lasting for some thousands of years. Again in its preliminary stages sand was probably deposited, and although the ice again carried away a great portion of the upper layers, there still remains a good residue. This long interval of warmth is generally known as the Inter-Glacial Period, and during it the district about Milton, in common with others, was doubtless the haunt of animals now totally extinct, or extinct so far as this country is concerned, such as the mammoth, rhinoceros, hippopotamus and others. Primitive man was also here, with other animals that still exist. A fossil tooth, the right lower canine of a horse, was found about ten feet below the surface in the railway sand-pit in Barn Lane just before these pages went to press. Remains of this period, known as the Inter-Glacial, have, however, rarely been discovered at Milton, but the neighbouring parish of Gayton has yielded them. In this connection, the following quotation from Baker's *Northamptonshire* (II, 271) under "Gayton," is interesting:

"Near the Banbury Lane wharf are rather extensive brick kilns. In those adjoining the wharf yard to the north is a diluvial bed from which my sister obtained in the winter of 1835 some interesting relics of mammalia—the humerus bone and fragments of the teeth of the Mastodon; the tibia of a full-grown, and portions of a tooth of a young Elephant; part of the tibia, teeth and tusks of the Hippopotamus; parts of the skull, humerus, tibia, vertebræ and teeth of an Ox; tibia and teeth of the Elk; horn and prong and portions of ribs of the Deer."

No record has hitherto been made of the discovery of remains of contemporary animals below the sand-beds we have referred to as occurring at Milton and a number of other places, hence the following is of particular interest.

In the spring of 1920, curiosity led me to the sand-pit close to the brick kilns since erected by Mr. W. T. Asplin. At the bottom of the pit was the dark gravel that had evidently formed the bed of the ancient stream that flowed there before the Glacial Period. Working at the foot of the high cliff of sand was one of Mr. Asplin's men, Mr. George Ager. As I watched him loading a cart with sand, and mused on the strange creatures that long ago had roamed near the bed of that river, I asked him casually if he had ever found any fossil bones while digging there. I was in the very act of speaking when he struck his spade into the sand and turned up a bone. Our astonishment at the coincidence was great, especially as he assured me it was the first bone he had ever discovered while thus employed. When first brought to light it appeared as fresh as if just taken from the animal and was actually covered with a greasy film, but after exposure to the air it gradually became chalky and showed its character. Fortunately, it had lain on the dark gravel at the bottom of the deposit, having been there some time before the sand made its appearance.

I submitted the find to Dr. A. S. Woodward, F.R.S., Keeper of Geology at the Natural History Museum, S. Kensington, and he wrote in reply : " It is the metacarpal of a rather large horse, evidently fossil."

So this solitary fossil bone, found as it was on

the surface of the river gravel beneath the sand deposit which, at that spot, was about thirty feet deep, indicates that horses existed in this district in those ancient days, about one hundred thousand years ago, or more.

The darker and coarser gravel-bed below the ordinary sand certainly points to the gravel being a real river deposit earlier than the infilling sand. If so, the bone that was found resting on it and beneath the sand may be considered Pre-Glacial, and consequently a very rare find.

Although the sand marks the course of this ancient river, it is not now one continuous bed. Various little brooks made their way across the sand and during the course of ages deepened their channels and formed valleys through atmospheric influences. Thus, wherever a break occurs in the line of sand, there will be found a little valley caused by a brook.

When the Glacial Period came to an end, possibly eighty thousand years ago, the geological formation of the district remained practically unchanged, to the great benefit of modern inhabitants in times of drought. Not only do the Marlstone beds yield a copious supply of beautiful water, but it must be remembered that the sand-beds rest upon the gravel strata above the clay. Now the sand being a water-bearing bed, and the clay impervious or watertight, the gravel between consequently abounds in springs, so there is always plenty of water to be obtained in Milton. During the great drought of 1921, when neighbouring villages ran so short of water that it was actually sold by the bucket, whilst the citizens of Northampton were rationed as to their water supply, there was always plenty and to spare at Milton.

Centuries roll by and the dawn of history brings its light to guide us. The woad-stained Ancient Briton, of the tribe of the Coritani, drove his scythed chariot along the valley, and the Druids practised their mysterious rites in the dense forests that grew here. Then came the conquering Cæsar, and the tramp of the Roman legions echoed along Watling Street not far away. Afterwards we read of the Saxon Conquest and then the incursion of the Danes, when we find the district forming part of the Danelagh. At last, when William the Conqueror comes with his organising skill, the light of recorded information breaks upon us clearly and surely, so that we begin to pick up with more certainty the particular threads that, woven in the loom of Time, form the warp and woof of the story of Milton Malzor.

CHAPTER II

THE STORY OF THE MANORS

For the first recorded notice of Milton we have to go back to the days of William the Conqueror and the great book he compiled, called *Doomsday*, or *Domesday, Book*, in which are set down the various Baronies held by his nobles, with the several Manors of which each consisted.

From its pages we find there were two Manors of Milton even then. Their story is a lengthy one, and to understand their significance it is necessary to see how they came into being.

After the Battle of Hastings and his subsequent coronation, William the Conqueror seized the lands of all who had opposed him. He also compelled those English lords who had submitted to him to surrender their lands, regranting them to their owners on their swearing allegiance. The King took care to look after himself first, and the lands he appropriated formed the Royal demesne. Of the rest of the confiscated lands he made grants to his followers, several of whom received each a great many of these estates. In disposing of them, the Conqueror was shrewd enough to realise that if he granted to anyone several estates so as to form one large, undivided portion of land, it might prove in course of time a source of danger to the Crown. Hence we find that, large as was the territory granted to any Norman, it was in several scattered portions, so that he could not become too powerful in one neighbourhood. These vast possessions were termed Baronies.

The King was then, not only in theory but actually, the owner of the land, the supreme lord, so that all who occupied land were his tenants. The great barons, or any other tenants who held direct from the King, were called tenants *in capite*. They held under the king a *fief, fee* or *feud* (hence the term *feudal* system), by which, in return for their right to hold the land, they swore to be faithful to the King and to perform certain services, such as providing knights or men-at-arms for his armies when necessary.

The barons, who had all come over with William, divided their vast possessions amongst other Normans, who were called knights or vassals. The estate granted to each knight became known as a *knight's fee*, because the knight held it under a *fief, feud* or *fee*, by which he was to do service to the baron.

The estate held through each knight's fee was called a manor, and he who held it was known as the lord of that manor. Each barony was also called an honor, because it consisted of several knights' fees and so conferred a position of honour upon its owner.

It is probable that the manor was the same as the old Anglo-Saxon *mark*, which was an area of territory occupied by a village community. It

THE STORY OF THE MANORS 29

consisted of the township or group of houses; the arable land, divided into several plots for growing crops, but used in common when fallow or between reaping and sowing; the meadowland, common to all after the hay had been carried, and the waste lands, over which the members of the township had rights of pasturage, taking wood, etc. Each mark was ruled by an excellent system of self-government in an assembly of freemen. It was, as a rule, of the same extent as the parish, and several marks made up what was called the hundred, which again was governed by the votes of the freemen. At the Conquest, we find that the old Anglo-Saxon independence came to an end, for in the manorial system the whole of the land in a manor was given to one man for his knight's fee, so he became its lord and all the people on that manor had to swear to do him service. As the King, too, was the supreme lord, every owner of land, whether he were " baron or squire, or knight of the shire," held it either directly or indirectly of the King. Therefore, for each estate, dues had to be paid annually to the Crown.

In course of time, William thought it advisable to find out exactly how much land each man had and what money should be paid to the Crown. So in 1080 or 1085 he appointed Commissioners who visited each county and every hundred and township. In each hundred a jury was empanelled who declared on oath the extent and nature of each estate, the amount of arable and pasture lands, the woods and mills, and the name of the owner of each, with the number of slaves that each man had. They also ascertained the value of the land both before and after the Conquest, with the amount due from it to the Crown. They found there were about 700 chief tenants and 60,215 knights' fees. These facts are all carefully recorded in *Doomsday Book*, which may be seen in the Museum of the Record Office in Chancery Lane, London.

As soon as the book was completed, William summoned all the landowners in the country to meet him at Salisbury in 1086, where all, whether his chief tenants or sub-tenants, had to swear allegiance to him. This was a most important step, for other feudal lords could only summon the aid of their immediate vassals, but William could now call not only upon his vassals, but the vassals of his vassals.

In these ancient pages of *Doomsday Book* we find that two men held lands at Milton as part of their baronies, William Peverel and Goisfrid Alselin. The records are in Latin and the following are translations:

"WILLIAM PEVEREL'S LAND.
IN FOXLEA HUNDRED

Ambrose holds of William four hides in Molitone (Milton). There is land for four ploughs. In demesne there are two ploughs, and three serfs ; and four villeins and five bordars with two ploughs. There are sixteen acres of meadow. It was and is worth four pounds. Gitda held these lands freely in King Edward's time."

It may here be mentioned that William Peverel was a powerful lord and was the founder of the Abbey of St. James, at Northampton. The land at Milton that formed part of his Barony was formerly held by Gitda " freely in King Edward's time." In all probability, this Gitda was Earl Goodwin's Countess, who bore the same name, and therefore would be the mother of King Harold, who was slain at the Battle of Hastings.

"GOISFRID ALSELIN'S LAND.

IN COLESTREV HUNDRED

Goisfrid Alselin holds of the king three hides and a half in Mideltone (Milton), and William holds of him. There is land for nine ploughs. In demesne there is one plough; and sixteen villeins, with the priest and five bordars, have seven ploughs. There is a mill rendering thirty pence, and two acres of meadow. Wood three furlongs in length and two furlongs and a half in breadth.

To this manor pertain two hides, less one virgate, in Colestrev (Collingtree). There is land for four ploughs. Two socmen and five villeins have these there. There are three acres of meadow.

In Torp (Rothersthorpe) there is half a hide belonging to Mildetone (Milton). There is land for one plough, which is there, with one villein. The whole was worth four pounds; now it is worth six pounds."

These extracts give us instances of the two kinds of tenures.

In the account of William Peverel's land in Milton, we read that " Ambrose holds of William four hides in Molitone." This means that Ambrose held one knight's fee at Milton, or in other words was lord of a manor, in extent four hides of land, situated at Milton and forming part of William Peverel's barony. Ambrose was a " Knight of the Honor of Peverel," and held this manor through his fief or fee, that is, his condition of service to William Peverel, his overlord.

In the account of Goisfrid Alselin's land we read " Goisfrid Alselin holds of the king," i.e. he holds *in capite*, being chief tenant. Further in the same " and William holds of him," means that William holds under Goisfrid Alselin one knight's fee, or was lord of a manor at Milton under the same conditions of service as Ambrose held under Wilam Peverel. William's manor consisted of three and a half hides in Milton, with the other lands specified in Collingtree and Rothersthorpe.

From this we see that there were two distinct manors at Milton, each with its lord.

Before we proceed to the story of the two manors, an explanation of some of the terms in the *Doomsday* extracts is necessary.

The " hide " was the unit of assessment, and was a measure of land equal to as much as a plough could plough in a year. Hence it varied, but generally consisted of about 120 acres.

The " virgate " was a quarter of a hide.

Of Ambrose's manor we are told " there is land for four ploughs. In demesne there are two ploughs, and three serfs." There was land sufficient for four ploughs. The demesne was the land kept by the lord of the manor for his

MILTON MANOR.

own use, and here we see it was sufficient to occupy two ploughs.

The " serfs " were no better than slaves. In Anglo-Saxon times they were probably the descendants of those Ancient Britons who, when the country was seized by the Saxons, had remained in the neighbourhood, unable to tear themselves away from the land of their fathers. In Norman times their number was probably increased by the poorer of the conquered Saxons.

The " villeins " seem to have been of a degree superior to that of the serfs, and were so called because they were attached to the " vill " or estate. They held a cottage and land, purely at their lord's will, and for this they had to render certain menial services. These services were mostly of an agricultural nature, but so uncertain that they never knew from one day to the other what might be required of them. The only claim that the villeins had to their land was the entry of their name on the Court Roll of the Manor. When, in course of time, it came about that conditions were modified, and they were able to sell their holding, their only title to possession was a copy of this entry on the Court Roll, hence we have " copyholders."

The " bordars " were apparently a degree higher than the villeins. They held a cottage and land on the condition of supplying the lord of the manor with small provisions such as poultry and eggs.

The " socmen " were tenants who held of their lord by soccage. By this, a man was enfeoffed freely, or in " fee simple," and his land could not be taken away at the will of the lord of the manor, as that of the lower degrees of tenants could. He was exempt from military service and paid a rent either in money or provisions. It was the duty of the socmen to sit as judges with their lord at the Court Baron of the Manor. In the socman's tenure of land, as well as that of the lords of the manor, we see the origin of freehold tenure.

There were two courts held by the lord of the manor, the chief being the Court Baron, in which the freeholders sat as judges with their lord. At this court, duties and customs were received, and surrenders of land considered and passed, as well as other business. The Court Leet was another ancient court at which people guilty of encroachments on land, using fraudulent weights and measures, committing nuisances, and so on, were punished. Of this court, the lord of the manor or his steward was the judge.

Notes on Milton were written between the years 1718–21 by William Taylor, the schoolmaster of Heyford. He was one of those employed by Dr. Bridges to collect information and transcribe inscriptions and records for his great *History of Northamptonshire*. These manuscripts are now preserved in the Bodleian Library at Oxford. In them is a reference to the Milton manorial courts :

"The Lord Leimpster (since Mr. Dry's decease) keeps two courts for this Town, at ye Cock in Cotton End, Northampton, but in the parish of Hardingstone :—First, called Easter Court

THE STORY OF THE MANORS 35

for swearing of parish officers :—the other called Cotton Leet, appointed for such as plow from One Another, and to Endict or present any one for ye Commission of trespasses."

Two of the old-time parish officers thus sworn in are met with in our records of Milton. They are the Hayward, and the Headborough, and their duties are explained in the chapter on the parish.

For a list of the lords of the two manors I am indebted to the *History of Northants*, by Dr. Bridges, who compiled the names of those who held them up to about the year 1720. In his list of the Lords of Milton, he begins with the Manor of Goisfrid Alselin, but assigns it to Collingtree from the reign of King John, while from the reign of King Henry III he deals solely with the knight's fee of the Honor of Peverel for Milton.

Dr. Bridges begins with the *Doomsday* account of Goisfrid Alselin's land already given, and then goes on to that of the Northamptonshire Survey.

" In the time of Henry II, Robert de Causho and one Geoffrey were certified to hold in Middelton 5 hides and one virgate amounting to the fourth part of one hide. In this account are included 2 hides and one virgate in Collingtree, which was then reputed a member of Middleton.

" From Geoffrey Alselin, this Manor with other Lordships in his possession, devolved to Ralph Hanselyn, his successor and descendant ; upon whose decease in this reign, without issue male, it fell to Thomas Bardolf, who married Rose, his sole daughter and heir, and became in right of his wife, the superior Lord of the fee."

Now he goes on to the Manor in the Barony of William Peverel :

"By inquisition taken in the reign of Henry III, John Malesoures was found to hold of William Bardolf one Knight's fee in Middelton and Colentre of the Honor of Peverel. This William was grandson of Thomas Bardolf by Down, his eldest son. In the 24th. year of Edward I this knight's fee was in the hands of William Bardolf, who held it of the king *in capite*. In the ninth year of Edward II John Malesoures was Lord of Middelton ; and in the 20th. year of Edward III, upon collecting the aid to make the king's son a knight, he accounted for one knight's fee in Midelton and Colyntre, as held of the fee of Bardolf. The successor of William Bardolf was Thomas his son, by whom this knight's fee, then in the possession of John de Malesores, was settled on Agnes his wife in way of dower ; and this Agnes surviving her husband, left it at her death, in the 31st. year of this reign, to John Bardolf, her son and heir.

"From John de Malesores the Manor of Milton descended to Sir Thomas Malesores, Knight, who by deed bearing date in the 35th. year of Edward III assigned it to Hugh Malesores his brother for the term of his life ; with remainder to Amicia, the daughter of the said Thomas and her heirs, and in case of failure of issue, to the heirs of Hugh Malesores aforesaid. Accordingly by inquisition taken in the 39th. year of the same reign it was found that Hugh Malesores was at that time in possession of this Manor ; and that the advowson of the church, with 4 acres of land, which were the glebe belonging to it, were in the hands of Thomas Wake, and held of the same

Manor by homage, fealty, and a certain annual payment. In the 12th. year of Richard II died Sir John Bardolf, seized of three parts of one Knight's fee in Midelton and Colingtre, then in the tenure of Robert le Veer, the husband of Amicia, or as she is called in this record, Anne, the daughter of Sir Thomas Malsores, and by virtue of his marriage with this lady possessed of the Lordship of Middleton.

" In the 7th. year of Henry VI Thomas Parwich[1] was certified to hold one Knight's fee in Midleton and Collingtre: and in the 10th. year of Henry VIII died Goditha Wigston possessed of this Manor which she had held of the King, as of his Manor of Shelford in Nottinghamshire, by the service of one Knight's fee. This lady was formerly the wife of William Perwich, son of William Perwich of Lubenham in Leicestershire, by whom she had issue Rose her only daughter and heir, first married to —— Kebull, and afterwards to William Digby of Kettleby in the same county. Her successor was John Digby, her grandson, a minor 11 years old, who inherited this Lordship as heir to Rose his mother. He married Mary, the third daughter and co-heir of William, Lord Par of Horton, who after his decease was remarried to Henry Brooker Esq. of Lubenham, and transferred the Lordship into that family. In the 7th. year of Edward VI. a fine was levied between Henry Brooke and William Digby of the Manor of Middleton-Malsor and Collingtre, with the advowson of the Church of Middleton. From this Henry they descended to Roger, the son of Roger Brooke his younger brother, who dying in the first year of Queen Elizabeth left them to Mary his daughter, a minor five years of age.

[1] See page 283.

38 THE STORY OF MILTON MALZOR

She died seized of them in the 16th. year of this reign without issue, nor did it appear who was her heir. But in another inquisition it is said that Andrew, John and Richard, the nephews of Henry Brooke, and her father's younger brothers, were heirs in remainder.

" The next possessor that we meet with of the Manor of Milton is Sir William Samwell, Knight, who by indenture bearing date the 1st. of April in the 11th. of James I conveyed the said Manor with its members and appurtenances, and advowson of the living, together with the Manor House, four yard lands and certain closes in Milton to Sir Sapcotes Harrington, who had married Jane his daughter, and his heirs for ever. Sir Sapcotes Harrington by deed of feoffment dated 11th. of August in the 18th. year of the same reign, conveyed the premises to Sir Francis Hervey and his heirs. From this gentleman they descended to his son Sir Stephen Hervey, Kt. of the Bath, who left them in the 6th. year of Charles I to Francis his son; upon whose decease without issue they devolved with a certain Manor or seignory in gross in Milton and Gayton, to Richard Hervey, Esq. his younger brother. In the 24th. year of Charles I this Richard Hervey in consideration of the sum of £1,500 sold and confirmed the Manor with its members and appurtenances to Richard Gleed and Edmund Gleed his son, and to their heirs for ever. This Edmund, surviving his father, became possessed of this estate; and by his last will bearing date 25th. April 1679, bequeathed it to Richard his son. He left issue Elizabeth an only daughter, wife to the late Richard Dodwell Esq., his successor in this inheritance and the present Lady of the Manor of Milton."

THE STORY OF THE MANORS 39

Thus far Dr. Bridges brings us in the list of Lords of the Manor of Milton of the Honor of Peverel. It remains to add that after the death of Mrs. Elizabeth Dodwell, in 1750, the manor passed to Mrs. Elizabeth Nash, who had a daughter named Mary. Mrs. Elizabeth Nash married John Darker, who, in his wife's right, was Lord of the Manor of Milton and Collingtrough and is so described in the Bill for enclosing the open fields and commons in 1779. At her death in 1788, her daughter, Mary Nash, became Lady of the Manor. She married William Blake the younger, of Danesbury, Welwyn, Herts. Their son, William John Blake, inherited it in 1852, and on his death in 1875, the manor passed to his nephew, Colonel Arthur Maurice Blake. In 1877 Colonel Blake sold the property to Mr. James Asplin, of Milton, who remained Lord of the Manor of Milton, of the Honor of Peverel, until his death in 1923.

In his account of the other manor, Bridges gives it under the head of Collingtree.

"At the general survey (*Doomsday*), Collingtree was certified to be a member of the Manor of Mideltone, and to contain 2 hides wanting 1 virgate, which were then held of the King by Geoffrey Alselin.

"In the time of King John the Manor of Colintre was in the hands of Will. de le Fremunt, who in the second year of this reign conveyed it, by licence from his majesty, to Simon de Pateshull and his heirs, with the moiety of the advowson of the churches of Middleton and Colintre. In the 5th. year of the same reign a fine was levied between this Simon de Pateshull and Margery the wife of Will. de le Fremunt[1] of a third part of his inheritance, which had been settled upon her, the said Margery, by way of dower. And in the 9th. year of Henry III a second fine was levied of the said 3rd. part between Walter the son of Simon de Pateshull demandant and Walter de Gatesbury and Emma his wife one of the sisters and co-heirs of Will de le Fremunt deforciants, to the use of the said Walter de Pateshull; with covenant that the service due from the said Walter to the king, from this his Manor of Colintre, should be performed by Philip de Quinton, the son and heir of Agnes the elder sister of the said Emma de Gatesbury.

"From Walter de Pateshull it descended to Simon, the son and heir of John de Pateshull, his grandson; upon whose decease in the 24th. year of Edw. I this Lordship came to John his son and heir, who was then in the 4th. year of his age. It was at this time certified to be held of Philip de Gayton. By inquisition taken in the same year John de Pateshull was found to hold one Knight's fee in Midleton and Colintre of Philip de Quenton (more probably de Gayton), who held the same of Robert de Everingham, who held it of the king *in capite*. In the 6th. year of Edw. II he levied a fine of the Manor and in the ninth of the same reign was certified to be Lord of Colintre. In the 20th. year of Edw. III, upon collecting the aid to make the king's son a knight, John de Pateshull accounted for half a knight's fee in Middleton and Colintre as held of the fee of Everingham; and dying in the 23rd. year of this reign left issue William, his successor in the Lordship of Collingtree. In the 33rd. year of Edw. III died Sir William de Pateshull seized

[1] See page 285.

THE STORY OF THE MANORS 41

of this Manor which he was found by inquisition to have held of Sir John de Meaux by an annual payment of xxiis. viiid., having no male issue his inheritance descended to his sisters ; a partition being made between them in the following year, the lands and tenements which had belonged to him in Middelton, Collingtre, &c., were assigned to Alice, the wife of Sir Thomas Wake of Blisworth. Upon the demise of this lady in the 22nd. of Richard II, the Manor of Colingtre devolved to her grandson Thomas Wake, the son of Sir Thomas Wake her eldest son. From this gentleman it descended in the 37th. year of Henry VI to Thomas Wake Esq his son, who left issue Roger Wake his successor in this estate.

" This Roger was a firm adherent to Richard III, upon whose defeat at Bosworth field his possessions were confiscated and in the 1st. year of Henry VII the Manor of Collingtre was granted to Sir Charles Somerset, who in 1488 presented to the living. But he was afterwards restored to his fortune and in the 20th. year of this reign died seized of the Lordship of Collingtre with the other possessions which he had formerly enjoyed. By his will, bearing date May 12th. 1503, he settles an annuity for life of X L issuing out of his Manors of Middleton beside Colingtre and of Colingtre, on William Wake his brother, pursuant to the will of Thomas Wake his father. To this he likewise added another annuity of V L arising from his lands and tenements in Middleton and Colingtre. His successor was Thomas Wake Esq., his eldest son.

" This gentleman appears to have sold the Manor of Collingtree soon after to Oliver Wode, who in the 6th. year of Henry VIII was seized of it with the advowson of the church. He left them at his death to Margaret his daughter, the wife of Sir Walter Mantell of Heyford in this county, and afterwards married to Sir James Hayles of Kent who was her third husband. This lady died seized of them in the 15th. year of Queen Elizabeth, and was succeeded by Matthew Mantell the son of Walter, the second son of Walter Mantell and Margaret aforesaid. From these possessors it had the name of Mantell's Manor ; and came afterwards into the hands of William Dry of Milton, who died possessed of it in 1637 and left it to his posterity.

" In the 25th. year of Queen Elizabeth certain lands and tenements in Milton and Collingtre were given to Theophilus Adams and Robert Adams. These were formerly belonging to Walter Mantell attainted, and are said in the grant to have been concealed lands."

This concludes all that we can learn of the two manors from Bridges' *History*.

From William Dry, whose tablet is on the vestry wall, this manor passed to his son, another William Dry, who died possessed of it in 1678. His epitaph, in rhyme, is on a stone in the vestry floor. In his Will, dated October 10th, 1677, he bequeathes as follows : " I do geve unto my Sonne Edward my Statute booke." This son Edward became the next lord of the manor, and was buried November 19th, 1707. According to the inscription on the tenor bell, he held the office of churchwarden in the year 1686 (page 131). Then in 1721 we find that the Lord Leimpster had the manorial rights, and held two courts annually for the manor (see page 34). This

THE STORY OF THE MANORS

Lord Leimpster was afterwards Earl of Pomfret, ancestor of Sir T. Fermor-Hesketh of Easton-Neston, Towcester. At that date, however, the owner of the manor was Mr. Edward Price, who had married Anne, the daughter of Mr. Edward Dry. From Mr. Price the manor became commonly known as Price's Manor, just as a century before it was called Mantell's Manor to distinguish it from the other. The next owner we meet with is James King, whose name occurs in the Enclosure Award. There we find that ten quit rents were yielded by him in return for various small portions of land. These are described as being formerly

" paid to James King as Owner or possessor of a certain manor in Milton otherwise Middleton Malsor and Collingtree otherwise Collingtrough aforesaid called Price's Manor."

The award was signed in 1780. A few years later this manor passed by purchase to Joseph Dent, Esq., from whom it has descended to Milton's illustrious son, Sir W. Ryland D. Adkins, K.C.

There are two manor houses in Milton. That of the Honor of Peverel is the gabled Tudor residence at the top of Pluck's Lane, called The Manor, with a very fine dovecote standing a few yards west of the house. In this house dwelt Sir Sapcotes Harrington and his young son, the talented James Harrington, the author of *Oceana*.

The other manor house is known as Milton Manor, and is the residence with the Georgian front near the main road to Northampton. In the house is a very fine carved staircase dating from about 1650. The older portions of the house date from Tudor times and earlier. Milton Manor is famous for its lawns well stocked with bulbs, which present a glorious show in spring, of which Sir Ryland Adkins is justly proud.

There being two manor houses, there should be, and there are, two dovecotes. One has been already mentioned. The other stands at the end of the line of buildings to the east of the " Grange." Because of this, it has been suggested that the Grange may have been the site of the old Milton Manor centuries ago. However, this need not necessarily follow, as the dovecote could be situated at some distance from the manor house.

With the exception of the Rector, none should keep doves but the lords of the manors, as they would not dream of allowing their corn to be eaten by their tenants' birds. Also, the doves in winter provided a welcome change of diet from the universal salt meat, for it was an expensive matter to keep beasts for killing as root crops were then not generally grown in England.

It should be noted that as two manors existed in the same place, there should be two mills. The sites where these stood are still distinguished by their names, Mill Banks, near Stockwell, and Mill Close, a little to the east of the church.

Some idea of the privileges of a lord of the manor may be gained from the Will of Edmund Gleed, April 25th, 1679, who bequeathed to his

THE STORY OF THE MANORS

son Richard the manor, with the commons and "rents customes services Court Leetes veiwes of ffrankpledge Courts Baron pr'gnisise profitts of Courts wayfes & strayes felons goods and all other Royaltyes franchises libertyes priviledges com'odityes & hereditam'ts whatsoever to ye said Manor or Seigniory . . . belonging."

In earlier days the lords of the manor exercised other rights, some of which cannot be written of in a work of this description.

The subject of the manors must not be left without a few words about the remarkable man, James Harrington, who as a boy lived in the old gabled Manor House at the top of Pluck's Lane. He was the son of Sir Sapcotes Harrington and his wife Jane, who was the daughter of Sir William Samwell of Upton Hall. Dame Jane's father bought Milton Manor and gave it to his son-in-law Sir Sapcotes Harrington on his marriage. Their eldest son James happened to be born at Upton Hall on the first Friday in January, 1610, and was baptised at Upton Church on January 16th. During his boyhood he lived at Milton.

He proceeded to Trinity College, Oxford, but left without taking a degree. During his continental travels he visited Rome and while there he refused the privilege of kissing the Pope's toe, which was the usual mode of expressing honour and reverence to the Pontiff. When King Charles heard of this he reproved him for his rudeness, but Harrington declared he would not kiss the foot of any prince after kissing his King's hand.

After his return to England, Harrington joined the Presbyterian Party, but took no part in the great Civil War. When King Charles, who had been captured by the Scots, was handed over to the English, Harrington was one of the commissioners who received him at Newcastle and brought him to Holdenby House, afterwards accompanying him to the Isle of Wight. Though a strong Republican, Harrington treated the Royal prisoner with such consideration and sympathy that a warm attachment sprang up between them. On one occasion in some dispute he took the King's part so stoutly as to cause great offence and he was told to leave his post, but he continued to serve Charles until at last he was forcibly dismissed. Harrington was allowed to attend the King to the last "memorable scene" itself, on the scaffold at Whitehall. Just before King Charles placed his head on the block, he gave Harrington a token of Royal favour in consideration of his friendship for him.

In 1656 he published his once celebrated book, *The Commonwealth of Oceana*, the manuscript of which is said to have been seized when at the press by Cromwell, but afterwards restored. At the Restoration he was thrown into the Tower on November 26th, 1661, because of his strong Republican views, but was eventually released and died of paralysis in London on September 11th, 1677. He lies buried side by side with Sir Walter Raleigh on the south side of the altar in St. Margaret's Church, Westminster.

Professor Saintsbury's criticism may be of interest : " His imaginary commonwealth,

Oceana, makes the subject of a very delightful though excessively odd book, wherein the project for a doctrinaire republic is worked out with all the learning, all the quaintness, and almost all the splendour of these mid-seventeenth-century writers, and with a profusion of fancy that never comes very far short of expression suitable to it."

CHAPTER III

THE NAME OF MILTON

"WHAT'S in a name?" Sometimes a great deal, and so it is with the name Milton Malzor. It carries us back to Celtic and Roman days, to the Saxon township and the great Norman lords.

The suffix "ton" is a little history in itself. It tells us that long before the Norman Conquest and before the incursion of the Danes, our village was surrounded by a strong fence and a ditch as a rough fortification. The name given to this fence and ditch was the "tun," from which we have "town" or "township," and hence Milton.

Why was it called Mil-ton? At first sight it would seem to be simply a contraction of its other name, Middleton, being the "middle town" of the neighbouring villages of Collingtree, Rothersthorpe and Blisworth, each of which is distant a little more than a mile away.

Another meaning, and probably the correct one, is suggested by the difference in spelling in *Doomsday Book*. There the name is given three times, and in each case differently—Molitone, Mideltone and Mildetone. Further, it will be seen that one item about Milton reads: "There is a mill rendering thirty pence." This is

THE MANOR, MILTON.

Drawn by Miss H. M. Asplin.

more than a coincidence with regard to the name.

The mill would make the village of great importance, for there the people of the district would bring their corn to be ground. It was no ordinary thing to possess a mill in those early days. In fact it was a great privilege which could only be obtained and maintained by special permission, for the lord of the manor was very jealous of his rights. The musty pages of history are occasionally illumined by curious stories of those who had the temerity to transgress these rights by building unauthorised mills. One instance tells us how Abbot Sampson of St. Edmundsbury (1173–1203) disposed of a mill erected without permission on land that was the builder's own freehold. He heard that Herbert the Dean had built a windmill, and Sampson gave orders to his carpenters to go and pull it down. Herbert, getting to know of this, went immediately to the Abbot to protest against such an act of injustice. He claimed that he could surely build a mill on his own freehold. He protested that the use of the wind ought to be free to everyone and that he had built it only to grind his own corn on his own premises. " By God's grace," roared the Abbot, " I will not eat bread till your mill is plucked up. Not even the king himself can do such a thing within the liberties of the Abbey. Away with you, and before you return home you shall hear what has become of your mill." Dean Herbert, however, forestalled the Abbot, for he rode posthaste to his house and when the carpenters arrived at the place they found no mill to put down. Richard de London, Abbot of Peterborough (1273–99), for a similar reason, destroyed a mill that had been erected at Oundle without his sanction, as it interfered with the profits of his own mill there.

From these instances we see that a mill, being of importance, conferred some distinction upon the place where it stood. As a mark of that distinction, our village was given the name of Milton, derived in the first instance from Molitone.

It is only fair to say that there is a difference of opinion as to the identity of the Molitone of *Doomsday*. It has been claimed as Mollington in Oxfordshire because the names Molitone and Mollington are somewhat similar. However, the similarity between the names Molitone and Mildetone, another of the names for Milton in *Doomsday*, must not be overlooked. I have also been told that since Molitone is given as being in Foxlea Hundred, it could not possibly be our Milton. To that argument it is sufficient to say that William Peverel's estates in Foxlea Hundred were situated at Brackley, Molitone and Courteenhall, and this particular manor of Milton could very well be in the same hundred as Courteenhall, as both parishes adjoin each other. Further, since Molitone forms part of William Peverel's barony, or the " Honor of Peverel," and we find that in the reign of Henry III John Malesoures held one knight's fee, or manor, in Milton and Collingtree " of the Honor of Peverel," it is clear that William Peverel had

THE NAME OF MILTON 51

land in Milton which is not catalogued in *Doomsday*, if Molitone is not our village. There is no reason for such an omission in this case.

The evidence certainly points to the fact that the Molitone of the Honor of Peverel in *Doomsday* is the Milton of the Honor of Peverel in the reign of Henry III, and the late Mr. Stuart Moore identified Molitone as " Milton or Middleton Malsor."

This being the case, Molitone gives us the key to Milton. There are three sources whence it could have been derived, the Celtic *melyn*, the Roman *mola* or the Anglo-Saxon *mylen*, all meaning a mill. Each source has its claim upon our attention.

The Celtic derivation is by no means an impossible one as there are other Celtic names in the district. Collingtree, for instance, is purely Celtic. The suffix -tree is a corruption of " trev," as may be seen from *Doomsday* and mediæval Wills, while the sound of the " v " survived even as late as 1779, for in the Enclosure Award it is spelt Colingtrough. " Tref " or " trev " is the Celtic for town, and we have a similar instance of its corruption in Coventry, which was originally Couan-trev. Add to this the fact that Collingtree Church is dedicated to St. Columba, sometimes known as St. Columb, a Celtic saint, and we have the name at once—Colum-trev, the town or place of St. Columb. This survives with very little difference as Colestrev in *Doomsday*. Another local instance of a Celtic name is that of the River Tove at Towcester, which is similar to the Welsh names

Teify, Tav, Taff and Towy. Hence, as names of Celtic origin are sometimes met with in the neighbourhood, it requires no great stretch of the imagination to derive Molitone from *melyn*, as it may well be a relic of Celtic times.

However, the Roman *mola* may seem phonetically to have even a stronger claim than *melyn*, to form a component part of Molitone, as only one letter needs to be changed,—Mola-tone. The Romans, as we know, were in the neighbourhood; their great road, Watling Street, is not far away, running through Towcester where they had a camp or station; and the Nene Valley was a favourite resort of theirs to judge from the number of villas and other traces of occupation that have been unearthed. So this conquering race may possibly have given the name to this village, because of its mill.

Finally, we have the Anglo-Saxon *mylen*, which would give us Mylen-ton, with an easy transition to Molitone or Mildetone and thence to Middleton and Milton. Where the mill was, there, too, was the village or " ton."

Milton is a very common name, and for this reason was probably found inconvenient by the powerful Malesoure family who were lords of the manor of the Honor of Peverel from the reign of Henry III to Edward III. Accordingly, they caused it to be known as Middleton or Milton Malesoure, afterwards contracted to Malzor. The same family stamped their name on one of the Thorpes in this county where they had a manor, so that it became Thorpe Malzor.

The Malesoures were descended from three

followers of the Conqueror, and were a proud and dominant family. John Malesoures, who first settled in Milton, seems to have been fond of litigation, for at the Northampton Assizes held on June 25th, 1247, he summoned the Master of St. John's Hospital for having sued him in a Court Christian. Four years later (1251) he brought another action against the Master of the Hospital, asserting his claim to a quarter of a knight's fee in Rothersthorpe as his by right.

Like many another old and powerful Norman family, the elder branches died out, leaving only the younger sons of younger sons to perpetuate the name. Consequently this great house is now represented by those who occupy much humbler stations in life, but the families named Malsher or Melcher in the neighbourhood are of blue-blooded Norman stock and can boast as ancestors those great lords who lent their name to the village where they once held sway.

CHAPTER IV

OUR CHURCH : ITS DEDICATION, ALTARS, SCREENS, ETC.

ACCUSTOMED as we are to speak of our parish church as the " Church of the Holy Cross," it seems strange at first to regard it as being dedicated to St. Helen. Such, however, is the case.

The earliest reference to the church by name occurs on the Coroner's Rolls for 1321 (see page 143), where it is called the Church of St. Helen. In pre-Reformation Wills it is referred to by the same name, as the following extracts show :

John Byllyng, 1526, " My body to be beryed in the churchyarde of Sayncte Ellyns in medelton aforesaid."

William Bowye, 1528, " My body to be buryed in the churchyard of Seynct Hellyn in medylton malsor."

It was called St. Helen's Church as late as the middle of the eighteenth century, because it appears under this name in the *Thesaurus Rerum Ecclesiasticarum*, page 495, published in 1742 by John Ecton, late Receiver-General of the Tenths of the Clergy. Browne Willis, in his *Survey of the Cathedrals*, etc., page 534, in the editions published in 1730 and 1742, also gives it as the Church of St. Helen. Hence it cannot for very long have been called the "Church of the Holy Cross." The mistake in the name was undoubtedly due to the evil days of sloth and indifference through which the Church passed during the latter part of the eighteenth century and to sheer carelessness on the part of bishops' secretaries about a century, or less, ago, there being a chapel of the Holy Cross at Milton, near Peterborough, with which our church probably got confused. It is true that Milton Feast is not held on August 18th, St. Helen's Day. This is probably due to an order of the time of Henry VIII that owing to the numerous feasts or wakes in connection with the annual festivals of the dedication of churches, many occurring at short intervals in the same neighbourhood during busy seasons, they were to be transferred to Michaelmas or some date near it. What new date near Michaelmas would be fixed on for the Feast, in obedience to the Royal decree? It would be most natural to choose a day near the Festival of Holy Cross, which falls on September 14th. Hence Milton Feast has been kept for centuries on the Sunday next after Holy Cross Day, so that it can be as late as September 21st. This is borne out by the following extract from our old register:

"Sarah Lister, baptized Sept. 21st, 1707, which was Milton Feast day."

A similar change occurred in the date of Collingtree Feast, which is held in October, although the festival of St. Columba, the patron saint, falls on June 9th.

Why, if the feast had to be changed from St. Helen's Day, would it be natural to choose a date near Holy Cross Day? The reason is not far to seek. According to tradition it was St. Helen who discovered the Holy Cross on which Our Saviour died. As she is our patron saint it would not be amiss to give here a short account of her life, or, rather, the traditions surrounding her name.

Flavia Julia Helena was born about the year 248–50 and died in her eightieth year about A.D. 328–30. According to Geoffrey of Monmouth she was of British birth, being the daughter of a chieftain named Coel, the " old King Cole " of the nursery rhyme, who founded Colchester. She became the wife of Constantius Chlorus, Emperor of Rome. Her husband died at York in A.D. 306, and there her son Constantine was proclaimed Emperor, to be known for all time as Constantine the Great, the founder of Constantinople, which he named after himself. About the year 325, after being warned in a vision, she journeyed to Jerusalem, which she found in ruins, and proceeded to search for the Holy Sepulchre. On the most likely spot there was a huge mound on which stood a temple to Venus. She demolished the temple and caused the mound to be removed, thus bringing to light the sepulchre. In it she found three crosses, the two on which the thieves died and that on which Our Lord suffered, together with the tablet on which Pilate had written in Hebrew and Greek and Latin, " This is the King of the Jews." There was nothing to distinguish the crosses, for the tablet was lying loose, so how could she tell which of the three was the Cross of Christ? Macarius, Bishop of Jerusalem, came to her aid and asked of God a sign. There was a woman lying at the point of death, and one after the other the crosses were laid against her. The first two had no effect, but when the third touched her, although she was in the very act of yielding up the ghost, yet, as an old historian tells us,

"she recovered and regained her former strength. After this sort was the Cross of Christ found out. The Emperor's mother built over the sepulchre a goodly and gorgeous Church and called that new Jerusalem which she had founded over against the old and waste. The one half of the Cross she locked up in a silver chest, and left there to be seen of such as were desirous to behold such monuments, the other half she sent unto the Emperor."

Such is the narrative related by Socrates Scholasticus in his *Ecclesiastical History*, I, 17, about A.D. 450. Other historians, Sozomen and Theodoret, who wrote about the same time as Socrates, but evidently independently of him, tell us much the same story, except that the former states that the true Cross restored a dead man to life. Eusebius, however, who was contemporary with Constantine the Great and evidently a privileged spectator of the events he describes, tells us plainly that it was Constantine who overthrew the temple of Venus and discovered the Holy Sepulchre when the mound was cleared away. He says nothing about the discovery of the Holy Cross. Eusebius began writing his Life of Constantine at the death of that Emperor in A.D. 337, so that we could wish for no better authority.

St. Cyril of Jerusalem, the next authority in point of time, states in a letter dated May 7th, A.D. 351, written to Constantius the son of Constantine, that the " saving wood of the Cross " was found at Jerusalem in the time of his father.

St. Ambrose, in A.D. 395, states that St. Helen found at Golgotha the three crosses and the nails, and that Our Lord's Cross was known by the title thereon.

After him we have St. Chrysostom who, in A.D. 407, mentions the discovery of the Holy Cross and states it was known by Pilate's tablet fixed to it. He says nothing about St. Helen.

Further than this it is not necessary to follow the story or the evidence, except to say that in course of time supposed portions of the Holy Cross found their way as relics throughout Europe and very likely a small piece was kept as a relic and venerated at Milton.

The church being the Church of St. Helen, the High Altar was dedicated in her honour. This of course stood at the east end of the chancel and close to it was a statue of the saint or else her picture on the wall. She is usually represented crowned, holding the cross in her left arm and with the nails in her right hand. Before the image, or picture, votive lights would be burning, for the maintenance of which money or goods were bequeathed.

Jayne Garnytt, 1532 : " To Seynt Helen light ijd."

Henry Davy, 1536 : " To Sent Hellyns lyghtt halfe a pownde of waxe."

Closely associated as St. Helen was with the story of the discovery of the Holy Cross, it is only natural to find that the Rood, or Crucifix, was especially honoured in her church here, for we find that Milton had the distinction of possessing not less than two Rood-screens. One, the High Rood, was in the usual place across the chancel arch. This was probably of wood with a door or gate in the centre through which communicants would pass to reach the altar rails. Above the screen stood the Crucifix, flanked by figures of the Blessed Virgin and St. John. The Crucifix stood immediately over the door in the middle of the screen, thus symbolising that the Blessed Sacrament was attained through the Cross of Christ. The second Rood-screen, or " Lesser Rood," was across the west end of the Lady Chapel in the north aisle, and is now represented by the vestry screen.

An examination of the ancient Wills in the Northampton Probate Office proves that here existed two Rood-screens.

Thomas Basse, 1521, in his Will mentions the High Rood, i.e. the one across the chancel arch, in the following bequest :

" To the hye rode lyght a stryke of barley."

Wm. Garnett (1531) mentions the Rood across the north aisle :

" To the rode in ye north yle ijd."

And thus Henry Davy, 1536 :

" To the roode lyghtt in the north ylle halfe a pownde of waxe."

Thomas Rage, 1523, who was a great benefactor of his parish church, refers to both Roods in his Will :

" To the hye rod a stryke of barley, also to ye rode yn the north hyle ij powndes of waxe in too torches."

Sometimes no particular Rood was specified, the bequest being simply to " the Rood," or, as in the case of Robert Stewynnys, 1518 : " to the crucyfyx ij stryk of barley."

So the evidence proves conclusively that there were two Rood-screens in our church, though now, alas, not a trace of them remains.

Either on the narrow platform that formed a canopy above the High Rood-screen, or on the floor of the nave close to the screen, stood the Rood Altar. That it existed is proved by the Will of William Bowye, 1528, which runs thus :

" I gyve and bequethe to the lyght before the rode alter a stryke of barley."

The Rector at certain services would ascend to the top of the Rood-screen, and so would the sexton every night and morning for the purpose of extinguishing and rekindling the lights. In some churches, as at Blisworth, may still be seen the staircase in the wall used by the priest and sexton, and high up in the wall is the door through which they came out to the Rood-loft across the chancel arch. The walls in Milton

Church show no trace of such a staircase built in them, nor do they appear to be thick enough to allow of one. How then did the Rector of Milton climb up to the roods ? Evidently by a wooden staircase fixed in such a position as to serve both the High Rood-screen and that across the north aisle. That position would be somewhere near where the pulpit now stands, and an examination of the demi-shaft or half-pillar between the chancel arch and the north aisle will provide evidence that such a staircase had once been fixed there. Scattered here and there on the shaft and that part of the wall close to it, will be found no less than eleven small square plugs let into the stone, the lowest one being near the floor and the highest near the capital. These plugs are very significant, for they are pieces of stone let in to fill up holes in which small wooden beams were once fixed. It seems conclusive that in this place, between the two roods, a wooden staircase must have been fastened to the wall for stability, hence the holes in which the supports were held. To confirm this theory, one of the topmost plugs is between the demi-shaft and the chancel arch, as if to support a platform by which the High Rood could be gained.

The Lesser Rood, we have said, stood before the Lady Chapel, at the eastern end of the north aisle. This was the usual position for the Lady Chapel, except when it was built to the east of the High Altar. In this chapel was an altar, with a statue of Our Lady or a painting of the Madonna and Child on the wall, before which candles would be burning. In the south wall of the chapel still exists a rather large piscina, the drain where the altar vessels were cleansed. Bequests were made to this altar, as for instance:

Thomas Rage, 1523 : " It. to our lade awter[1] a stryke of barley."

And for the lights that burned before the statue :

Henry Davy, 1536 : " Unto our Ladys lyght a pownde of waxe."

At the east end of the south aisle there is another chapel, which, if the " wheel window " is a sure indication, was originally dedicated to St. Catherine. Here again stood an altar, with a statue or picture of the saint, while the piscina still remains in the south wall.

Thomas Rage, 1523 : " It. to Seynt Cateryns awter a quarter of wax."
Lawrence Davey, 1526 : " Item to Saynte Nicolas and Seinte Katerins altarez in the same churche to eiche off them oone stryke Barley."

Again, for the lights before the statue :

Wm. Garnett, 1531 : " To Sent Katheryn light ijd."

As her chapel is now in frequent use, a brief life of this saint may be given here.

The festival of St. Catherine, or St. Katharine, falls on November 25th. She was a Virgin and Martyr, but there is very little reliable information respecting her. It is said she was

[1] Our Lady's altar.

of royal descent and was born in Alexandria in the early part of the fourth century. Being a Christian, she was brought before Maximin the Emperor, and in his presence had to dispute her case with heathen philosophers. However, she was of such great learning and ability that she not only confuted her heathen opponents but was the means of their conversion. The Emperor, when he knew that the philosophers had confessed Christ, ordered them to be burnt to death, but reserved St. Catherine for a further trial. Steadfast in her faith, she refused to sacrifice her chastity to the tyrant's lust and was condemned to death. She was first torn to pieces on four revolving wheels to which sharp spikes were fastened, and then what little life remained was mercifully ended with the sword's keen edge. In the eighth century her body was taken by holy monks to the monastery of Mount Sinai, but mediæval legends say she was borne there by angels. St. Catherine is the patron saint of secular learning and her name was highly venerated in East and West. In statues or pictures she is represented crowned, bearing in her hand either the martyr's palm, a book, or a sword, and having the spiked wheel by her side.

The positions of four altars in our church have now been identified. These are the High Altar, dedicated to St. Helen, the Rood Altar, Our Lady's Altar and St. Catherine's Altar. There was a fifth altar, that to St. Nicholas, as we see from Lawrence Davey's bequest above, and also from others, e.g. :

Thos. Rage : " Also to Seynt Nycolas awter a stryke of barley."

Where, then, was the chapel of St. Nicholas ? Speculations as to whether a small chantry chapel once stood here between two pillars, led me to examine carefully the stonework of the columns. Evidence was soon forthcoming. In the south arcade, in the two pillars to the east of the porch, are several stone plugs, inserted in holes that once very probably held wooden beams. In the aisle wall may be seen, directly opposite these two pillars, the places where holes for two beams have been plastered up. The positions of these plugs and plastered holes seem to indicate that a screen stood between the two pillars, and between each pillar and the wall of the south aisle, thus setting apart a portion of the aisle as a chapel. A position near the font would be very appropriate for this chapel, as St. Nicholas is a patron saint of children, for this reason. We are told that one day he heard a man say he would have to sell his three little daughters as he was too poor to keep them. So St. Nicholas threw three bags of gold that night through their window. Here we have the origin of hanging up our stockings on Christmas Eve, for St. Nicholas is better known, perhaps, by the popular title of Santa Claus. This change of spelling easily came about, because there is very little difference in sound between Sant Nic'las and Santa Claus. His Festival is on December 6th.

In his chapel stood his altar, with his statue or picture, in front of which were lights.

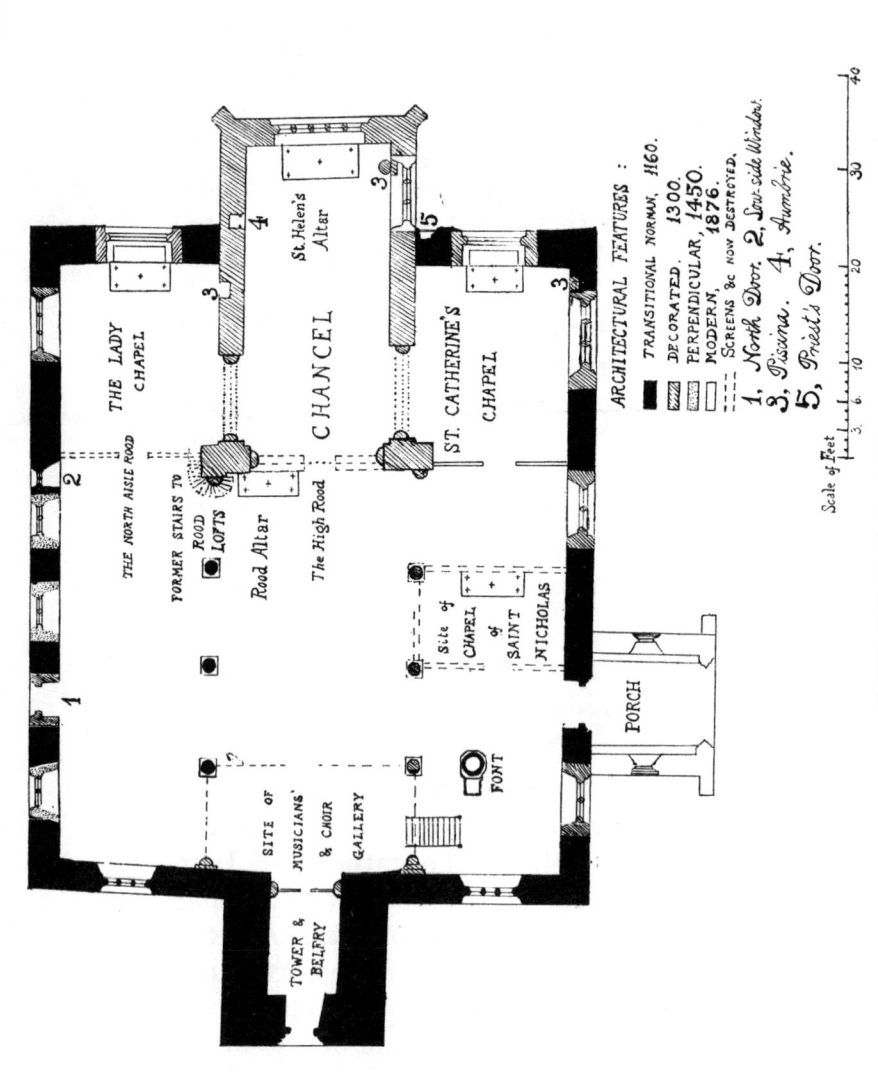

GROUND PLAN OF MILTON CHURCH.
Showing ancient features.

Wm. Garnett, 1531 : " To Seinte Nicholas light ijd."

Wm. Bowye, 1528 : " It. I gyve and bequethe to Seynct Nicolas Lyght a stryke of barley."

Though probably extinguished at night for safety, lights were burning every day before images of saints. From bequests made in old Wills for the maintenance of such lights we find that there were other saints specially venerated in Milton Church, although there was no altar in their honour.

There was a statue of St. Christopher, or probably a painting of that saint, on the wall of the north aisle and, as near as possible, opposite the south door. This position was usually chosen because this saint was the protector of travellers, and it was considered of great benefit merely to take a peep at the saint's picture through the open church door when passing by.

Lawrence Davy, 1526 : " Item to Sainte Christoferus lighte the oone strike off Barley."

Richard Knight, 1529 : " Item to Seynt Xrsfer lighte a stryke of Barley."

There were at least two more statues in our church. They were of St. John the Baptist and St. John the Evangelist. The statue of St. John the Baptist was probably attached to the pillar close to the font, and that of St. John the Evangelist either on the wall of the north aisle or one of the pillars in the north arcade, the north side being the Gospel side of the altar. Before these statues votive lights were kept burning.

Thos. Rage: "Item to Seynt John the Baptyste and to Seynt John Eva'gelyst a pownde of waxe."

From the testamentary extracts already quoted we see that bequests were made for the maintenance of lights to be kept burning before various images, altars and roods in Milton Church. There was another light, that before the Easter Sepulchre, about which a few words of explanation may be given here.

The Easter Sepulchre was in use only between Maundy Thursday and Easter morning. After the Mass on Maundy Thursday, the Host, i.e. the consecrated wafer, was placed in a silver pyx, or box, together with a small cross, and "buried" in a small wooden chest or some other receptacle. This was the Easter Sepulchre, and in some churches there still remain beautiful specimens elaborately carved in stone. That in Milton was most probably of wood, since nothing remains to show that one of stone ever existed here. The usual place for the Easter Sepulchre was against the north wall of the chancel, near the altar. After the Host was deposited therein on Maundy Thursday, lights were kept burning before it day and night until dawn on Easter morning. Then the Rector took the Host out of the Sepulchre, and after carrying it in a joyful procession round the church, replaced it upon the High Altar. This was a dramatic way of impressing upon the minds of the people the death and burial of Our Lord and His glorious Resurrection.

Bequests were made for the light burning before the Easter Sepulchre.

John Byllyng, 1526 : " To the sepulker lighte ij stryke of barley."

Wm. Harbord, 1532 : " It. to Seyntt pulcar's lygt xjd."

A curious bequest to the Sepulchre light is made by Robert Stewynnys in 1518, which is as follows :

" It. to the sepulcur lyght of the churche of mydulton a cowe."

In this case it is obvious that the cow was intended to be sold and the money used for the benefit of the light before the Easter Sepulchre, but this bequest recalls an interesting fact that cattle were very often given to the church and were added to the stock that the Rector let out to the poor for hire.

In the same way, of course, the strikes of barley bequeathed to various lights or altars would be sold and the money disposed for their maintenance. On the other hand, the wax bequeathed would be given to the parish officials, who would make it into candles for the altar or statue mentioned in the Will.

The " strike " was a measure of two bushels, according to an old table of measures. It is interesting to know that the name " strike " was also given to a stick, commonly used up to fifty years ago, to level the grains heaped up at the top of the bushel measure. This stick, or strike, was drawn across so that the superabundant grains were swept off. The late Mr.

James Asplin, Lord of the Manor of Milton, informed me that it fell into disuse because dishonest persons had their strike thicker in the middle instead of straight, so that it swept away more than was just.

Another favourite bequest was for the maintenance of a funeral custom. This was for the burning of " torches," or " serges," as the great candles were called, at the side of the coffin during the funeral service in church and at the Requiem Mass. People who could afford to do so provided their own torches for their funerals, but the poor had to depend upon those belonging to the church, for the maintenance of which the rich gave wax or money in their Wills. The torches were very big, and each would be several pounds in weight. Bequests towards torches for Milton Church are frequently found, some giving the price to be paid for them.

Robert Stewynnys, 1518 : " It. to the forsayd churche (Milton) a torche prise vjs viijd."

John Lawrence, 1530 : " To helpe to by a torche xxd."

Thos. Rage, 1523 : " Also too torches of iiijs a pece, a torche to Medylton and a nother to Colentre churche."

Though not in itself a benefaction to any particular altar or light, the " obit " is of great interest and demands a brief notice. It was a bequest made to a church either in a lump sum of money or in rents of houses or lands, usually for the purpose of providing a curate and for charitable purposes at the disposal of the Rector in return for an annual Mass. A lamp was kept

OUR CHURCH 69

perpetually burning in church to symbolise the constant prayers of the faithful for the soul of the donor. In connection with this, the Will of Lawrence Davy, 1526, is most interesting, but unfortunately is in a torn condition. However, in the following extract I have attempted to fill up the blanks, the words or letters in italics showing where the page was torn.

" Then I will that the foresaid Johanne my wife if she supervive my said *decease* haveyng no issue shall have the said messuage in middelton aforesaid for the term of her live and *with it* to make and kepe yerely an obbett in Medelton aforesaid to the value of XVId, and after the dec*ease* off the seide Joh'ne my wife then I will my seide *assigns* shall stande and be seased off and in the said messe (i.e. messuage) and lands with there app*ur*tenance to the use of the parish church of Medilton aforesaid for ever and the church wardens of the same for the tyme *being* to kepe yerely for my fay (i.e. father) and mother my s*oul* and all Xren sowles an yerely obbett in the sa*id* churche and the same obbett yerely to be keppid *for* ever and off the profetts and issues of the sam*e I* will VIs. viiid. sterlyng to be distributed yerely *to* pr'ste, clerks and among the parishioners there. The residue off all my goods &c."

This was in the reign of Henry VIII, but that money does not now belong to Milton. Towards the close of his reign an Act was passed (37 Henry VIII, cap. 4), in 1545, by which all grants for religious uses, if considered superstitious such as chantries, obits and so forth, were vested in the Crown. An inventory of all such was made, and the parchment rolls may be seen at the Record Office. From the list for Northamptonshire I have copied the following :

Lands & Rents
{ Given by dyvers persons to churches to maynteine certeyne Obits, Lights Lampes & such like things, bying in dyvers townes viz. in Welton xiiijd, Grendon viijd. Milton iiijs iijd & Blysworth vid.   vjs vijd.

CHAPTER V

OUR CHURCH'S STORY—TO THE REFORMATION

As we have seen from the record in *Doomsday Book*, there was a priest at Milton in the time of William the Conqueror, and where there was a priest, there, too, was his church wherein he could minister. Of that little church no trace remains.

The present church was begun about the year 1160, during what is called the Transitional-Norman Period in architecture, exhibiting features both of the Norman and the Early English styles. The two lower stages of the tower are late Norman—the set-back of the two stages, the " battered " or tapering walls and their enormous thickness of over five feet, all go to prove this. It would seem as if there had once been a big window, or a great west door, in the tower, indicated by the round Norman arch in the wall, but this was changed for the present Early English doorway. The font is probably of late Norman date, the axe-work with which the sides were rounded off being plainly discernible. Its interior diameter is twenty-five inches, broad enough for a baby to be dipped in it as is ordered by the Prayer Book.

Of the same period as the tower are the walls of the nave and the lower part of the pillars in the north arcade. Two of these pillars are of white limestone for six feet from the base moulding, about two-thirds of their height, and the original capital rested where the first course of brown stone begins. The piers are one foot eleven inches in diameter, and are massive for pillars of such short height as they were originally, and typically Transitional. The bases of the three piers have the trough moulding, an

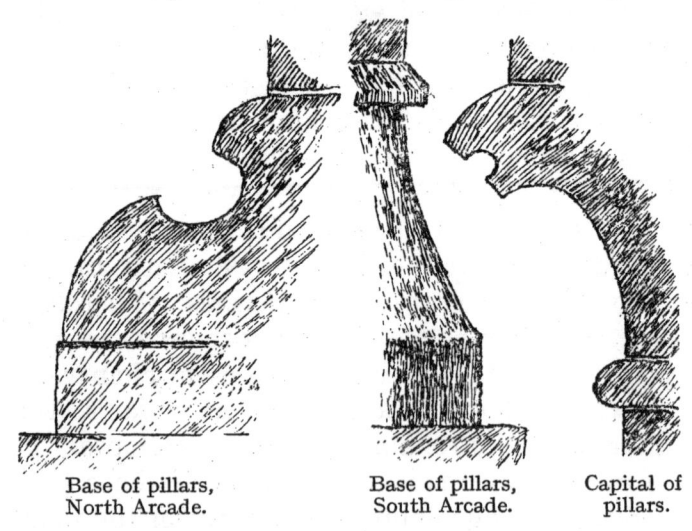

Base of pillars, North Arcade.   Base of pillars, South Arcade.   Capital of pillars.

Early English feature. These massive pillars on such moulded bases are similar to those in the choir aisle in Christ Church Cathedral, Oxford, which date from 1160. From the same period we can date the walls of the nave, which are devoid of buttresses.

Two of the original windows remain to us, these being the two Early English west windows, each of three lancet lights, while the little Priest's Door in the east wall of the south aisle dates also from very early in the Early English period.

We must conclude from the foregoing that the church was at first not so lofty as it is now, since the pillars were only as high as the two taller white portions.

One feature must be carefully noticed. The chancel walls are not bonded with the east walls of the north and south aisles, which proves that the present chancel was not built at the same time as the nave, while the fact that there is a buttress at each of the eastern angles of the chancel, and no buttress anywhere else, proves that the chancel is of more recent date than the nave.

The inference to be drawn is that the church ended in an apse, as was customary in the Norman and Transitional Periods. Therefore the nave must have been longer than at present, and extended as far into our present chancel as the east wall of the aisles, that is, as far as the altar rails. Probably the apse collapsed in course of time, as it did in other churches.

Such was our church until early in the fourteenth century, a witness of many notable events, and taking its due share in the life of the nation.

Then in 1236 something occurred which is of interest to us. It must be remembered that the water for Holy Baptism was kept in the font and renewed each Easter, being probably added to from time to time. Now, it would seem that people took away by stealth the baptismal water with which to practise incantations, or for other sacrilegious uses. Therefore, by the constitutions of Archbishop Edmund of Canterbury, issued in 1236, it was ordered that all fonts should be provided with a fitting cover, and that they should be kept locked as a precaution against sorcery.

Accordingly in that same year the Rector interviewed the village blacksmith, who came to the church and drove a staple into the stone of the font, to which the cover could be padlocked. There it remains to this day for all who wish to see, while the strong arm that fastened it in position is long since dust. On the opposite side of the font can be seen the end of a piece of iron driven into the stone, forming part either of another staple or of a hinge for the cover.

Five years after this, on February 13th, 1241, we find the great Bishop, Robert Grostete, of Lincoln, paying a special visit to Milton on his itinerary. As we know that Henry de Wycheton, Sub-Deacon, was instituted to the rectory that year, it is possible that the Bishop performed the duties of induction and institution himself at Milton, but nothing is said in the records as to the object of his visit.

About sixty years later great building operations were begun, which very probably originated through the collapse of the apse at the east end. An entirely new chancel was built, projecting into the nave, and at the same time the north arcade was made higher, three feet six inches being added in brown Duston stone to the old white limestone pillars, and they were finished off with octagonal capitals. The pillars in the

The North Door, Milton Church.

Moulding of Jamb, North Door.

south arcade were entirely rebuilt of brown stone, with octagonal capitals and with bases somewhat similar to the capitals, inverted, upon a single plinth. All the arches are acute. The difference in the styles of the bases is readily apparent, for those in the north are moulded and rest on double plinths.

About the same time, 1300, the tower received further attention. Already, a little less than a hundred years before, an addition had been built in the Early English style above the second stage. Now the octagonal lantern was built on squinches at the top and finished off with a low crocketed spire. This style is called the Decorated. The four pinnacles at the top of the tower are probably later.

Of the same style, and dating from about 1320, is the north door. This has an acutely pointed arch with very good moulding in the Decorated style.

Most of the windows in the church are of this period. The Early English windows in the west wall were left alone, but the great east window, those in the south aisle, and the large window in the Lady Chapel, the present vestry, were constructed about this time.

A singular and interesting window is that in the north wall close to the screen against the choir vestry. Such a window is commonly called a " Low-Side Window," but it used to be popularly known as a " Leper's Squint." Various theories as to the use of these peculiar windows will be found on page 236.

In the north wall of the chancel there still

exists an Aumbrie, or cupboard formed in the wall. Here in olden days were kept the chalice, paten, cruets and other things for the altar when not in use. The door is modern.

The existence of the Priest's Door in the east wall of the south aisle seems to point to the fact that the present south chapel was originally used as a vestry, for this reason. The rectory, up to 1779, was situated in a parcel of ground called Anchor Close, to the north-west of the church, where Anchor Terrace or Barrack Yard and the Post Office now stand. To reach the church, the Rector passed through the field behind his house and probably entered the churchyard through a small gate in the east wall. He would come first to the north aisle, but the Lady Chapel with Our Lady's altar stood there, so the Rector would pass on to the south aisle, where there was no altar. It is interesting to note that the right of the Rectors to take this path through the field remains to this day, the right-of-way established then still existing in a path and stile.

From the fourteenth to the seventeenth centuries the weaving industry flourished in the neighbourhood. Accordingly, a place had to be found in Milton Church for an altar to St. Catherine, on whose festival the weavers made holiday. So the ancient vestry at the east end of the south aisle became the Chapel of St. Catherine. As this saint was put to death on a wheel, what more fitting than that her emblem should be perpetuated in the stone tracery of a window above her altar? Therefore it was done, and the beautiful " Catherine Wheel " window took its present shape, a wheel within a square. As this part of the aisle had been screened off for a vestry, it already had, of course, a piscina fashioned in the wall. A piscina is a niche, ornamented according to the period, the bottom being in the form of a shallow basin with a hole leading through the wall into the earth. Down this drain was poured the water after cleansing the altar vessels, and hence a piscina is always found close to the altar or where an altar once stood, generally in the south wall, and also in mediæval vestries.

We can fix the date approximately when the chapel was formed by the tracery of the window. The style is Curvilinear, and the date is 1340 or thereabouts. It is mentioned in Bloxam's *Principles of Gothic Architecture*, Vol. I, page 231.

Such a perfect gem as this exquisite window that graces the Chapel of St. Catherine, was not to be alone in its beauty. Another round window, of a somewhat similar design, was put in the east wall of the north aisle above the altar in Our Lady's Chapel, where the vestry and organ chamber are.

This window in the north aisle perished in course of time. It may, of course, have been a Wheel Window such as is now there. I am, however, inclined to the opinion that the original was a Rose Window of very delicate tracery, for the reason that the Wheel Window blazons St. Catherine's emblem and so would be meaningless in the Lady Chapel, while a Rose Window would symbolise Our Lady, the *Rosa Mystica*. During the interval between its final removal and Mr. Montgomery's gift of the present window, men's memories would become hazy as to its exact design, but they would remember it was circular and so conclude it was like the other—a Wheel Window. This, however, is mere conjecture and it is quite possible it was of a Wheel pattern.

At what time the Rood-screens were erected we cannot tell, because nothing of them now remains, but it was probably during the Perpendicular Period. Had they been erected during the Decorated Period, in which the chancel was built, provision would doubtless have been made in the wall for a staircase.

Then in 1348 the terrible Black Death swept over the country and spared no class. It brought the Decorated Period to an abrupt end, for Gothic art in building received a distinct check in England. Like other places, Milton must have suffered terribly, and we find nothing more was done to the church for over a century. At last, about the year 1450, the three windows of the " Perpendicular " style were inserted in the wall of the north aisle. It is manifest that these windows were not in the original plan, for it will be seen that the most western of the three is on a lower level than the other two, in order to allow of sufficient masonry above the window to support the corbel of a roof-beam. This is interesting, as it tends to show that the north wall possessed until then the original windows of the narrow lancet pattern that first gave light to our church. As these Perpendicular windows are of the same period as the Tudor front of

The Manor, probably the same masons were employed in both places.

With the reconstruction of English life after the ravages of the Black Death, there arose a greater devotional spirit among the people, and this was manifested chiefly in the foundation of Guilds and Chantries, while the veneration of saints took on a new importance. This led to the erection of additional altars in the church, and so about this time was formed the Chapel of St. Nicholas in the south aisle (see page 64). Statues of various saints were also put up in the church (see page 65). The Rood-screens, too, were most probably erected about this time.

A feature of the church which has long since disappeared was the stone seat similar to those that are in the porch. This was about eighteen inches high and ran around the walls inside, providing seating accommodation for the congregation. Traces of its position are still left, for when the stone seat was removed the walls were plastered to meet the old plaster, as in the north and west walls where the line of demarcation is distinctly seen, or left bare as in parts of the south wall. There were no pews in those days, nor church chairs, but the people could use this stone seat, or sit on the base of a pillar, or squat on the rushes with which the floor was strewn. Sometimes they would bring cushions or stools with them to church on which to sit, and we have the historic instance of Jenny Geddes hurling her three-legged stool at the Dean in St. Giles' Cathedral, Edinburgh.

MORTIMERS, MILTON.

Very beautiful must have been the interior of the church in those days. The windows were filled with glass of glowing colours. Upon the walls were frescoes, paintings depicting some sacred story or legend. Here and there the statues of saints seemed to keep solemn watch and ward, while the lights of many candles and torches were reflected in the rich gilding of the Rood-screens.

There were many visitors to Milton who came in monkish garb to collect rents and other dues from lands given to them. About the fourteenth century the powerful Malesoure family had granted certain lands to the Abbey of St. James, Northampton, a monastic house of the Austin or Black Canons, and therefore one or more of the Regular Canons would come at times to the village on the business of the Abbey and say his office in our church before returning home. This land and its value are entered in the *Valor Ecclesiasticus* as being worth 41s. and 4d. per annum.

Another house of a religious character in Northampton that possessed land in Milton was the Hospital of St. John, that ancient building at the bottom of Bridge Street. The Master and Brethren of the Hospital owned the house now known, after a family who lived there, as Mortimers, with thirty acres of land. Before the Enclosure Award, part of their land was at Stockwell. From old plans of the house and stables I am inclined to the opinion that Mortimers was probably an offshoot of the Northampton Hospital of St. John at one time, for the house is shown as being 97 ft. long and 20 ft. 9 ins. broad, while the stables are 73 ft. long and 19 ft. 3 ins. broad. These dimensions are more suitable for a building of a monastic character than an ordinary dwelling. Parts of the house are very ancient, some of the work in the cellar windows being of fifteenth-century date, and others much older.

For some years up to the early part of last century this ancient house was partitioned off and inhabited by three families. Then it was taken by the Montgomery family, who restored it to its former dignity and afterwards purchased it from St. John's Hospital. It descended, through his mother, to the present owner, Edward Montgomery Alexander, Esq., who in recent years has greatly improved the house as a dwelling by shortening its unusual length and introducing modern conveniences, so that it is now a well-equipped country house of a convenient size. There is a fine staircase of early date in the hall.

It is almost certain that this property was held by St. John's Hospital in 1305 because in that year there is an account in the Lambeth MSS. (244, f. 72) of an ecclesiastical lawsuit in which they were involved. A dispute had arisen between St. John's Hospital and the Rectors of Blisworth and the united parishes of Milton and Collingtree, and the matter was referred to the Dean of Arches, who decided in favour of the Rectors of Blisworth and Milton. The Hospital authorities were dissatisfied with his ruling, and appealed to the Archbishop of Canterbury, who, in his sentence promulgated on April 27th, 1305, upheld the decision of the Dean of Arches, which was to be enforced by ecclesiastical censure. A copy of the record in the Lambeth Register is given on page 293. The sequel is interesting. The Master and Brethren refused to give way and had to suffer. In August or September the Archbishop solemnly excommunicated them, and as they still proved obstinate they were handed over to the secular arm, after being more than forty days under the sentence of excommunication. The Archbishop's writ to the King, dated October 29th, 1305, is still in existence and is preserved in the Public Record Office. An order was accordingly sent to the Sheriff of Northampton, and the Master and seven Brethren were thrown into prison, but on November 12th they were released until April 28th because the King learnt they had appealed to the Pope against the Archbishop's sentence as an unjust one. As they had not prosecuted their appeal, the sheriff rearrested them on May 4th, 1306, and they remained in prison for two months, being released in July, 1306, on their exhibiting letters in Chancery that they had taken steps to further their appeal to the Pope. What the result was is not known, as that is the end of the story so far as the records are concerned. I have corresponded with the sub-librarian of the Vatican at Rome, but a search in that famous library has proved fruitless. It is quite possible, however, that the Rectors of Blisworth and Milton still won their case, though it must have cost them a lot. What it was all about in the first instance is not mentioned, and the records for that period of the Court of Arches have perished, but very likely it was a question of tithes due to the two Rectors on the lands in their parishes owned by the Hospital of St. John.

Some few years after this dispute there are records, that seem strange to modern minds, of cases of sanctuary in the churches of Milton and Collingtree. For a full account of these see Chapter IX.

During the next century something of great interest and importance occurred. Up to 1441 the rectories of Milton and Collingtree were one, the two rectories being regarded as two moieties. After that date they were separated and became two distinct parishes.

Another century rolls by, and we come to the reign of Henry VIII. This was the time of the rejection of the Papal Supremacy. Up till then, the profits of an ecclesiastical living for the first year after a vacancy were paid to the Pope. These are still known as the First-fruits. The Tenths, another charge on the clergy, is a tenth of the annual value of the living. Henry VIII saw to it that the First-fruits and Tenths were vested in the King, and in 1535 he caused a new valuation to be made, called the " Valor Ecclesiasticus," according to which assessment the clergy are still rated for these payments. They formed part of the Royal revenue until the second year of the reign of Queen Anne, who restored to the Church what had been taken away from it. She granted a charter by which the First-fruits and Tenths are vested in trustees for the augmentation of poor livings. This is now known as " Queen Anne's Bounty."

To obtain the necessary particulars for King Henry VIII, his officers visited every monastery and parish church, making a list of the income payable to abbots and parish priests, and thus compiled the *Valor Ecclesiasticus*. In this book are various items relating to Milton, all of course written in Latin. The following translations give an account of what St. John's Hospital and St. James' Abbey possessed in Milton:

The Hospital of St. John in Northampton.
Richard Birdsall, Master.

Annual value of rents and woods in divers towns and hamlets in Northamptonshire.

	£.	s.	d.
Milton	—	xxij	—
Deduct rents paid to the King and divers other persons, viz. The heirs of Walter Mauntell for land in Milton	—	iiij	—

The Abbey of St. James, near Northampton.
John Basset, Abbot.

	£	s.	d.
Colingtre	—	xvij	—
Milton	—	xlj	iiij

It is interesting to note that some two centuries before, this property had been given to the abbey by the powerful Malesoure family, who were lords of the manor.

The account for Milton is translated as follows :

MIDDELTON ALIAS MILTON, RECTORY.
EDWARD WIGAN, DOCTOR, RECTOR AND INCUMBENT THERE.

	£	s.	d.
Value in tithes and offerings, annually		xvij	vj	iij
Thence in synodals and procurations paid to the Archdeacon of Northampton, annually			x	vj
And there remains .		xvj	xv	ix
Thence for tenths .			xxxiij	vij

So we see that in 1535 the net value of the living of Milton was £15 2s. 2d. per annum, after 10s. 6d. was paid for Procurations and 33s. 7d. for tenths each year. In 1254 it was valued at six marks and a half. The procurations and tenths are still paid by the rector to the Archdeacon and Queen Anne's Bounty respectively, and the First-fruits are duly forfeited by each new rector.

Procurations represent the ancient liability of incumbents to provide hospitality on the visitation of the Archdeacon and his retinue to the church. In course of time, a fixed money payment was charged on the benefice in place of the original indefinite liability.

A few years later, 1539, saw the dissolution of the monasteries, and the lands at Milton belonging to the Abbey of St. James were confiscated to the King. A Latin charter by which Queen Elizabeth makes a grant of these lands, called the " Prior's London," or Prior's Lands, is

OUR CHURCH'S STORY

preserved in the British Museum, and a translation will be found on page 286. St. John's Hospital did not lose its lands, but retained possession of Mortimers until it was sold to the Montgomery family some few years ago.

There is a mystery with regard to monastic lands in Milton. The Abbey of Peterborough was of course involved in the general confiscation and its lands disposed of. Now the *Valor Ecclesiasticus,* in its list of the property of Peterborough Monastery, does not mention any revenue of any sort derived from Milton. However, in the parish chest are receipts which go to show that in the reign of King Charles II the churchwardens of Milton paid rent for the occupation of land situated in the parish and which formerly belonged to Peterborough Monastery. The receipts are seven in number, for the years 1661 to 1667 inclusive, the first being reproduced here in full.

Certain lands bying in Milton.
{ —Received the 2nd. day of October Anno Dom. 1661 Annoque Regni domini nostri Caroli, Regis Angliae, &c. decimo tertio of John Manas & Edward Parker for Rent, due to the King's Majesty, for the year, ended at the feast of St. Michael th' Archangel last past, the sum of 5lb.   05. 0. 0.
  per me John Ellis, D. Receptor.

The Latin portion of the receipt refers to the date and means " In the year of our Lord 1661 and in the thirteenth year of the reign of our sovereign lord Charles, King of England, &c."

" D. Receptor " at the end stands for Deputy Collector.

What is striking about these receipts is the marginal note on each made by the clerk. The first, as above, simply refers to certain lands at Milton. The others are given herewith :

    1662. P'r —— in Collingtree & Milton p'r cell de Peterbor monaster.
    1663. For rent or Xths (tenths) for ye Manor of Collingtree and Milton.
    1664. For rent or Xths. of lands in Collingtree and Milton.
    1665. Peterborowe, for Xths in Collingtree and Milton.
    1666. Peterbor Monaster for rents in Collingtree and Milton.
    1667. Peterburgh Monaster for rents in Collingtree and Milton.

All the above are receipts for £5 except that for 1666, which is for £10. Four of the seven refer to the property belonging to the great Abbey of Peterborough, but an exhaustive inquiry has failed to show that Peterborough had any possessions here. It may be contended that the marginal notes were written by a careless clerk and that the lands should have been described as formerly belonging to the Abbey of St. James. This, however, is not very probable, as those lands had been granted to others, and, besides, there were men then living who must have heard from their grandparents what properties the different abbeys held in the parish.

    Much of the monastic land throughout

England was given away to his courtiers, but some of it Henry devoted to good uses, one of which was the founding of the Regius Professorship of Divinity in the Universities of Oxford and Cambridge. Who was to be the first Regius Professor at Cambridge? Henry had his man in view. This was Eudo Wygan, sometimes called Edward Wigan, by which name he is recorded in the *Valor Ecclesiasticus*. He graduated B.A. at Cambridge in 1508/9, M.A. in 1514, B.D. in 1521 and proceeded to D.D. in 1524, being then sub-dean of the Chapel of Cardinal Wolsey. He had evidently been of great service to the King at the University of Cambridge by strongly supporting the cause of his divorce from Katharine of Arragon. In 1526 Henry VIII appointed him to the Rectory of Milton, the living being then in his gift. When the Regius Professorship was endowed at Cambridge, the Royal messenger arrived at the little rectory of Milton in 1540 with a letter from the King, inviting Dr. Wigan to be the first to hold the post. This was accepted, but the learned professor continued to be Rector of Milton for another five years, being assisted by his curate, Dom. John Carter. Dr. Wigan resigned the rectory in 1545, but held the professorship until his death, which occurred in or about the year 1550.

King Henry then turned his attention to a pressing need in the Church, which was the creating of new dioceses. While the majority of the great monasteries, through being totally deprived of their revenues, were brought to an end and fell into ruin, the noble monastic church of Peterborough was spared the general fate by virtue of its being the burial-place of Queen Katharine of Arragon, and entered upon a new phase as a cathedral. So in 1541 Milton, with the rest of Northamptonshire, severed its connection with the ancient and vast Diocese of Lincoln, now to form part of the new Diocese of Peterborough. Formerly, people left money or other gifts by will to Lincoln Cathedral, the " mother church " of the diocese, as we see from the will of Thomas Rage in 1523 :

" I bequeath to the mother yn Lyncoln iiijs."

After Peterborough Abbey Church was made a cathedral in 1541, we find that Alice Campyan, of Milton, on September 18th, 1546, made the following bequest :

" I give and bequeath unto ye mother church off Pet'brough ijd."

Other Milton people made bequests to the new cathedral, and things seemed to go on much in the same way. Changes there were, it is true. The Litany was said in English and the Bible had been translated, but the Mass was still said in Latin and votive lights were still burning before the images of the saints. The authority of the Pope had been shaken off and the new diocese had been carved out of the old, but otherwise there was little to warn the people of Milton of the tremendous upheaval that was to take place in the near future.

CHAPTER VI

OUR CHURCH'S STORY—FROM THE REFORMATION TO THE PRESENT TIME

KING HENRY VIII died on January 28th, 1547, and was succeeded by his young son, Edward VI. He was only ten years of age when he came to the throne, so his uncle the Earl of Hertford became Protector, with the rank of Duke of Somerset, and governed in his Royal nephew's name.

In 1549 was published what is commonly known as the "First Prayer Book of Edward VI," by which the services were to be rendered in English. Then in 1550 a Commission was appointed to visit each parish and make an inventory of the church goods. This was followed by a second Commission in 1552 which was more thorough in its work. The inventories were made and most of them still exist, being preserved in the Public Record Office. Unfortunately some of the returns are missing and it is much to be deplored that the inventory of Milton Church is amongst the number, so that we cannot now tell what altar vessels, vestments and other church ornaments and furniture were used here.

A great change occurred in the parish churches, for the work of the Commissioners was complete and drastic. The stone altars were demolished and the mensa, or top slab, of each was placed in the floor of the church or porch to form part of the pavement to be trodden on and so desecrated. One such slab marked with crosses may be seen in the floor near the south chapel in a neighbouring church. The images of the saints were broken up and, with the various stands for lights, were thrown out of the church. From our two Rood-screens were hurled down the Crucifix that stood on each, and as the lights of beautiful coloured glass in the " storied windows " depicted some episode in the lives of the saints, they were regarded as objects of superstition and so were smashed to atoms. Much other deplorable damage was committed and Milton Church must have suffered badly.

It was a time of great distress amongst the poor, for the old order of things was passing. A law to suppress chantries, obits and so forth had been passed in the reign of Henry VIII, but so far it had not been acted upon, or if at all, very indifferently. However, this Act was rigorously enforced by the Duke of Somerset. The yearly rents from the endowments of the chantries and obits, part of which went towards the relief of the poor, were confiscated and devoted to other uses. We have seen on page 70 how the obits of Lawrence Davy and others were included in the King's list. It is probably for the house or land bequeathed to Milton Church for an obit and valued at four shillings and three pence annually that a quit rent was paid by the churchwardens of Milton

OUR CHURCH'S STORY 93

to the King. Receipts still extant in the Parish Chest for the years 1652 to 1656 and 1660 to 1667 show that the churchwardens paid a rent of four shillings a year for what is variously described in the marginal notes as " Chantry Lands," " The Chantry House " and the " Town House in Milton." From 1660 to 1667 it was paid to King Charles II, but in 1800 it was paid under the name of a Fee Farm Rent to Lord Fitzwilliam and from 1814 onwards to the Earl of Pembroke. The last payment was made by the church-wardens in December, 1896, after which they refused to pay it any more, as nobody seemed to know what the rent was for.

Such was the fate of lands and houses left to the Church for religious purposes, and not only was the Church deprived of this income, but the poor were robbed of their share as well. So in the reign of Edward VI an Act was passed by Parliament (5 Edward VI, Cap. 2) for the collection of alms for the poor in every parish. The contributions were nominally voluntary, but payment might be enforced by the reproofs of the clergy, the censures of the Church and by punishment at the discretion of the bishops. It is interesting to note that Milton was well in advance of this Act. A poor box was set up in Milton Church for this purpose which was supported not only by the alms of the living but by the legacies of the dead. In the Will of Agnes Billing of Milton, October 2nd, 1547, a bequest is made as follows :

" Item. I bequethe to ye poore men's chyst iiijd."

And again, among many others, Robert Dunckly, on August 16th, 1559, directs thus:

"I also bequethe to the poore men's box of ye churche of Milton iiijs iiijd."

When Queen Mary succeeded her brother Edward in 1553, an attempt was made to restore the old religious practices. The living of Milton was in her gift and she presented it to John Roote, who was inducted on October 27th, 1553. He seems to have been by no means a supporter of the Reformation, and so we come across a hint of restorations in Milton Church. He certainly had the Rood with statues of St. Mary and St. John, replaced in their original positions on one of the screens, for we find bequests made in the old manner. William Mole of Milton, on March 8th, 1556, states in his Will:

"Item, I give unto the Rood lyght a stryke of barley."

We have something similar in the Will of Thomas Malshare of Mydelton, May 21st, 1557. This name is of interest, as he was probably a humble descendant of the great lords of Milton. His Will runs:

"Item, I geve to the rod lighte for wast and ware (waste and wear) at my buriall iijs."

So the people of Milton evidently reverted to the old ways under the ministrations of their Rector, John Roote, who said the services in Latin as before, until some time in the reign of Queen Elizabeth. Then in 1571, as he still refused to conform to the authorised usage, he became what was called a Recusant and was deprived of his benefice. Other people of Milton suffered pains and penalties for adhering to the old rites and ceremonies.

Up to this time, the Probate Office is one of the few sources of information respecting the people of Milton, but now something of great interest and importance appears. That is, the Parish Church Register.

It was Thomas Cromwell, Vicar-General in the reign of Henry VIII, who saw the importance of such an official record being kept and, in 1538, he issued the first mandate for keeping registers of baptisms, marriages and burials in each parish. As there are very few registers that go back to such an early date, it would seem that not many saw fit to comply with the order. The mandate was repeated in more rigorous terms in 1558 when Elizabeth came to the throne. This again was not generally obeyed, so it was ordered in 1597 that a register of parchment should be provided at the expense of each parish, and in it should be transcribed all the names from the older books, which were mostly of paper, from the year 1558. John Roote was Rector of Milton on the accession of Elizabeth, and he must have obediently begun his registers in 1558. Then when the order came in 1597 that the names in the old paper books should be transcribed in new ones of parchment, we find them in our register copied out for the forty years in the neat handwriting of the curate, " Thomas Mayo, Mynister there."

Unfortunately the top right-hand corners of

the first six sheets were destroyed by fire at some date after the year 1741. The heading runs as follows, the words in brackets being those that I have supplied in the burnt portion :

> " The Register (Book)
> of the parishe Church of (Milton alias)
> Myddleton Malsor, con(taining the)
> names and surnames of a(ll who have)
> byne baptized, married (and buried)
> wthin the sayd parishe from (the viith)
> daie of August, in the ffirst year (of the)
> Raigne of our most gracious Soūaigne Ladie
> Queene Elizabeth yt nowe is. Ao Dni 1558.
> Recorded By Thomas Mayo. Mynister there."

The work of transcribing was evidently finished in 1598, because up to that date for sixty-five pages the entries for each year are tabulated under the different headings of baptisms, marriages and burials. From March 25th, 1599, the events are chronicled as they occurred.

An entry in the old register about this time (1611) deserves notice.

" Robert Heward was married to Dorothy Willet the xxvjth day of March. Licentiā obtent."

The two Latin words at the end mean that they obtained a Licence, and a search in the Bishop's Book of Licences at Peterborough shows us how very stringent the proceedings were in order to obtain a Marriage Licence. The entry runs :

" 1611. xxvth of March at Milton. Robert Heward of Milton at own disposal, 50, and Dorothy Willet of Milton, widow. Samuel

MILTON CHURCH, INTERIOR.

Photo, J. L. Hopkins, Esq.

Greenough attests. Bondsmen, Samuel Greenough and John Denton of Milton."

From the Wills in the Probate Office we have a hint that by this time the church was in bad repair, probably suffering from the excesses committed during the Reformation, for we find that on April 10th, 1610, John Stephenson of Milton in his Will directs :

" Item. I give towards the repare of the churche chansey (i.e. chancel) xijd to be paid to the Churche Wardens at such tyme as the said chansey shall be amended."

During the Commonwealth an Act of Parliament was passed which placed the parish registers in the custody of laymen. Accordingly, in the year 1653, we find the following note entered in the old register :

" Edward Parker of Milton in the County of Northampton was according to the Act of Parliament in that case provided elected and chosen by the maior part of the parishioners of Milton aforesaid in the County aforesaid to be parish Register there, who according to the said Act tooke his Corporall Oath the 22th October in the yeare of our Lord 1653 before mee William Ward."

This William Ward was a magistrate of Northampton. The registers were in lay hands until November, 1660, after the restoration of the monarchy, when they came once more into the Rector's keeping. A curious, smudged scrawl at the close of the entries for 1655 arouses curiosity. The word KING can plainly be discerned through the smudge in big Roman characters, written at least twice. As the register was then in the hands of one appointed by the magistrate, we wonder whether it was some loyal member of his family who wrote KING in such bold letters to the consternation of Mr. Edward Parker, who came across it while the ink was still wet and smudged it over. Mr. Edward Parker, here mentioned, afterwards became churchwarden.

In the same year we have an instance of a " Brief." The rubric after the Nicene Creed tells us that at that point in the Holy Communion Service, " Briefs, Citations and Excommunications " shall be read. A Brief must have been issued by Oliver Cromwell in 1665, which was duly read in Milton Church, asking for collections, and the following is the receipt :

" The XVIth. day of July 1655.

Received then of ffrancis Atterbury, Minister, John Woodwerts and John Palmer, Churchwardens of the parish of Milton in North'tonshire ye sume of ffifty ffower shillings and seaven pence, being so much by them collected for the relief of the poor Protestants within the Dominions of the Duke of Savoy, according to a Declaration and Instructions from his Highness the Lord Protector, of the 25th of May last. We say Received

    Chas. Packe, Milles
    Tho. Vyner Treasurers. Liiijs vijd."

Oliver Cromwell was made Lord Protector, December, 1653, and was succeeded by his son Richard, September 3rd, 1658.

From the following document we see that the

election of churchwardens during the Commonwealth had to be approved and confirmed by the magistrates.

"North.ss. We whose names are subscribed, Justices of Peace within this County of Northampton, doe approve and allow of Rogger Seabrooke and Thomas Palmer of Milltone in the said County to be new Church-wardens for the said Parish, for the space of one yeare next ensuing the date hereof, According to the Ordinance of Parliament in that case made and provided. In witness whereof, We have hereunto set our hands and seales the 4th day of Aprill 1656.
William Ward   George Benson."

The following note is at the foot of the document : " the ould ones are to paye to the newe ones the sume of £3-6s-9d."

The year 1660 saw the restoration of the Monarchy, when the "Merry Monarch," Charles II, entered London on May 29th. An erroneous idea of life in those days would tempt us to think that ordinary people paid little heed to the rules of the Church with regard to fasting and days of abstinence. However, the Book of Licenses of the Bishop of Peterborough gives us light on the subject in the form of a dispensation :

" 1662/3. Feb. 25th. License to Mrs. Dorothy Dove, widow, to eat flesh, together with her family, in Lent, *proviso id sobrie et tecte faciat ad evitand' scandalum.*" (i.e. " on condition that she does it moderately and discreetly to avoid giving offence.")

From this date very little is known of the church for more than a century. The bells were recast in 1686, as we know by the inscription on them. Then in the year 1779 came the Enclosure Commission. Up to that time the Rector derived his income not only from the Glebe lands, some of which had belonged to the Rectory since 1366 and earlier, but also from the greater and lesser tithes. In lieu of tithes, a small proportion of each commoner's grant of land was awarded to the Rector. Certain small tithes remained, amounting to 12s. 1d. a year, and Easter Dues, which consisted of 4d. from each householder, but if holding a pew in church then it was 1s. The ancient Mortuary Fee remained and was 10s.

The tithes and dues were to be paid in the church porch according to the Enclosure Award, and there is extant a notice by the Rev. John Castleton Miller, D.D., to the effect that the dues were to be paid there on August 13th, 1827. The church porch was in ancient times the scene of many public transactions, and even as recently as 1821 a public auction was held there, as the following Vestry Minutes show :

1821. Thursday, March 29th. At a public Vestry : " Agreed at the same that the Church and Poors Land should be let by auction at the Church, on Monday next for one year."

1821. Monday, April 2nd. " Agreeably to proposals at the Vestry the 29th March, The Church and Poors Land was Lett at the Church."

No irreverence or disrespect was meant by this, of course, as it was merely a survival of what was once customary. Indeed, the disunion of the purely secular from the religious is even now by no means complete, for in the church porch may still be seen, nailed upon a board, notices of rates and other mundane affairs.

The Mortuary Fee that has been mentioned was a survival from Pre-Reformation days, and was once an excuse for unreasonable extortion by the parish priests. It was not a burial fee, but was a payment demanded at the death of any person, as compensation for any church dues he probably had forgotten and left unpaid during his lifetime. Formerly, it was the custom to pay to the Rector as a Mortuary Fee the second best animal owned by the dead person, the best being reserved for the lord of the manor as heriot. If there was no beast, then the second best garment was claimed as Mortuary.

The taking of Mortuaries by Rectors was much restricted by an Act (21 Henry VIII), which ordered that payment was to be taken in money at a fixed rate. The highest sum that could be charged was ten shillings, but even that could not be demanded unless the deceased had left goods to the value of forty pounds.

We find this fee mentioned in early Wills.

Jayne Garnett, 1532: "Item, I give and bequeathe for my mortuary all ye law will."

Agnes Cooper, 1572: "And for my mortuarie that right ys."

Occasionally an entry occurs in the registers when the mortuary fee happened to be paid:

1746. "Henry Watts was Buried January 11 —for w'm I recd. a mortuary 10s."

1770. " Received 10 sh. of Francis Evans of Collingtree, being a Mortuary due on the death of his mother. June ye 26th. 1770."

1806. " Thomas Gleed—mortuary 6s : 8d.—non parishioner. April 27th."

A Terrier of property and dues claimed by the Rector of Milton, dated 1739, gives the following as the Mortuary Fee :

" A Mortuary is ten shillings paid for one that dies possess'd of a personal estate of forty pounds and upwards, and a noble for one that dies possess'd of a personal estate of thirty pounds but under forty pounds, ten groats for one that dies possess'd of a personal estate of twenty pounds and under thirty pounds."

A Terrier was compiled by the Rev. T. A. Kershaw in 1855, and in this the Mortuary Fee is stated to be 10s., but it has not been demanded for a great many years. This fee and the few Rectorial tithes, as well as the Easter Dues, have been swallowed up in oblivion. In ancient days the payment of tithes was regarded as a strict duty, so much so that people on their deathbed were fearful as to the consequences of any omission of such payments, whether through forgetfulness or other cause, and endeavoured to make reparation. So we find such expressions in the Wills of Milton people, the phrase being frequently in Latin, " *pro decimis oblitis* "—" for tithes forgotten."

Lawrence Davy, 1526 : " Item to the high altare in mydelton for my thithes forgotten and not dewly . . ."

John Lawrence, 1530 : " Item I bequethe to

the hie aulter a stryke of barley pro decimis oblitis."

William Garnett, 1531: "Item to the hie aulter of myddilton pro decimis oblit's vjd."

John Bugg, "of Melton," July 23rd 1547: "I bequethe to the blessyd sacrament of mylton alijs Medyltō pro decimis oblit's viijd or ells a stryke of wayt (wheat)."

As a strike was a measure of two bushels, we may safely conclude from the above bequest that the price of wheat was fourpence per bushel in 1547.

A glance at the ancient tithes due to the Rector (see page 294) will show there was some excuse if any had been forgotten or overlooked. Those days are long past, but we find both tithes and other dues to the Rector perpetuated in the Enclosure Award.

Some few years after the enclosure of the Commons, a note was written on the fly-leaf of Register No. 3 by Wm. Walmsley, M.A., who was curate here and took a delight, good man that he was, in chronicling various items of interest. The note says:

"During the summer of 1796 the chancel was new leaded and the Church white washed and ornamented at the same time."

So another coat of whitewash was laid over previous ones that had obliterated the ancient paintings with which the walls were adorned.

Early in the last century extensive alterations were made in the furnishing of the church. A new pulpit was bought in 1809, and about the same time a gallery was erected, as is shown by the Churchwardens' Accounts, between the north and south pillars at the west end :

"1817, Octr. 4. Settled with Richard Froane the money he laid down when the Galiary was bilt & other bills he Paid . . . £28–12–0."

This gallery did not extend over the aisles, but across the nave only, and was reached by a staircase behind the font. A new weathercock was put up in 1820 and the church was entirely reseated about 1824, the pews being painted and numbered. Then in 1826 the parishioners thought it would be a good thing to have the pillars brightened up, so they were " coloured a stone colour and the ceilings white washed." I presume the ceilings were those of the aisles.

Up in the newly erected gallery sat the musicians and the choir, and underneath, in a smaller gallery on the nave floor, sat the children.

A few words may be said here about the instrumental music in the church. Our first record is in the Churchwardens' Accounts :

"1813, Sept. 16th. Pd for green bag for the bas viol 7/–."

Then we read in the Vestry Minutes for January 30th, 1828 :

"Mrs. Frone to be paid for a Violincello (purchased by her late uncle) by the Churchwardens."

There were violins also.

"1823. Sep. 6th. Pd Mr. Crosby for set of best strings for a violin, 4/6."

In 1852 a small organ was introduced to swell the harmony. Probably this was a harmonium, and we find that the organist was paid five shillings per year:

" 1852, April 6th. Richard Robinson for Playing the Organ, 5/–."

The tuning of the organ was an expensive item, for in 1852 sums of £1 5s. and 10s. were paid for this purpose. Having seen what could be done with a small organ, the authorities in 1866 purchased a larger one from London, which cost £54 14s. The blower was paid 10s. a year, but the organist seems to have given his services voluntarily.

Old Mr. Wm. Oxley, who died in 1923, aged eighty-five, gave me the names of some of the musicians who played in the church gallery when he was a boy.

His uncle, Wm. Oxley, played the Bugle.
His father, Ben Oxley, played the Flute or Flageolette.
His uncle, Joseph Twiselton (father of Reuben Twiselton), played the Big Drum.
Henry Palmer played the Clarionet.
John Pell played the Serpent.
A man from Wootton played the Trombone.
Thomas Caswell, uncle of William Caswell, played the Bass Viol.
Wm. Dunkley played the small organ.

In addition there were violins, as we know from the entries relating to purchase of strings, but Mr. Oxley did not remember any more names.

The Psalms could not be accompanied in their Psalter form by the band, so Tate and Brady's paraphrase must have been used, in which the words are written in four-line verses like hymns. Thus we find, probably for the use of the band, this entry with its old-world atmosphere :

" 1825. July 2nd. Six extracts of the Psalms for the Church 10/-."

During those days there was a custom in church that seems strange in our eyes. When the hymns and Psalms were sung, the congregation stood and turned facing the gallery at the west where the choir and band were.

An interesting record occurs in 1814, when the churchwardens paid £1 7s. 9d. to James Johnson " for lathing the gallery and putting a new window in the church." I am inclined to think that at this time the stone tracery of the wheel window in the present vestry had become so decayed that it had at last fallen to pieces. So, as the church officials were busy with the church furniture and had funds only sufficient to proceed with the new gallery and pews, they commissioned James Johnson to put in a temporary " churchwarden's window " of two lights. A " churchwarden's window " is probably so called because it is built with the limited funds for church expenses, and so is usually a cheap makeshift by no means remarkable for beauty of design. At all events, a picture of the church now in the possession of Mr. J. C. Emery shows the east end as it was about 1850 with only one wheel window—that in the south aisle. In the north aisle is depicted a window of two lights. That this two-light window was a temporary substitute for a circular or wheel window that had perished is proved by a Parish Vestry minute. In 1856 or 1857 the wheel window was restored, and on April 13th, 1857, being Easter Monday, it was resolved " that the best thanks of this vestry on behalf of the parish of Milton be tendered to Wm. Montgomery, Esq., for the handsome and liberal manner in which he has at his own expense restored the Wheel Window at the east end of the north aisle in the parish Church."

During the centuries that had passed since the church was first built, there was the significant alteration in the level of the churchyard. After some thousands of interments, the ground had gradually risen until it was at last as high as the church window-sills. Representations were made to the Rector, in 1820, that this was detrimental to the fabric, so the Vestry ordered that the earth should be removed to a width of four feet from the church walls and carted away. About the same time the churchyard was drained.

Here may well be mentioned an ancient superstition regarding the choice of a position for a grave. In olden days, people had an idea that the devil lurked in the churchyard to the north of the church. This belief may have arisen from the fact that when, in certain services, the evil spirit was exorcised, the north door was opened to drive him forth. That particular door thus gained the unenviable title of the " Devil's Door " and was seldom used. Indeed, to this day, in almost every ancient church, the principal door will be found in the south wall, or sometimes the west, very rarely in the north wall. Prompted by the same idea, the people said that the reason why the priest at Mass read the Holy Gospels with his face towards the north, was to show his defiance of the devil. Consequently, as may well be imagined, competition for the choice of burial sites to the north of the church was by no means keen. There are elderly people in Milton who can remember that there were very few graves on the north side of the churchyard up to 1860 or 1870, for even then people did not like that part. The south side was in olden days considered very much safer, being far enough away from the ill-omened portion of the churchyard. The most coveted spot was the south-east, or, failing that, due east of the church, so as to be close to the High Altar dedicated to the patron saint and therefore nearer her protection. Thus it happens that in Milton the level of the ground has been raised to a considerable height east and south-east of the churchyard, but towards the west it is lower, whilst to the north and north-west it actually slopes down from the church.

The next date we have to record is 1850. Presumably the font had by now got into a bad condition, for a Mr. Sealey was paid £5 5s. for restoring it.

An important event took place in 1863, when the Vestry authorised the churchwardens to purchase an eight-day clock, " only with two dials provided the consent of the owner of the orchard in Mr. Fisher's occupation be obtained as to the removal of two trees growing therein."

As the owner would not allow the trees to be removed, only one dial was obtained. The clock was purchased from Mr. Joyce, of Whitchurch, for £87, but the cost of erecting it came to £50 more. Soon after it was placed in position a boy named Will White climbed up to the clock face and fell to the ground. He escaped marvellously with only a broken leg, which became shortened so that he always used a patten afterwards.

Some particulars as to the clock may prove interesting. The diameter of the face is 4 ft. 6 ins., the minute hand is 2 ft. 3 ins. long, and the weight weighs 250 lbs. It was overhauled in 1891, when the hands and figures were re-gilded.

In 1870 we find this resolution of the Easter Vestry, "that the offer of the Rev. Robert Montgomery to glaze the two wheel windows with stained glass in Milton Church be accepted with many thanks for the same." However, the work was not then done, but was left for his relatives, Miss Montgomery and her sister Mrs. Watts-Manning, to do.

The year 1874 saw the beginning of the great work of restoring Milton Church. In June of that year a faculty was applied for to restore the chancel and the work was proceeded with. The Rector at that time was the late Rev. John Brown. There were some important alterations: the floor of the chancel was raised a step higher, additional light, which must have been badly needed, was provided by a new large window on the south side, and a new pulpit with base and steps of Caen stone was fixed at the chancel steps. The old Jacobean altar rails, which were probably in very bad repair, had to be discarded, unfortunately, and eventually found their way to a house in Gayton.

The Rev. John Brown, to whose energy the preservation of our church is undoubtedly due, did not rest here. Having put the chancel in order at his own expense, he now turned his attention to the rest of the building. The same year, the late Mr. E. Law, architect, was called in to report on the state of the fabric of the nave and tower. He found the structure in a very bad condition. The clerestory windows of the nave were in a very dilapidated state, with " vile and badly constructed wood windows " on the south side. He found the tower out of the upright, leaning seven and a half inches towards the west, but as the spire did not incline to anything like the same extent he thought the inclination of the tower might be partly owing to faulty construction when first erected. This conclusion was confirmed to a certain extent " by the dipping of the courses of the walling stone and the inclination of the string courses, which do not tally one with the other, and some of which it is clear never were placed in a perfectly horizontal position." He considered that the inclination of the tower was partly due to its being built upon a clay foundation and on the side of a hill. After severe drought, the clay would contract and so cause a movement. However, he reported, " inasmuch as the tower having been originally erected with battered or tapered walls the settlement has not at present scarcely brought the upper face of the structure beyond a perpendicular line, so that in fact, even now, after the lapse of ages, it scarcely overhangs the base."

In the summer of 1876, encouraged by the amount of subscriptions received, the work was taken in hand. The church was put into thorough repair : the porch was entirely rebuilt, the inside arch of the north door was raised, an extra clerestory window was inserted and the wall of the north aisle was raised to suit the arcade. The whole cost £2,154 17s. During the restoration, the services were held at the school, whither the organ had been transferred. On July 12th, 1877, the church was reopened.

In 1891 the Rev. A. W. Gross, Rector, who was a keen musician, generously presented to the church the organ now in use, and in 1894 he raised the sum of £200 to provide the stained glass for the great east window, the subject being the Crucifixion. This was dedicated on Thursday, December 16th of that year. A few months afterwards, Miss Montgomery and her sister, Mrs. Watts-Manning, filled the wheel window in the south aisle chapel with stained glass, and in 1901 the wheel window in the north aisle was filled with stained glass at Miss Montgomery's expense.

We have now reached the present century in the story of our church. Two things remain to be chronicled that were brought about by my immediate predecessor, the Rev. A. C. Neely, now an Honorary Canon of Peterborough. First, the restoring of St. Catherine's Chapel to its original purpose, the faculty for which was applied for in 1909, and, secondly, the extension of the churchyard by the addition of the Hempland, the odd piece of glebe, in 1916.

The writer gratefully records the gift of the oak War Shrine in 1917 by Mrs. C. T. Craig, then of Milton Manor, and of an oak Litany Desk and a Credence Table in 1918 by H. B. Ermen, Esq., formerly of the Grange, in memory of his wife.

Some features of the church not already mentioned deserve notice. The length of the aisle walls is 63 ft. 8 ins.; the breadth of nave and aisles is 52 ft. 9 ins. The length of the chancel is 32 ft. 6 ins., its breadth 15 ft. 6 ins., and it projects 21 ft. 6 ins. into the nave. The church will seat about 450.

The big east window consists of five trefoil-headed lights with reticulated tracery forming quatrefoils. The west window of each aisle is of three lancet lights within a pointed arch. Externally they are surmounted by a dripstone terminating in small heads. At the east end of north and south aisles is a circular window in a square frame, already noticed. In the south wall are two good decorated windows of two trefoil-headed lights with a quatrefoil above, and in the south wall of the south chapel is a window of three cinquefoiled lancet lights. The north chapel, now used as a vestry, has in the north wall a window of three trefoil-headed lights with tracery of three quatrefoils above. In the wall of the north aisle, close to the vestry screen, is a small low-side window, explained elsewhere, filled in with decorated tracery and glazed. In

JAMES HARRINGTON.

From a Print in the British Museum, engraved by M. Van der Gucht
after a painting by Sir Peter Lely.

OUR CHURCH'S STORY

the same wall are three windows of the Perpendicular Period, each of two trefoil-headed lights. These are square-headed without but arched within. The chancel has three clerestory windows on either side, quatrefoil in shape, and the nave has four trefoil windows in its clerestory on the south.

There are three piscinæ in the church. The largest is in the old Lady Chapel, now the vestry, and has a trefoiled arch and plain circular basin. That in St. Catherine's Chapel in the south aisle has a lancet arch, cinquefoiled within and a plain circular basin. In the south wall of the chancel the piscina has a semicircular arch with a swelled chamfer, and trefoiled within. It has a large projecting, circular basin, but the wall-shaft, through which the drain was pierced, has disappeared. In the north wall of the chancel is an aumbry with a pointed arch.

The tower is at the west end, surmounted by an octagon terminating in a low, crocketed spire. There is a pinnacle at each corner of the tower.

For use at the Holy Communion service the church possesses some valuable plate. This comprises an Elizabethan communion " cup," a silver paten with foot, a silver flagon and a silver-plated alms-dish.

Major C. A. Markham, F.S.A., thus describes the cup in his book on the church plate of Northamptonshire :

" This cup has a conical bowl with slightly hollowed sides ; round the upper part is the usual strap ornament, enclosing foliage and crossing four times by hour-glass curves. The stem is evenly balanced, with circular knop on flat fillet; it is connected with the bowl and foot by horizontal mouldings. The foot is domed, on flange, which is ornamented with the egg-and-tongue pattern. Weight 6:9. Height 5⅝. Diam. of bowl 3¾, of foot 3. Date 1570 (Elizabeth). Hall marks: (1) Small black-letter N. (2) Leopard's head crowned. (3) Lion passant. (4) Fleur-de-lys, without shield.

Silver Paten.—Weight 10:4. Diam. 7¼. Diam. of foot 3¼. Height 2¼. Date 1700 (William III). Hall Marks: (1) Court hand E. (2) Lion's head erased. (3) Britannia. (4) H O, with pellet above and below, in ellipse. This paten is plain.

Silver Flagon.—Weight 32:9. Height 12. Diam. of centre 5. Date 1772 (George III). Hall marks: (1) Capital black-letter R. (2) Leopard's head crowned. (3) Lion passant. (4) C W in oblong—Charles Wright, Ave Maria Lane. This was evidently a jug made for domestic purposes. Round the spout is bead moulding, the lid has a knob at the top, the neck is fluted, round the body are festoons of flowers which are repeated round the foot, the lower part of the body has upright leaves. The whole is much ornamented."

Since the above was written, Mrs. C. T. Craig presented the church with a beautiful silver cup, embossed with flowers and foliage, the bottom part of bowl and stem being fluted. Height 6⅝, diam. of bowl 4, of foot 3⅝. Date 1810. Hall marks: (1) A.F. in oblong, (2) lion passant, (3) leopard's head crowned, (4) capital Roman letter P, (5) duty mark, King's head. Weight 9 ounces.

William Taylor, the master of Heyford Grammar School, gives us the following information about the plate in his notes about Milton Church:

" Mrs. Elizabeth Watts, born in this Town, gave a Silver Plate for the Bread, and a silver Cup for the Wine Came at ye same time by her Orders, to be used at ye Celebrating the H : Communion."

Mrs. Elizabeth Watts was buried February 1st, 1657.

In a Memorandum of Requisitions for Milton Church passed at a Vestry Meeting on November 9th, 1826, it was ordered that a " Chalice for Sacramental Wine " be procured, the estimated cost being £20. There is no record in the accounts that this was done. It is evident there were two chalices and one got lost about this time, which explains the vacant space in the communion plate box.

In the chancel are the graves of many rectors, while in the nave and aisles lie buried many of the Dry and Samwell families. There are a few mural tablets, one being of more than ordinary interest.

North wall, vestry :

Near this place are deposited the remains of the Rev. Francis Montgomery, Rector of Harlestone, in this County ; who departed this life Jan. 4th 1831, in the 76th. year of his age.
Also
Mary, his wife, who departed this life Oct. 30th. 1840, Age 71.

The Rev. Francis Montgomery for many years was Curate of Milton until his death, and seems to have been in charge of the parish for some years during the absence of the Rector.

In remembrance of Louisa Montgomery, daughter of the late Revd. Francis Montgomery and Mary his wife, who departed this life 24th March 1853, aged 58.
   The Christian when life's trials close
   Sleeps in refreshing calm repose.

Here under lyeth the body of William Dry, Yeoman, who was Lord of a Manor in this towne called Mantell's Manor, who married Ursula one of the daughters of Will. Tibbes of Bugbrooke, by whom he had issue eight sonnes and two daughters. He deceased the twenty third of Sept. Anno Dom. 1637.

In the floor below is a rhyming inscription :

    HERE LYETH INTERRED
    IN THIS TOMBE THE BODY
    OF ONE WILLIAM DRY WHO
    LED HIS LIFE TO GAINE A ROOME
    IN HEAVEN TO ALL ETERNITY.
          1678.

North aisle wall :

Sacred to the memory of John Cooper, Quarter Master Sergeant of the Northamptonshire Militia and for many years School master & Churchwarden in this parish. He died on the 2nd. day of Feb. 1831, much lamented & universally respected.
   Also Hannah his wife who died on the 18th. day of Feb. 1834 in her 62nd. year.

In memory of Frederick Norton Manning M.D. eldest son of John & Eliza Manning of Milton Ham who died at Sydney, June 18th. 1903 aged

64, & was buried as he wished in the burial ground adjacent to the Gladesville Hospital where he had lived many years. He held for some years the appointment of Inspector General of the insane for the colony of New South Wales, and under his able guidance the lunacy department was raised to a high state of efficiency. He was beloved by all who knew him.

This tablet is erected by his brothers and sisters.

The Manning family is an old one, a " John Manning, Yeoman," being here in 1698.

On the north wall of the chancel :

Sacred to the memory of John Castleton Miller, D.D. of Queen's College in the University of Cambridge and Rector of this parish. Born March 14th. 1775. Died Aug. 18th. 1828.

Also Sarah A. Wooldridge, widow, sister of the above, who died 25th Oct. 1855. Aged 73.

Mary, the beloved wife of Thomas Atherton Kershaw M.A. Rector of this parish. Died 17th. May 1854 aged 29 years.

On the south wall of the chancel :

> HERE VNDER LIETH THE
> BODIE OF DAME IANE,
> DAVGHTER OF Sr WILLIAM
> SAMWELL KNIGHT, & LATE
> WIFE TO Sr SAPCOATES
> HARINGTON OF MILTON
> KNIGHT, BY WHOM HE HAD
> ISSVE 2 SONNS & 3 DAVGH
> TERS (VZ) IAMES, WILLIAM,
> IANE, ANN, & ELIZABETH, wch
> LADIE DIED MARCH 30 1619.

For an account of James Harrington, whose name is on this tablet, see page 45.

On the north wall of the chapel :

Memoriae sacrum
Richardi Dodwell, Armigeri, Filii natu maximi
Richardi Dodwell ex Agro Oxoniensi, Generosi,
Quem
Pater primae Eruditionis commodi non ignarus
Ad Scholam adhuc tenerum misit Etonensem
Eo Literarum rudimentis feliciter imbutum,
Linguarum praeter Aetatem avide peritum,
Nativi quasi soli amatorem
Oxonia cito recepit
Ad quam etiam et mores formari,
Et animum tutissime dirigi
Non vana sibi persuaserat,
Ubi & Londinensis Hospitii Curae
Tanta cum sagacitate legibus invigilavit
ut apud forum postea non immerito disertum
improviso litigantibus private judicem
Sese frequenter exhibuit
Vultus firmitate non indecora
Indefesso probitatis tenore
Inconcussa erga amicos fide
Innocua cum omnibus libertate
Per omnes vitae partes
Semper emicuit
Diuturna Phthisi tandem correptus
Obijt
Tertio Die Maij
Anno { Domini MDCCXXVI
{ Aetatis XXXVI

[Translation]

Sacred to the memory of Richard Dodwell, Esquire, eldest son of Richard Dodwell, of

Oxfordshire, gentleman, whom his father, mindful of the advantage of an early education, sent while still of tender age to Eton school. There happily instructed in the elements of Letters, eagerly expert beyond his years in languages, Oxford speedily received him, a lover of its soil as being his own, for not falsely had he persuaded himself that his character was trained and his mind directed most profitably in accordance with its standard, and there and at the Inns of Court in London he applied himself diligently with such shrewdness to the laws that afterwards at the Bar he often shewed himself deservedly an eloquent arbitrator in private suits when men were unexpectedly involved in litigation. His face was strong though not without charm. His honesty was ever unquestioned. His loyalty to his friends never failed. He was open in his dealings with all men and harmed none. In every stage of his life he always made his mark, but at last, overtaken by a consumption of long standing, he died on the third day of May in the year of our Lord 1726 and of his age 36.

His gravestone lies in front of the chapel screen.

On the Lectern :

Given by Thomas Herbert and Edwin Montague Kershaw in memory of their father the Revd. Thomas Atherton Kershaw. December 1874.

On the Litany Desk and the Credence Table :

To the Glory of God and in cherished memory of Gwladys Mary the dearly loved wife of Hugh B. Ermen, who fell asleep January 28th. 1917.

CHAPTER VII

THE RECTORS OF MILTON

FROM the ancient records of Acts of Institution in the Lincoln Registers, it appears that the churches and rectories of Milton and Collingtree were united and held in two moieties. This was probably due to the fact that Collingtree formed part of one of the Manors of Milton, and so the rectories would form two moieties of that manor. In very early times these two moieties were held by one rector, as is shown by the following extract from the Lincoln registers, of the sixth year of Robert Grostete (1241). This is the earliest record extant of an institution to these rectories.

COLYNTRE. Henricus de Wycheton, sub-diaconus, presentatus per Symonem de Pateshull ad medietates de Colyntre et de Middelton (etc.) in eas canonice rector institutus. Et mandatum (etc.).

The following is a translation :

COLYNTRE. Henry de Wycheton, sub-deacon, presented by Simon de Pateshull to the moieties of Collingtree and of Middleton (etc.) was canonically instituted rector therein. And it was ordered (etc.).

Owing to the difficulty of singling out any particular parish of Milton from the many others of the same name, some expedient had to be devised by which records of induction to the living would not give rise to any future question of identity. Therefore the two rectorial moieties of the manor were called by the name of Colyntre, a part of that manor, to obviate confusion with the twenty-five other Middletons and twenty Miltons in other parts of the country. So in ancient ecclesiastical documents we must look for Milton under the head of " Colyntre." In the Lambeth MSS. recording the case of the dispute between the Master of St. John's Hospital and the Rectors of Milton and Blisworth, the Rector of Milton, who at that time was John de Clopham, is called " John de Colyntre."

During the incumbency of this John de Clopham, a second rector seems to have been appointed, and from that time up to 1441, or a few years later, there were two rectors, though the rectories were still united. From 1464, the rectories and churches were separated and held by the various Rectors of Milton and Collingtree respectively.

The two benefices having been united for so long a time, the two rectors lived at Milton even after the separation of the parishes. The site of the ancient Rectory of Milton was in the garden behind the present post office, in a plot of ground called Anchor Close. Tradition says this old rectory was burnt down some time early in the last century. Not far away, on the other side of the road, there stands an ancient tenement known as Collingtree Rectory which, up to about thirty years ago, belonged to the Rectors of Collingtree, and here, it is said, they once resided. This tradition is supported by entries in the Milton church registers :

"1600/1. Gye Smyth the sonne of Mr. Willm. Smyth p'rson of Collingtre was bapt. the vjth. Daie of ffebruarie.

1600/1. Gye Smyth the sonne of Mr. Willm. Smyth p'rson of Collingtre was buried ye ixth. Daie of ffebruarie."

From these two entries of the baptism and early death of his son, it is evident that in those days the Rector of Collingtree lived in Milton. The infant being but weakly, it was too far to carry him from his home at Milton to his father's church at Collingtree for baptism. Three later entries up to December 28th, 1604, record the baptism in Milton Church of two other children of the same William Smyth and the burial of one, which affords sufficient proof, I think, that Collingtree Rectory was once in our village. Indeed, the path by which the Rectors of Collingtree made their way thither through the fields from their home in Milton, still exists as a right of way. A further explanation of this is given in the chapter on the parish. Owing to the two Manors of Milton, the parishes were intermixed.

In the entries above, William Smyth is correctly and legally described as "parson" of Collingtree, for he was Rector, and only rectors in Holy Orders are parsons. A vicar or curate is not, strictly speaking, a parson. This is a title of honour given to a rector because he was

"Collingtree Rectory," Milton.

the " persona," or principal personage in the ecclesiastical parish. A vicar could not be so described, for as a rule he was inducted in place of a rector who was unable to perform the religious duties himself, such as an abbot, who had his abbey to attend to.

Information as to the institution of the various rectors is gleaned from many sources, including the Lincoln Registers, the Lambeth Registers and finally the Peterborough Registers. A list of rectors so far as is at present known is given here.

	Date of Institution.	Patron.
A Priest (at Milton) in 1085.	*Doomsday Book.*	
To Both Moieties		
Henry de Wycheton, Sub-deacon.	1241.	Simon de Pateshull.
John de Harvey	1280.	
John de Clopham	Oct. 1291.	
John de Clopham was the Rector concerned in the dispute with the Master and Brethren of St. John's Hospital (see pages 83 and 293).		
Thomas de Maleshoures		
Henry de Cliffe, M.A.	June 18th. 1307.	Rex.
To the First Moiety only		
John de Hemyngbury, Deacon.	Nov. 23rd. 1308.	Rex.
Simon Est, Priest.	March 3rd. 1352.	Abbot & Convent of St. James, Northampton.
Will. de Depyng.		Rex.
Ric. Donne, Clerk.	Aug. 13th. 1361.	
Dom. Thos. Rage, Priest.	Feb. 18th. 1409/10.	
Dom. Joh. Ingrith, Priest.	April 21st. 1411	
Henry Hanslop.		Thos. Wake.
Joh. Tewe, Priest.	March 2nd, 1428/9.	Rex.

THE RECTORS OF MILTON

Name	Date	Patron
Ric. Bate, Priest.	March 10th. 1437/8	
Henry Dyssell, Priest	June 6th. 1441	
Joh. Lychebarow, Priest	July 13th. 1441	

He had the degree of Bachelor in Decrees, and was the Bishop's Commissary General in the Archdeaconries of Northampton and Leicester.

Name	Date	Patron
Will Harcourt, Priest.	Oct. 28th. 1441.	

To the Second Moiety only

Name	Date	Patron
Joh. de Tyddeswell, Acolyte.	March 5th. 1317/8	Joh. de Pateshull.
Joh. Vivien, Acolyte.	April 23rd. 1330,	
Joh. de Beryndon, M.A., Acolyte.	Feb. 2nd. 1330/1.	Joh. de Pateshull.
Alex. Mount-Fichet, Priest.	March 12th. 1340/1	Will. de Pateshull.
Will. Baldewyn, Priest.	June 1st. 1357.	
Will. Donne de Yelvertoft, Priest.	June 1st. 1357	Rex.
Joh. de Depyng, Priest	Nov. 30th. 1364	
Will. de Rondon, Priest	March 19th. 1368.	
Joh. Turnpenny, Priest.	Aug. 16th. 1393.	
Laurence Hawkyn, Chaplain.	May 22nd. 1399.	
Henry Redman, Priest.	Oct. 28th. 1400.	
Will. Stoke, Chaplain	Feb. 8th. 1400/1.	
Alan de Thame, Priest.	Aug. 11th. 1401.	
Dom. Thos. Kyrkeby, Priest.	Aug. 12th. 1405.	
John Parmenter, Priest.	Apl. 29th. 1421.	

Rectors of Milton only

	Date of Institution.	Patron.
Will. Ingylton,	Feb. 8th. 1464/5.	Rex.
Robert Ingylton, Clerk.	Dec. 18th. 1470.	
Dom. Robert Barker, Priest.	Nov. 23rd. 1489.	
Dom. John Parker, Priest.	June 24th. 1494.	
Joh. Alyson, Priest. M.A.	June 21st. 1506.	
Edward Wigan, D.D.	1526.	

Was the first Regius Professor of Divinity at Cambridge (see page 89). His curate was Dom. John Carter.

Thos. Follwell, Clerk.	Sept. 5th. 1545	John Dygbye, Armig.
John Roote, Priest.	Oct. 27th. 1553.	Queen Mary.

He was deprived in 1571 (see page 95).

Giles Sharrock.	March 8th. 1571	

The registers are signed by his curate, "Thomas Mayo, Mynister there."

Reginald Sharrock.	Feb. 8th. 1609/10	Sir Wm. Samwell.
Lawrence Howlett,	May 7th. 1625.	Stephen Harvey, Armig.
Francis Atterbury, M.A.	Apl. 6th. 1627.	Sir Stephen Harvey, K.C.B.

His curate was Andrew Groobye.

THE RECTORS OF MILTON

In his notes on Milton written for Dr. Bridges, 1718–1721, William Taylor states: "I have been somew't particular in relacion to the Family of the Atterburies, inasmuch as ye present Lord Bishop of Rochester is a Branch of this Family, whose uncle for several years was Rector of this Parish: &c.: (& if we may credit some people) was very Instrumental in promoting his Relations."

Nicholas Clerke Benjamin Twigden, M.A.	Aug. 7th. 1673. Sept. 9th. 1679.	John Clerke. Richard Gleed, John Twigden & Giles Twigden.
Previously Vicar of St. Giles, Northampton, 1676–1679.		
Nicholas Twigden, B.A. Fullwood Haden, M.A.	Sept. 16th. 1724. Feb. 25th. 1745.	Giles Twigden. Edward Price, Esq.
Mrs. Elizabeth Dodwell, widow of Richard Dodwell and daughter of Richard Gleed, tried to recover possession of the advowson of Milton Church and took proceedings against Edward Price in the High Court for that purpose. *Additional MSS.* British Museum. It had been bequeathed to Mr. Price by the Rev. Nicholas Twigden.		
Thomas Backhouse, B.A.	Aug. 28th. 1754.	Rev. George Backhouse.

Curates: Joseph Backhouse, Richardson Wood, C. Justinian Rainsford, Vincent Green, Thomas Corbye, Ed. Gillespie, and William Walmsley, M.A.

128 THE STORY OF MILTON MALZOR

	Date of Institution.	Patron.
Simon Pagett, B.A.	April 6th, 1796.	Rev. Wm. Pagett.
John Castleton Miller, D.D.	Oct. 18th, 1799.	Wm. Pagett, Esq.
George Wilson Sicklemore, M.A.	Feb. 11th, 1829.	Louis Hayes Patit & John Geo. Children.
George Oakes Miller, M.A.	June 7th, 1830.	Louis Hayes Patit & John Geo. Children
Edward Robert Butcher, D.C.L.	Dec. 17th, 1840.	Rev. E. R. Butcher.

Aged 78 at his induction. Had as curate Wm. Walmsley, M.A.

Dr. Miller had his grave dug in the chancel during his lifetime, and it is said that going there one day to see the man at work upon it he thought it was not long enough. The sexton maintained that it was, so Dr. Miller got into the grave and lay down at the bottom, and found the man was right.

The Curates of Milton were: Thos. Hornsby, M.A., J.P. (1801–1806), Francis Montgomery and Henry Flesher. The Rev. Francis Montgomery lived here and acted as curate until his death in 1831.

Curates: Edward Robert Butcher, D.C.L., and William Butlin.

Dr. Butcher changed his surname to Pemberton on April 21st, 1842, by Her Majesty's Royal Licence, in accordance with the Will of his mother. Before being instituted to the Rectory of Milton he had been Vicar of St. Sepulchre's, Northampton, from 1821–2, Chaplain of the Chapel Royal, Brighton, 1822–30. In 1835 he became Curate of Milton.

MILTON RECTORY.

THE RECTORS OF MILTON 129

He resigned the Rectory of Milton in 1842 for All Saints', Wandsworth. He died Rector of North Huish, Devonshire, in 1879.	
Thomas Atherton Kershaw, M.A. June 4th. 1844.	Rev. T. A. Kershaw.
He built the modern part of the Rectory, facing the lawn.	
John Brown, M.A. June 26th. 1872.	Executors of the late Rev. T. A. Kershaw.
Mr. Brown was inducted to the Rectory of Didcot in 1890, and died there in 1923.	
Alfred William Gross, M.A. July 30th. 1890.	Pickering Phipps, Esq.
He was Vicar of Whittle-le-Woods, Lancs., from 1883 to 1890. After resigning the Rectory of Milton in 1903, he was for some time chaplain of Luxor, Egypt, from 1904.	
Andrew Cavendish Neely. Jan. 8th. 1904.	Executors of the late Pickering Phipps.
Was Vicar of Denford with Ringstead, 1894–8, and Rector of Islip, Thrapston, 1898–1903. He was inducted to the Vicarage of St. Mary's, Peterborough, in April, 1917, and was installed Honorary Canon of Peterborough Cathedral in 1921.	
Benjamin Edward Evans, M.A. June 9th. 1917.	Executors of the late Pickering Phipps.
Minor Canon of Peterborough Cathedral 1910–1917, Sacristan 1910, Precentor of Peterborough Cathedral 1911 to 1917. The glebe, all but two acres, was sold in 1919.	

CHAPTER VIII

THE BELLS

A CLIMB up the perpendicular iron ladder fixed against the tower wall brings you through a narrow trap-door into a small chamber. From here another short climb, then a scramble over massive woodwork, and you are at the top of the tower amongst the bells in the octagon, with the wind blowing keen and chill through the louvres of the unglazed windows.

The bells are five in number, and are hung in two tiers, two above and three below, the smallest being No. 1 and leading up to No. 5, the big tenor bell. From their inscriptions we know the date when they were cast, and from the names upon them we can tell that they are Northamptonshire bells, cast in the county by Northamptonshire men. The following are the inscriptions on the various bells; the figures giving the date of the casting:

1. CANTATE DOMINO CANTICVM NOVVM. 1686. (This is the Latin for " O sing unto the Lord a new song," the opening words of Psalms XCVIII. and CXLIX.) The figures give the date of the casting. In diameter, this bell is 30 inches.

2. HENRY BAGLEY MADE MEE. 1686. Diameter 32 inches.

THE BELLS

3. MATTHEW BAGLEY MADE MEE. 1686. Diameter 34 inches.

4. HENRY BAGLEY MADE MEE. 1686. Diameter 36 inches.

5. EDWARD DRY AND STEPHEN MILES. CHURCHWARDENS. 1686. O. Diameter 40 inches.

The Edward Dry, churchwarden, commemorated on the big bell, succeeded his father as lord of the manor and was buried November 19th, 1707. Stephen Miles was the son of a benefactor of the parish. See page 265.

The Bagley family were bellfounders of Chalcombe, in Northamptonshire, so we read in *The Church Bells of Northamptonshire*, by Thomas North, F.S.A. Matthew Bagley, of that village, a blacksmith by trade, died in 1649, leaving two sons, Henry, who was born in 1608, and John, who was born in 1618. Henry became the first bellfounder there, and opened his foundry about 1632. He died about 1676, and was succeeded by his two sons Henry and William, and his nephew Matthew, the son of his brother John. Their names are not found together on any single bell, but their individual names appear on different bells in the same ring or peal cast by them.

There were bells in Milton Church long before 1686, and it is probable that the date they now bear tells us when they were recast. In those days, we know it was the custom in most places for men to mount to the bell-chamber and strike the bells with sledge-hammers instead of ringing them, and what was done in other places may have been done at Milton. Cracked and dented by being badly used, their pealing was inharmonious until they were melted down and recast, once more made tuneful and ready to " sing unto the Lord a new song."

Milton people have always had a warm affection for the bells of their parish church. In Pre-Reformation times bequests were made in money or kind for their maintenance.

Lawrence Davey 1526. " Item to the bellis in the same churche halffe a quarter barley."

Henry Davies, 1536. " Also I give to the use of the bells iiijd."

Nicholas Byllyng 1545. " Item I bequeth to ye bells iiijd."

Alice Campyan 1546. " Item I bequath to ye mayntenyng of ye bells iiijd."

Thomas Johnson 1552. " I bequethe to the repacon[1] of the bells a strike of barley."

Wm. Garnett, 1576. " I geve to the repaire of the bells of Milton iiijd."

A search through the Wills of Milton people will furnish evidence that some made bequests not only to the bells of their own church, but also, because the parishes were intermixed, to those of the sister church of Collingtree, and some Collingtree people on their death repaid the compliment :

John Smythe of Collingtroughe, 1557, " Also I geve to the mayntenance of the belles of Collingtrey viijd also I geve to the belles of Mylton viijd."

[1] Reparation or repair.

Several old customs in the use of the bells are still observed at Milton.

Upon a death, the great tenor bell is rung out, three strokes for a man and five for a woman. Then the age is given, the number of strokes being the years the deceased had lived, so by this means the villagers can give a reasonable guess as to who has passed away. After a slight pause, the bell is then tolled for some minutes.

With regard to the " three for a man," according to North's account the older custom at Milton was three times three, a slight pause occurring after each third stroke. The old saying that " nine tailors make a man," considered derogatory to those who provide us with our Sunday clothes, has really nothing to do with the knights of the needle. It should be " nine tellers mark a man," the " tellers " being the strokes of the death bell. And why the nine, or three times three ? In my opinion, we must go back to Pre-Reformation times for the reason. During the Mass, i.e. the Holy Communion, at the time of consecration the tenor bell was rung three times at the elevation of the Host, three times at the elevation of the Chalice and three times at the close of the consecration prayer. The broken bread being the Body of Christ and the outpoured wine His precious Blood, signified the Death of Our Lord, and thus the " three times three " of the Mass became the " nine tellers " that mark a man, otherwise signify his death.

On Shrove Tuesday, the shriving bell is still rung at 11 o'clock in the morning, the bell used from time immemorial being No. 3. " Shrive " is an old Saxon word for confession to a priest, and as the week before Lent seems to have been specially marked for confession of sins, we therefore have Shrove Tuesday, or Confession Tuesday. The rector would await the penitents in church, and to let them know he was ready a bell was rung. In this way originated the Shrove Tuesday bell. It is now called the " pancake bell," and it may possibly have been so called in days of yore, but what have pancakes to do with Shrove Tuesday and the confession of sins ? Nothing at all, except that next day Lent, the great season of fasting, would be ushered in, when there must be no meat eaten and no rich foods. This meant that all fats, such as butter, lard and dripping, had to be used up, so the housewife made pancakes and other rich delicacies to be eaten the same day. Hence the 11 o'clock shriving bell became also the signal for the preparation of pancakes, and so might well have been known even in those far-off days as the " pancake bell." In *Poor Robin's Almanac*, published in 1684, we read :

> " But hark, I hear the pancake bell,
> And fritters make a gallant smell."

On the three last Mondays in Advent, peals are rung on the bells before sunrise, usually about half-past five. Thomas North in *The Church Bells of Northamptonshire* mentions this practice in some other villages, but does not include Milton. This must have been an oversight on his part, for old ringers have told me that the early morning Advent ringing was customary here long before 1878, when North published his book. The custom probably originated through St. Paul's exhortation in the Epistle for Advent Sunday : " Now it is high time to awake out of sleep."

At noon a bell is still rung daily, the one used being No. 2. It is commonly called the " dinner bell," as it summons the labourers home from the fields to their midday meal. Quite possibly this is a survival of a Pre-Reformation Angelus rung at midday, for that religious custom would have its secular value as a signal of time when there was no clock. On the other hand our " dinner bell " may be of purely secular origin, though possibly in use for centuries.

The church bell being found so convenient a signal for workmen prompted a more frequent use of it, for we find it was rung at Milton no less than four times daily. In the minute books of the Public Vestry of Milton the following resolution is recorded :

" 1829. Thursday, March 5th. John Cherry to ring the Bell for the Labourers to return from Breakfast at half past eight o'clock in the morning."

John Cherry had already been ringing the bell at other times, as the following month it is recorded he was paid wages for so doing.

" 1829. Thursday, April 2nd. John Cherry to have a pair of shoes, and five shillings given him for ringing the Bell at eight, half-past eight, twelve and one o'clock."

John Cherry seems to have been the general factotum of the parish, as his name occurs frequently in the Churchwardens' Accounts. At any rate, he must have done his work very well for his wages were raised, as under date October 1st of the same year we read :

" John Cherry to have 7/9 for the half year for ringing the bell &c."

At what time the bell was discontinued as a signal for the workmen, except at noon, it is impossible to decide, as the entries are rather vague, but it was probably when the striking clock was put up in 1863.

At times of national rejoicing or mourning our bells have patriotically given tongue. In this respect the following extracts from the Churchwardens' Accounts are of interest :

1820. Apl. 18th. Paid Richard Robinson for tolling the Bell at the King's funeral 2/–
1827. Feb. Paid the ringers for a dumb Peal and Tolling the Bell the day the duke of York was buried. . . 3/6
1830. July 15th. Paid Richd. Robinson for tolling the bell at the King's Funeral 2/–
1861. Richard Robinson for Tolling Bell, Prince Consort's Funeral . . 2/–
1862. Ringers (on Prince of Wales's Marriage) 10/–

The bells were also rung at the Jubilee and Diamond Jubilee of Queen Victoria, the Coronation of King Edward VII and of his son George V, and the last time on a national occa-

THE BELLS

sion in joy and thankfulness when the Armistice was signed on Monday, Nov. 11th, 1918.

Some of the accounts prove quaint and instructive reading.

1803. Apl. 12th. Pd. new set of Bell Ropes	£1 7 0
1805. Feb. 13th. Pd. Jno. Fox for repairing the Bells, for new brasses & lineing the gudgeons .	£5 5 6
1806. May 23rd. Pd. James Palmer Bell Role	1/–
1834. July 17th. Menden a bell rope	6d.
1834. Sept. 20th. Shuting a bell Rope	3d.

Being in such frequent use, the bells have from time to time required attention. Among the Vestry Minutes we find the following resolution as to their condition :

1847. April 5th. " That a competent person be forthwith engaged by the Church Wardens to put them in a state of safety and repair."

Fifty years afterwards they were again attended to and rehung in time for the celebration of the Diamond Jubilee of Queen Victoria.

The subject of the bells must not be left without a word as to the hand-bells that are in the charge of the captain of the belfry. They are ten in number, the ringers using them one in each hand, and with such a range of notes they are able to play many melodies, with which they give much delight at Yuletide.

The last team of ringers was depleted by some

leaving the village. They rang together for the last time at the Armistice, and their names were :

Charles Tack (Captain), Samuel James Turner, William Stockford, Arthur Robinson and William Clarke.

In the spring of 1921 a new team was formed. By diligent practice they have so mastered the art that their performance is a source of delight to all who love the sound of the bells.

It is a noteworthy fact that on Thursday, March 8th, 1923, just two years after the band had been formed, they rang a peal of Doubles, 5,040 changes, at Milton in three hours and sixteen minutes, being 30 six-scores of Grandsire and 12 of Plain Bob. The peal was conducted by Mr. John A. Townsend and not only was it the first recorded peal on our bells, but the first recorded peal by a local band, all being natives of Milton. The names of these enthusiastic devotees are :

Albert Turner (1), Charles Yates (2), John A. Townsend (Captain) (3), Raymond Asplin (4), Philip Asplin (5) and Willie Stockford, supernumerary.

Long may they flourish and speed by their art the message of the bells.

> " Ring out, wild bells, to the wild sky,
>   The flying cloud, the frosty light :
>   The year is dying in the night ;
> Ring out, wild bells, and let him die.
>
> Ring out the old, ring in the new,
>   Ring, happy bells, across the snow :
>   The year is going, let him go ;
> Ring out the false, ring in the true."

CHAPTER IX

SANCTUARY SEEKERS

IN barbarous ages when each man was a law unto himself, the ancient dictum that " whoso sheddeth man's blood, by man shall his blood be shed " was usually fulfilled by the vengeance of the next of kin. Hence the need for some place where an offender could dwell in security for awhile and be afforded time to provide for his own safety or the welfare of his dependents, or, indeed, to compound for his offence.

Such privileged places existed from very early times. The Hebrews had their six cities of refuge, the Greeks had the asylums afforded by certain of their temples, and the Romans could find safety in the sacred precincts not only of the altars in their temples but also of the statues of their emperors.

The fear and reverence that made heathen temples a place of refuge ; the awful sanctity of the Holy of Holies, where the Sheckinah quivered above the Mercy Seat ; all this was reflected in after-days in the Christian Church.

Where the altar stands at the east end of the church is still the Sanctuary. At the altar is enacted the holiest of all that is connected with the Christian religion, to which the penitent sinner, however great his crime may have been, is allowed to draw near, but where the unhallowed feet of the avenger thirsting for blood might not approach. Hence it was natural that the church should be a place of refuge for a fugitive, whether he were an unwitting one fleeing from vengeance or a downright criminal. By degrees there came into being the right of "Sanctuary," as recognised by law.

The usual privilege of Sanctuary was in some cases considerably extended by Royal Charter. Hence the prominence given to the rights possessed by certain chartered sanctuaries such as the great Religious Houses of Beverley, Durham and Hexham, has caused such confusion that we have lost sight of the privilege of Sanctuary that pertained in ancient times to the ordinary parish church.

All consecrated churches possessed this right from very early times. From the laws of Ethelbert, King of Kent, drawn up soon after his baptism by St. Augustine in 597, we see that the violation of church " frith," or peace, was heavily punished. The laws of Ina, King of the West Saxons, drawn up about the year 680, also make it clear that even the right of every consecrated church to afford Sanctuary was well established, whilst in the ninth century a period of Sanctuary extending to seven days and seven nights was granted to any fugitive seeking refuge in a church.

The church's peace, or "frith," was denied to none save those guilty of heresy and thus without the pale by the nature of their offence.

Though the period of Sanctuary was so limited

it was a decided advantage because it obtained a remission of part of the punishment. No bloodshed was allowed by the Church, and so the fugitive within her borders could not be condemned to death, but a more merciful punishment, or perhaps even a fine, could be imposed.

In successive reigns we find the time of grace extended a little. Definite rules, and scales of penalties for violation of church " frith," were drawn up. It was provided that those in Sanctuary were not to be removed except by the priest or his ministers. No fugitive was to retain stolen property, but was to restore it to its owner. Finally, any fugitive who took refuge repeatedly in a church was to forswear the province, and if he presumed to return no one was to shelter him, except by the consent of the King's justices.

This last clause is the earliest known reference to the formal Abjuration of the Realm made by the Sanctuary fugitive, which became customary from about the middle of the twelfth century.

By the time of King Henry II (1154-1189) the laws relating to the Church's asylum for offenders were strictly defined. A person accused of felony, or in danger of such accusation, could flee to any church for Sanctuary, and having reached consecrated ground he was allowed to stay there for forty days. While he was in Sanctuary the church authorities were responsible for his maintenance, which meant that the parishioners supplied him with food. If the parish authorities neglected this merciful provision, sentence of excommunication could be pronounced against them, as was once done in such a case by William of Wykeham, Bishop of Winchester. The parishioners were responsible for the fugitive's safe keeping in another way, for if he escaped they were heavily fined. So, during the period of Sanctuary, a careful watch was kept around the church to prevent an escape or rescue, the four neighbouring vills, townships or parishes providing a guard.

Before the expiration of the forty days of grace, the man in Sanctuary was expected to send for the coroner and then, in the presence of the sheriff, confess his crime at the churchyard gate and take an oath to quit the kingdom for ever. If, at the end of the forty days, he refused to abjure the realm or to quit Sanctuary, what was to be done? No layman must interfere with him. The priest alone could endeavour to persuade him to leave the sacred precincts, but if he should fail, then the supplies of food would be cut off and the fugitive would be forced by hunger to surrender.

In the Assize Roll, 632, for the County of Northampton, being the Pleas of the Crown and Gaol Delivery, under date 3 Edward III (1329), which covers a period of thirty years, we have two local instances of fugitives abjuring the realm. One was at Milton and the other at Collingtree, which at that time was still regarded as part of Milton.

M. 59. " The Hundred of Wymersle come by twelve."

M. 60. " Rob'tus Burdeuill' de Burstall' in

Com' Leyc' posuit se in eccl'ia S'ce Elene de Midelton' & Ibide' recogn' se esse l'rone dem plur' latrociniis & abjur' regnu' Angl' cora' Coron' Cat' eius ijs vn' vic' r' Et quia even' de die & villat' de Colentr' no' cep' ip'm Io' in m'ia."

[Translation]

" Robert Burdeville of Burstall, in the County of Leicester, placed himself in the Church of Saint Helen at Midelton and there acknowledged himself a thief of many thefts and before the Coroner abjured the realm of England. His chattels were worth 2s., whereof the Sheriff answers. And because he fled of the day and the vill of Collingtree did not take him, therefore it is held in mercy."

M. 60. D. " Walt'rus fil' Will'i de Brinton' p'rcussit Thom' Baroun de Dayhugton in Campis de Colentre cu' quod' bac'lo q'd statim inde obiit Et pr'd'cus Walt'rus statim post fam' posuit se in eccl'ia s'ce Columbe & ibidem recogn' se int'fecisse pr'dcm Thom' & abiur' regnu' Angl' cora' Coron' Cat' eius ijs. vjd vn' vic' r'."

[Translation]

" Walter, the son of William of Brinton, struck Thomas Baroun of Dayhugton with a stick in the fields of Collingtree, so that he instantly died thereof. And the aforesaid Walter at once, after the deed, placed himself in the Church of Saint Columba and there acknowledged that he had killed the said Thomas, and abjured the realm of England before the Coroner. His chattels were worth 2s. 6d., whereof the Sheriff answers."[1]

[1] For other local items of a different character on this Roll, see page 286.

When a Sanctuary man summoned the coroner and abjured the realm, the mode of procedure was as follows: In the presence of the coroner the criminal admitted his guilt. The coroner then summoned a jury from the four nearest townships, that in which the fugitive had taken Sanctuary being always one of the four. A second jury representing the whole Hundred, was occasionally called together, and the verdict was then said to have been found " by twelve sworn men, together with the next four vills." These twelve men and four vills seem often to have been regarded as two distinct bodies, and their verdicts were in some cases evidently given separately.

Having agreed to quit the realm, the ceremony of abjuration usually took place at the churchyard gate or stile. There the fugitive took the oath in the presence of the sheriff, coroner and jurors. The Northamptonshire form of the oath, and therefore the one administered at the churchyard gate of Milton, was as follows:

" Thus here, Sir Coroner that I, ——, am a felon of our Lord the King and felony I have done like. as I have confessid to you (here he states the crime). Wherefore I forswere the realm of England and that I shall hie me to the port of ——(Dover, Bristol, Portsmouth or Yarmouth were the usual ports)—the which ye have given me. And I shall not goe out of the King's Hie way and if I do I will that I be taken as a felon of our said lord the King. And at the said port I shall ask passage. And I shall not abide there but a flood and an ebb if I may have passage. And if I may not have it in forty days

MILTON CHURCH PRIOR TO 1856.
From a painting in the possession of Mr. J. C. Emery.

next I shall admit me to the church again as a felon of our said Lord the King so help me God and all the Saints &c."

The fugitive was to cross the seas to some other Christian country within a given time, and accept banishment for life, and the port authorities had power to compel ships, on leaving, to give him a passage. Standing there at the churchyard gate, penniless, clothed in sackcloth and carrying a cross of white wood, he was assigned a port and a reasonable time in which to make the journey, usually from three to fifteen days in consideration of the age of the fugitive and the distance to be traversed. In early days he had to discard all his clothes, which became the perquisite of the church officials, and wear a single garment of sackcloth, but this strict rule was abrogated as time went on and shirt and breeches were generally allowed. The abjuror was strictly forbidden to leave the King's highway. The penalty for infringing this order was death by beheading. He was not to spend more than one night in any one place and was passed on from constable to constable, each place being bound to furnish him with a minimum of food and shelter. During all this time he had the protection of the law and the Church, provided he kept to the King's highway. Indeed, it was a grave offence to interfere with fugitives on the way to the coast and was equal to breach of Sanctuary such as dragging a man out of church. The fugitive would be of course unarmed, as in the first place he could not seek Sanctuary if he bore weapons, but would have to discard them before entering the sacred precincts.

Occasionally it would happen that the abjuror on his way to the coast would seize some favourable opportunity to escape. At other times the fierce behaviour of the crowd of spectators would constrain him to leave the King's highway through fear of being molested. In either case, if caught, he would be at once beheaded, because he was then an outlaw. A notable case occurred at Wootton early in the fourteenth century, being of great interest to us as the final act occurred in the fields between Collingtree and Milton.

Early in the year 1322, Henry Felip, of Stoke Bruerne, was found dead in the parish of Courteenhall and an inquest was held on Wednesday, March 24th, 1322. It was found that he had been attacked and murdered by certain thieves. His son, who was with him, escaped and raised the hue and cry, with the result that five of the robbers were captured, but one of them, named John of Ditchford, escaped to the Church of Wootton and took Sanctuary there. On the same day that the inquest was held, the fugitive summoned the Coroner, Richard Luvell, and before him and a jury of the four nearest townships, he confessed that he was guilty of the robbery and murder, and abjured the realm of England. The port of Dover was assigned to him and his chattels were a sword, a knife and a " courtepy," valued at eighteen pence.

On the following Friday, March 26th, Richard

Luvell, the Coroner, was again called to the district on a grim business, for a dead man had been found with his head cut off " in the fields of Collingtree." An inquest was held by oath of twelve men and the four nearest townships, viz. Collingtree-cum-Middleton, Courteenhall, Wootton and Rothersthorpe. It transpired that the body was that of John of Ditchford who on the preceding Wednesday had abjured the realm of England before the Coroner. On the same day, he violated his oath by abandoning the King's highway and the warrant of Holy Church and fled towards the woods. Hue and cry was immediately raised against him. He was pursued by the people of Wootton and others until at last they caught up with him in the fields between Collingtree and Milton, and he was beheaded while still fleeing. The Coroner probably commended the beheading as a just act because he ordered the severed head to be carried by the four townships to the King's Castle at Northampton.

It is quite possible that poor John of Ditchford having left the churchyard gate of Wootton on his way to Dover, was terrified by the demeanour of the exasperated people, who had probably known Henry Felip for many years. With threats and execrations ringing in his ears he made a dash for freedom. Consequently, as soon as he ran beyond the roadside he became an outlaw and the prey of any man.

Such was the penalty for a breach of the rules. It must have been pitiful to see the wretched abjuror on his journey, perhaps at times full of anxiety because of the badly defined roads and the stern necessity of keeping to the King's highway. On more than one occasion it is recorded that a fugitive had the good fortune to meet with the King, who, moved to compassion, granted him a full and free pardon.

When abroad, the banished men sometimes joined the King's armies in the wars against France and frequently some were pardoned and could return home. Return of an abjuror without permission was sternly punished.

A man who had taken Sanctuary was not compelled to summon the coroner and admit he was guilty. One who was accused of any crime of which he was perfectly innocent would take Sanctuary and remain there until he had obtained evidence or arranged his defence. He could then surrender himself "to the King's peace," or in other words, go to prison, stand his trial and take his chance of being acquitted. If he felt the evidence against him was overwhelming, he would summon the coroner, admit he was guilty and abjure the realm.

Sometimes the rights of Sanctuary were violated. The well-known instance of the murder of St. Thomas-à-Becket in Canterbury Cathedral will occur to all. Those who offended in this way, however, were severely punished by the Church, being usually excommunicated until they made their peace.

That the Church was right in sternly upholding her rights of Sanctuary will be acknowledged by all when it is remembered that there were some who sought her protection through fear of being falsely accused of some crime.

Certain of the great Religious Houses, such as Durham, Beverley, Westminster and Hexham, had special privileges conferred by Royal Charter. At Beverley, for instance, Sanctuary extended for a radius of a mile and a half from the minster church. A fugitive in one of these chartered sanctuaries was not compelled to abjure the realm, but could elect to live within the boundaries of the Sanctuary.

When Henry VIII dissolved the monasteries the case of these fugitives, who thus dwelt in Sanctuary, gave rise to curious situations. So in 1540, on the abolition of the chartered sanctuaries, and also because of the remonstrances of foreign powers who objected to criminals being dumped on their shores, the custom of abjuring the realm was abandoned and eight towns were declared to be places of permanent Sanctuary. These were: Westminster, Northampton, Wells, Norwich, York, Derby, Manchester and Launceston. Needless to say, these places were by no means pleased at being thus distinguished, and many and bitter were the complaints that reached the Council.

Good as were its intentions, this Act of Henry VIII's was not a success, and after several vain attempts to improve it, all rights of Sanctuary for persons who abjured were abolished in 1603, during the first year of James I. The rights of Sanctuary pertaining to churches and churchyards still remained, though Sanctuary for serious crimes such as murder had already been abolished by Henry VIII. At last the end came in 1623 by the Act of James I, 21, Cap. 28, when all forms of Sanctuary in church or churchyard were swept away. Strange to say, however, one small privilege survives, a faint shadow of the old-time right of Sanctuary, in that a writ served in church has no legal force.

CHAPTER X

MILTON PAROCHIAL SCHOOL

THE education of children in England was in the first instance begun and continued by the Church, and the earliest record we have is Alcuin's capitulary issued in 787 and a second in 789. In this specific directions are given : " Let every monastery and every abbey have its school where boys may be taught the Psalms, the system of musical notation, singing, arithmetic and grammar."

During the Middle Ages it is highly probable that almost every parish church had its school, for it was necessary that the priest should have boys in church to sing the responses, which were of course in Latin. Care was therefore taken that the Latin tongue should be taught, and side by side with this went arithmetic and grammar. There can be no doubt that such a school existed in Milton in those days.

The first record that we have of a schoolmaster at Milton is under date March 22nd, 1720, when the church registers tell us that John Wells, Schoolmaster, was buried. We have no earlier record for the simple reason that the occupation and rank of different people were seldom entered in the registers.

In the Will of Elizabeth Gaffield, 1746, who

charged certain lands with the payment of 52/- yearly for educational purposes, we have a reference to the school. The rector and churchwardens were " to sett six poor children to school belonging to the aforesaid parish . . . to learne to read and to give two pence a week with each and to pay the Master once a quarter as they shall receive it " (see Chapter XIV).

Our next records are of Joseph Froan, schoolmaster, buried May 12th, 1775, and of his widow, Ann Froan, schoolmistress, buried July 13th, 1793. Of the latter, a note written in the register by William Walmsley, the curate, informs us : " She was a skilful woman in her profess'n, a good Xt'n and a useful mem'r of society."

From the Minute Books of the Parish Vestry we learn that on November 7th, 1823, it was resolved " William Caswell's wife to have the Charity School," and on November 18th, 1825, " Mary Lambert to have the girl's free school." Probably this Charity School and the Free School were one and the same institution, but, if so, it was quite distinct from the Parochial School, for in 1823 John Cooper was schoolmaster. In 1830 the eight poor children were taught by a schoolmistress.

I have been informed by some old inhabitants that about 1850 a day school was kept by " governesses " in the first three houses of Workhouse Yard, which may have been a survival of the Charity School.

Mr. William Clarke informed me that the school of which John Cooper was master was

MILTON PAROCHIAL SCHOOL

held at The Hollies, a large house not far from the present school, and here the vestry meetings were occasionally held :

1824. Apl. 1. " At a public Vestry held this day at the School Room."
1826. March 30. "At a Public Vestry held this day at the School House."

Mr. Cooper was a former Quartermaster-sergeant of the Northamptonshire Militia and became Vestry Clerk, Overseer, Assessor of Taxes and Churchwarden of Milton. His multifarious duties must have harassed the poor man, for in an address read at the Public Vestry on March 3rd, 1828, he states he has been Overseer for the last eight years and says that the work calls him so much from his school duties that he cannot do it again under the restrictions imposed.

Seeing his signature frequently occurring in the Minute Books I was startled to find the old soldier describe himself as " John Cooper V.C." years before that coveted decoration was first awarded. Then it dawned on my understanding that it was a short way of writing " John Cooper, Vestry Clerk."

Mr. Cooper died on February 2nd, 1831, and on his mural tablet is described as " for many years schoolmaster and churchwarden in this parish."

On September 18th, 1848, Mr. William Montgomery conveyed to the Rev. T. A. Kershaw 315 square yards or thereabouts

" as a site for a schoolroom for poor persons of and in the said parish of Milton . . . such school to be for the education of the poor in the principles of the Established Church and according to its principles and to be under the exclusive management and control of the Rector of Milton aforesaid for the time being."

Our information about the school is scanty until we come to 1862, when the Code of Regulations ordered that every school receiving a grant should keep a log book. From that year onwards we have a full and particular list of masters and their assistants.

The children were supposed to pay their school pence weekly, at the rate of twopence each. The boys and girls had to take it in turn to sweep the school and, in the winter, see that the fires were lighted and kept going. The following entries are illuminating :

1866. Oct. 1st. " School fee is 2d. per week. One boy pays 3d. and is excused school sweeping. Mary H—— does not take her turn at school sweeping."

1870. Jan. 18. " No fires to-day and yesterday, the boy whose duty it is to see to the fires did not attend to them."

Later, the children in Standards I to III paid twopence per week, in Standards IV to VII threepence, but in October, 1891, the Managers adopted " free education."

The school was at first very small and uncomfortable. The floor was of brick and at the west end of the main room was a small classroom with a room above. The window of this little upper room still remains high up in the wall, and here the master lived. In 1873 the classroom with the room above were removed, a new classroom built for infants at the other end of the main room and a boarded floor was put down. Further alterations, including the cloak-rooms and an addition to the infants' room, were made in 1895, at a cost of £400.

The dimensions of the school are : main room, length 42 ft. 6 ins., width 17 ft. 4 ins., accommodation 72. Classroom, length 26 ft., width 18 ft. 10 ins., accommodation 54.

From the Log Book also we learn of the existence of another school, held in a room belonging to the Baptist Chapel. The first reference is in 1863, but the school was discontinued in 1880.

The following list of masters, compiled from various sources, may prove of interest :

1720. " John Wells, Schoolmaster, buried." Church Register.

1775. " Joseph Froan, Schoolmaster, buried." Church Register.

1793. " Ann Froan, Schoolmistress, buried." Church Register.

1823. Mrs. William Caswell, Mistress of the Charity School. Parish Vestry Minutes.

1823. John Cooper, Schoolmaster. Parish Vestry Minutes.

1825. Mary Lambert, Mistress of the Girls' Free School. Parish Vestry Minutes.

1844. " William Mansfield, Schoolmaster." Church Reg.

1858. June 28th. George Winter, Certificated Master. Log Book.

From this date, the particulars are all taken from the school Log Books.

1866. Jan. 15th. William John Sutton.
1867. March 28th. D. Evans, Certificated Master.
1868. Jan. 6th. Henry Padfield.
1869. Apl. 5th. Joseph Bancroft.
1871. July 4th. J. Wakem.
1872. Jan. 22nd. Benjamin Bassford.
1872. Feb. 25th. J. Horton.
1872. Apl. 26th. Henry Charles.
1872. Sept. 30th. John Bennett, Certificated Master, 1st. Class.
1876. July 1st. William Rediough, Certif. Master, 1st. Class.
1885. Sept. 28th. G. H. Lander.
1886. Jan. 4th. Geo. Henry Langley, Cert : Master, 2nd. Class.
1887. Jan. 3rd. Alfred Brown, Certif : Master, 2nd. Class.
1896. Feb. 24th. Samuel H. Bowden, Certif : Master, 2nd. Class.
1900. Sept. 10th. J. Brenig Jones, Cert : Master, 1st. Class.
1902. March 11th. Robert M. Anthony, Certif : Master.

CHAPTER XI

THE PARISH

WE have seen that, for the sake of convenience and to avoid confusion since the name is so common, Milton was often entered in ancient records under the heading of Collingtree. That part of the manor was also responsible for the name of a Hundred in the time of William the Conqueror, which was no mean honour (see page 31). Mr. Horace Round, M.A., in his article on "Doomsday Book" in the *Victoria County History of Northamptonshire* (Vol. I, p. 296), says that in these ancient pages

" an interesting Hundred makes its appearance, as it would seem, there only. This is the Hundred of Collingtree, ('Colentreu,' 'Colestreu') to which are assigned the adjoining vills of Collingtree, Milton (Middleton Malsor) Rothersthorpe, Blisworth and Courteenhall, on the west of Wymersley Hundred. In the Northamptonshire survey (12th century) this Hundred disappears."

This seems to point to the fact that Milton in those days was a place of some considerable importance, since it had the distinction of having a Hundred named after a portion of one of its manors. Had the Hundred been called "Milton Hundred," the question would at once arise, "Which Milton?"

From the *Doomsday* account of the lands of William Peverel and Goisfrid Alselin, there seem to have been at least thirty-five families and the priest at Milton. The names of only the two chief tenants, Ambrose and William, are recorded. The others are unknown to us by name, but they here lived their simple lives near a thousand years ago in their reed-thatched huts of wood and dutifully put out their fires when the curfew sounded from the belfry of the little Saxon church.

From early times there were no definite boundaries between the parishes of Milton and Collingtree. They were apparently interwoven with one another, a state of affairs undoubtedly due to the uneven distribution of the lands of the two manors, and the fact that the two churches were originally in two moieties and so attached to one another. Dr. Bridges hints at this in his observations on Collingtree Church: " It appears to have been for some time united to the church of Middleton, now called Milton. The tythes of these two parishes are still intermixed with each other, in about an equal proportion."

As a rule, up to about the sixteenth century, the parish was simply an ecclesiastical district, the extent of which was decided by that of the manor, and the civil business of which was conducted by the Manorial Courts. From 1535 onwards, the civil parish as we now know it gradually came into existence, the boundary between Milton and Collingtree not being finally settled until 1780.

The following extracts referring to the village

THE PARISH 159

and parish are interesting, as they illustrate the prevalent confusion. The first two are from Wills:

John Wright, Dec. 6th., 1553, " of the towne of Myddelton Malsoure and of the p'rishe of Colentrye, husbandman."

John Stephenson, April 10th., 1610, " of Milton alias Midleton Malsor in the parishe of Colingtrough."

From the Milton parish registers we have:

1603/4. " Robert Nut of North'ton in the p'rishe of All Seyntes and Anne Sare al's Seares of this towne in the p'rishe of Collingtree were married the fourth daye of Marche. Licent' obtent." (i.e. by licence).

The above entries seem to show that those persons lived in some part of Milton regarded as a portion of Collingtree parish, that is, they were probably tenants of part of Mantell's Manor, as it was afterwards called. That portion of Milton belonging to the other manor was considered as being strictly in Milton parish, as we gather from the register:

1606. " Edward Tym'es of Blaxley and Joan Genyans of this parrishe were married the sixt daye of October."

1609. " Walter Greene and Joan Brumley both of this towne and parishe were married the —15 Daye of Oct."

The boundaries of the two parishes of Milton and Collingtree were finally settled by the Enclosure Award in 1780.

Notes descriptive of the parish and village of

Milton were written between the years 1718–21 by William Taylor. Owing to their interest they are given here:

"The farthest extent is from Thorp Brook to Courtenhall Grounds, and is 2 Large Miles: Bounded by Collingtree *alias* Collingtrough, Cortenhall, Blisworth, Thorp and Wootton:— Collingtree East: Thorp West: Wootton North Cortenhall South.

"No of houses is 65 :—Houses for ye Poor, 3 : —all which are now inhabited except 2 Farm Houses.

"Seats: Mr. Dodwell's, Mr. Duncomb's, Mr. Price's.

"Hills: 1, Mill Banks Hill: 2, Capbush Hill: 3, Hanging Hedge Hill: 4, Blandern Hill: 5, Lady Bridge Hill.

"Rocks: 2—1st. of Gravell, called ye Gravell pitts, but has One Course of stone, which is very thick & of a reddish colour, a Durable stone, and not to be rejected for Building: The 2nd. Rock lyes hard by this, which is a very hard stone, of a Brown Colour, impenetrable by Cold or Heat.

"They both lye a little below the Town.

"Brooks—1, Thorp Brook. 2, Wootton Brook, which is a mound (boundary)—to this Field (i.e. the open country) for 2 miles. 3, Blysworth Brook. The 1st. of these rises from Gayton Fish pond and joins the River Nyne at Upton Mill :—The 2nd. takes its rise from ye Dykes in Horton, so comes down by Peddington Field, and there join'd with other little waters, then is mett by Quin Bridge, and other waters from Wootton, so composes a Brook, and meets Thorp Brook at Upton Mill aforesaid :—

MILTON HOUSE, BEFORE THE ROAD WAS LOWERED.
From a painting in the possession of Mr. E. M. Alexander. The block lent by the Editor of *Northamptonshire Notes and Queries.*

THE PARISH

The 3rd. rises from Dykes and small springs in Blisworth field, Drives an Overshott Mill, makes a small Brook on ye West side of this Town, and joins the River Nyne with Wootton Brook at Upton Mill aforesaid.
"Springs—1, Holler's Spring : 2, Clanwell Spring : 3, at Ham Willows : 4, Fishpool Spring : 5, Lady Bridge Spring : 6, Root's Gutter Spring : 7, Long Land Spring :—all simple."

The parish is 1426 acres, 2 roods, 7 perches in extent. In 1923 the gross value was £8,185 6s. 2d., the rateable value of the land was £1,878 5s. 3d., and of buildings £4,463 1s. 6d.

Some of the place-names given by Taylor are now forgotten, but most are still known to the old folk. Mill-banks Hill is a sloping field not far from Stockwell, Hanging Hedge Hill is a field on the left-hand side of the road leading to Collingtree, and Clanwell and Root's Gutter are in the same neighbourhood. Capbush forms part of what was once the glebe farm. Blandern Hill I have not identified, and the same must be said of Holler's and Long Land Springs. Ham Willows, Fishpool and Lady Bridge are names still commonly known.

Other names in the village are of interest. Stockwell, or the "Bottoms," sometimes the "Willows," is the north-east corner of the village. Little Street leads from Stockwell to the corner of the road to the church. "Little Town" is another name for the houses on Little Green, near the War Memorial. Half Craft is the field by the Greyhound. Hobb End is the corner of the road leading to the Towcester Road, by Milton Manor.

In 1821 the number of houses had increased to 108 from the 65 in Taylor's day, and now in 1923 they are 143, partly by building and partly by the unfortunate expedient of making several small cottages of one large house. Three houses bear dates respectively of 1638, 1656 and 1701.

Apart from the Church and the Manors, little is known of the life of our particular parish in mediæval days. There is no record of the Wars of the Roses relating to Milton, but doubtless the village must have been stirred by the Battle of Northampton on July 10th, 1460, when King Henry VI was taken prisoner. In the Pipe Rolls and Subsidy Rolls preserved in the Record Office, lists of inhabitants are given who paid taxes at various times. It would be of little interest to publish all, but two are given here as examples:

LAY SUBSIDY ROLL. 155/125.

CO. NORTHANTS. 15 HENRY VIII. (NO HEADING.)

Hundred of Wymersley. Mylton.

	Assessment.	Tax.
John Wake, in londes.	x Li	x S
William Guner	xx S	iiij D
William Hodgkyn	xx S	iiij D
Rob. Whyte	xx S	iiij D
John Cowper	x Li	v S
Richard Harbard	xl S	xij D
William Harbard	xl S	xij D
Richard Knyght	xx S	iiij D
Thomas Craswell	xx S	iiij D
William Buge	iiij Li	ij S
John Byllyng	x Li	v S

THE PARISH

	Assessment.	Tax.
Nicolas Byllyng	iiij Li	ij S
William Byllyng	vj Li	iij S
John Wryght	xx S	iiij D
Richard Park	xx S	iiij D
John Idyll	xx S	iiij D
William Garnytt	iij Li	xviij D
Thomas Horbye	iiij Li	ij S
William Harbard	iiij Li	ij S
William Brokesham	xx S	iiij D
Thomas Mirrell	iij Li	xviij D
Robt. Lyng	iiij Li	ij S
Thomas Rage	viij Li	iiij S
Henry Draycote	xx S	iiij D
(Part of Roll is wanting here.)		
—— Byllyng	: :	: :
Henry Hart	: :	: :
Thomas Cleveden	xx S	: :
Thomas Craswell	xl S	: :
John Heyreke	: :	: :
Thomas Miles	: :	: :
Lawrence Roote	: :	ij S
Lawrence Davye	vij Li	iij S vi D
John Wayte	xx S	iiij D
John Waryn	xx S	iiij D
John Stephyn	xx S	iiij D
Thomas Langford	iij Li	xviij D
Summa iij Li.		

The Collingtree portion of the above Roll is given on page 283 because one person named therein was very evidently an inhabitant of Milton.

156/266.   3 Edward VI.   1549–1550.

Thomas Houghton	xiv Li	xiv S
Stephen Gilbert	xj Li	xj S
Robert Dunckeley	x Li	x S
Will Leeke	x Li	x S

This assessment was on goods and not on real property.

From Wills made about this time we glean some knowledge of the state of the country in Tudor days. The roads seem to have been chiefly maintained by private benefactions and legacies, which would not be sufficient to keep them in repair. Hence the state of the highways, as would naturally be expected, was very bad, being chiefly distinguished from the broad, hedgeless fields and the unenclosed Commons by the deep ruts made by the ponderous wheels of wagon and cart. Time after time loads of stone would be spread over them to fill up the ruts, but the roads were without foundation of any kind (except the old Roman roads) and so the metal was soon lost in the soft earth. It was long before the time of Telford or Macadam.

To provide for the maintenance of the highways was considered a pious duty and meritorious before God, quite as much as caring for the poor, because men saw in this a real charity for certain unfortunate people who were compelled to travel.

Thomas Rage in his Will (1523) orders that a house should be sold, the money " to be given to churche and to hyeway and to pore people where nede ys as God put them in mynde."

William Garnett, husbandman (1576) : " I geve three stryke of barley, that is one stryke to the repaire of the highe waies in Mylton or Mylton fielde and ij strykes to my sonne in lawe."

In the reign of Edward VI the trustees of the Milton Church charities diverted the rents :

THE PARISH

"to the use of the town of Middleton for the relief of the poor, for the repair of the King's highways in that place, or for the payment of a tax of one-fifteenth to the king."[1]

Notwithstanding these and other occasional gifts the roads must have been in a perpetually bad state, veritable quagmires where they led through dense woods, and almost undistinguishable in other places when bordered by ploughed unenclosed land.

Much has been written about the scanty and Spartan way in which dwellings were furnished in Tudor days, but things had not much improved in this respect during the Stuart period. The following inventory appended to the Will of Roger Gaffield will throw some light on the subject:

"An Invotary of the moovable goods, Cattels & Chattels of Roggar Gaffield husba'd'an late disseased in Milto' take' this 25th. daye of Aparill 1631, the praisers names Richard Wright, Robert Johnson, Thomas Sebrooke.

IN PRIMIS IN THE HAULE.

One Olde Cubbard	4s.
One Old Chear	1d.
One table and frame One forme one bench and benchbord One ffalling table	6s.
One salting trof	3s.
4 Stooles w'th other implements	1d.
3 peeses of putar[2]	2s.–6d.

[1] See pages 255 and 284.
[2] Pewter.

one lethare bottell
one spit and cobirens [1] } . . 4s.
with all other Implements
4 Peeses of Bras . . . . 10s.

IN THE OVER PARLAR.

2 Barrels
One Cimnell [2] } . . 6s.–8d.
One Wollan Wheele
w'th other Impleme'ts

IN THE NETHAR PARLER.

One joyned Bed with the bedding
   belonging to it . . . 26s.–8d.
One standing Bed w'th the bedding
   belonging to it . . . 10s.
One pare of sheets 3 Napkins one
   pillowbier [3] . . . . 8s.
2 Coffars one chest one boultingtub [4] 8s.
his waring apparrell . . . 20s.
One cow . . . . . 33s.–4d.
the Crap of a quartere land [5] sold
   for one y'er . . . . £5–2s.–6.
     summ' totali . . Xij li–iiijs–xd

    Roger Gaffield was a man of substance, for he not only owned land and houses, which he bequeathed to his eldest son, but made one bequest of £20, five of £10 each, two of 20/-

---

[1] Cobirens, otherwise "cobirons," were andirons, the irons in ancient kitchens which supported the logs used as fuel, or the spit for roasting.

[2] Cimnell, also Kimnell, is any kind of tub for domestic purposes.

[3] Pillowbier, also "pillowbear," a pillow-case.

[4] A bolting tub was a tub in which to "bolt" or sift meal, to separate the bran from the flour by shaking the mass backwards and forwards in a cloth of loose texture.

[5] A quarter land means a quarter of a Yard land. A Yard land was thirty acres.

each and one of 2/- to his other children and relatives. Money in those days had a considerably greater purchasing value than it has now, hence there are frequently found explicit directions as to the bequest of a few shillings. Comparing Roger Gaffield's bequests with the following items, we gather that the inventory of his belongings must describe the household effects of a man in very comfortable circumstances :

Joan Sare al's Seabrooke. Oct. 16th, 1621, Wyddow. " To Henrie Seabrooke my sonne the sume of sixe shillinges of lawfull english money."

Francis Palmer, husbandman, Dec. 31st. 1640. " I give and bequeath to ye poore of Milton ffive shillings to be distributed to them by ye overseers for ye poore within tenne dayes after my decease."

Stephen Watts, Cottager, Sept. 21st. 1650. " Item, I give to my sonne Thomas Watts for a legasie ffive shillings to be payd him by my hereafter mentyoned executrix uppon his demandinge of it, after my decease."

In 1642 the Great Civil War broke out between King Charles I and the Parliament, but no Milton entries refer to it.

Amongst the documents that have been preserved in the parish chest are three ordering the appointment of Overseers for the Poor in the time of the Commonwealth, dated 1649, 1650 and 1656.

" North'ton ss. Wee whose names are heereunder subscribed Justice of Peace w'thin the County aforesaid doe Authorise and Allow of

John Bude & John Pell to bee Overseers of the poore for the p'rishe of Miltone for one whole yeare next ensueinge, Comandinge them togeather with the Churchwardens to pr'vide for the poore of their p'rishe Accordinge to the Lawe in that case pr'vided, Heereof faile not att yo'r p'rills, Given under o'r Hands and Seales the 4th. day of Aprill 1656.
William Ward.   George Benson."

A line scrawled at the bottom of the document reads : " The ould ones to paye to the newe ones the sume of 1£, 2s. 1d."

The following notice that was sent to the Parish Constable bears on the same subject, and is signed by William Dry, the Lord of the " Manor called Mantell's Manor " in Milton. The first two words stand for Wymersley Hundred.

" Wim'sley Hundr. To the Constable of this towne of Milton.

By vertue of a Warrant to me directed from Willm. Ward & Georg Benson Esqrs. Justices of the Peace &c : Theis are to will & require you to geve warning to the Churchw : & Overseers of the Poore of this p'rish p'rsonally to appeare before them at the signe of the Crowne in North'ton upon wensday in Easter weeke next, & that they bring with them their sev'rall Accounts fairely written in severall books, what money they have disbursed & what remaines in their hands, with 4 of the most substantiall mens hands in this p'rish to their severall Accounts. And you are likewise to geve notice to the Inhabitants of this p'rish to make choyse of. 2. or. 4 honest & able Inhabitants to be Overseers of the Poore, & also : two to be Church-

wardens for the ensuing yeare & that you returne the names of them in writing at the time & place aforesd., And hereof faile not at yo'r p'rill.
  Dated Aprill 8 : 1658. William Dry."

Another interesting document preserved from the seventeenth century is of a military nature :

" Recd. the 18 of May 1660 of Thomas Geese of Milton the sume of ij lb–4s–9d. wch is for one mounthes tax for the militia. I say recd.   lb. s. d. ij – 4 – 9
  By me John Billing."

In those days all owners of property had to furnish horses, men and weapons for the militia according to the value of their property. Thomas Geese probably had neither horse to spare nor arms to lend, and to avoid serving in the militia himself he paid the equivalent for another man and horse.

From the register we see it was customary to bury a body very soon after death. It was carried to church in a coffin kept for funerals, taken out at the grave and buried in its shroud. Hence the rubric in the Burial Office : " while the corpse is made ready to be laid into the earth."

" Anne the daughter of Richard and Mary Wells dyed the 26th. of June in the morning and buryed the 27th. of June 1696."

It is occasionally found of some value when the occupation is appended to any name entered in the old register, but this only too rarely occurs. Fortunately there is one such entry preserved which is of great interest because it relates to an old-time parish officer.

"1728. John Blunt, the Haward of the Town, was buried March 28th."

Haward is clearly a variant of Hayward, though *Cowell's Law Dictionary* gives it as "Haward *alias* Hayward." The word is probably derived from hay, a hedge, and -ward, the custodian. In early days a horn was always worn by the Hayward, who used to blow it to warn off people from straying in the crops. *Jacob's New Law Dictionary* gives the following meaning:

"Hayward is one that keeps the common herd of cattle of a town and the reason of his being called Hayward may be, because one part of his office is to see that they neither break nor crop the hedges of enclosed grounds, or for that he keeps the Grass from hurt and destruction. He is an officer appointed in the Lord's Court, and is to look to the fields and impound cattle that trespass therein, to inspect that no Pound Breaches be made, and if any be, to present them at the Leet. There may be a Custom in a Manor to have a Surveyor of the Fields or Hayward and for him to distrain Cattle Damage seasant, but he must avow in the name of him who hath the Freehold."

We find references to this officer in early poems:

"Claryce of Cockeslane, the clerk of the church,
 An haywarde and an heremyte, the hangeman
    of Tyborne."
            Langland. *Piers the Plowman* (c. 1350).

"The shepheards and haywards assemblies and meetings, when they kept their cattel and heards."
            Puttenham. *Art of English Poesie* (1589).

THE PARISH

The entry in the register of John Blunt's burial provides the only reference we have to the ancient and interesting office of Hayward in our village. As there is no other record extant, it is impossible now to know whether this ancient office did or did not survive until the Enclosure of the Commons, but in all probability it did.

The other parish officers at this time were the Pinnier (see page 207), the Headborough and the Parish Constable. The last named is still with us, but the other officers were discontinued about the middle of last century.

The duties of the Headborough had become little more than that of the constable. *Jacob's New Law Dictionary* gives us the following explanation of the title:

" Headborow. Him that is Head of the Frankpledge in Boroughs. and had the principal Government within his own Pledge—also called Thirdborow and Tithingman in different places. These Headborows were the chief of the ten Pledges. Headborows are now a kind of Constables."

Several appointments to this office are recorded in the Parish Vestry Minute Books. The earliest preserved is that for 1815 when, on Easter Monday, Thomas Cockerill was appointed to the office of Headborough as well as Overseer.

" 1826. Thursday, March 30th. William Marriott to serve the office of Constable and Thomas Cockerill, Headborough, for the ensuing year."

" 1826. June 1st. Thomas Lever was nominated to serve the office of Headborough for the year ensuing, Thomas Cockerill having allowed a prisoner under his care to be rescued."

In 1827 and at the Easter Vestry, April 3rd, 1828, Thomas Lever again accepted the office of Headborough, after which date we have no further record of it. Probably it became merged in the office of constable, for in 1845 we find two, and in 1849 no less than three parish constables appointed.

In 1727–8 there were considerable timber-stealing riots in Whittlebury and Salcey forests. About 147 people, amongst them being five persons from Milton, were bound over to the Assizes for unlawfully cutting down and carrying away several trees out of the respective forests of Salcey and Whittlewood, belonging to His Majesty. They had an idea that the timber could be taken without payment.[1]

As the eighteenth century advanced there was some building activity in Milton, the larger houses being added to or otherwise improved. At this time the Georges reigned, and the houses or house-fronts then erected are generally of a simple dignity characteristic of the design which is nowadays called Georgian. Towards the middle of the century both manor houses received each a new front, that of Milton Manor built on the side facing the road and that of the Manor being the east garden front. Milton House, too, was greatly improved a few years later, about 1777, by adding to the older portion

[1] *Northamptonshire Notes and Queries*, Vol. I, p. 197.

an entirely new wing facing south, so as to form a more imposing front.

Up to the close of the eighteenth century there were vast commons around Milton, as in other parts of the country, where certain people had rights. These rights of Common varied according to the tenement or the amount of arable land cultivated, to which the right of Common was attached by the custom of the manor, for there were some few tenements that had no such rights whatsoever. With reference to this it is interesting to note the gift made by Thomas Rage to the church, in 1507, of a " Toft and seven acres of land" (see page 251). According to *Wright's English Dialect Dictionary*, a toft is, or was, " a homestead, a messuage, really a small holding, which had right of common. Since the enclosure there are no tofts." As will be seen further on, there were only twelve tenements in Milton the occupiers of which had no rights of Common.

There were various kinds of common rights, such as Common of Pasture, Common of Estovers, or the right of taking wood for repairs, and Common of Pannage, or the right by which swine could be turned on to the land to eat the acorns and mast. These rights of Common varied in different parts of the country, being regulated by the customs in force on each manor, and there being no hard and fast rule to guide us, we know really very little of what customs prevailed at Milton. The old Court Rolls of both manors are lost, and until they come to light again we have to glean what information we can as to the commons from the

Wills, aided by knowledge of the customs generally in force throughout England.

First of all, we have the usual rights of Common of Pasture Appendant, where the right was granted in the first instance to one who held manorial copyhold or freehold in arable land. By this, the commoner had rights for as many animals as he could properly keep and as many as he required for ploughing and manuring his land. The arable land to which this Common of Pasture was appendant when first granted, could afterwards be converted into meadow or even built upon, but that would not affect the right of that freeholder to the common. This particular right was only in respect of horses, oxen or sheep; it could not be exercised for pigs, goats, geese and other animals or birds. Thus, George Norman, Yeoman, of Milton, in his Will dated December 20th, 1638, bequeaths as follows:

"ffirst I give to Margarett my wife three quarters of lande with the Cropp of graine thereon, hay, chaffe, comons for horse, cowes, sheepe, and all other profitts and emoluments thence groweinge and ariseinge."

There we have the three classes of animals specified for which he had rights of Common of Pasture appendant to his three quarters of a Yard of land.

One more instance. Robert Dunckley, Yeoman, of Milton, on September 9th, 1708, bequeaths:

" Unto my sone Robert Dunckley, all yt my house and homested & one yard land, with two little Closes & one Cottage w'ch I purchased of Thomas Green of Milton, w'th one Cow Common & two Sheeps Commons lying & being in ye parish of Milton a fore said."

All bequests were not so explicit, e.g. in the Will of John Hardinge, "Shepheard," of Milton, April 1st, 1615:

" I geve and bequeath unto Luce Gibbes ... my cottage and tenam't with all and singular the commons, premisses and theire appurten'nce thereunto appertayninge whatsoever, set situate lying and beinge in Milton al's Middleton Malsor aforesaid."

Again, John Langford of Milton, Taylor, on April 5th, 1686, bequeaths to Rebecca his wife:

"All my house homestall & cloase with all their appurtenances in Milton. Also I devise & give to her my two quartern lands, being of arable land leyes meadow & pasture ground with the Com'ons & appurtenances thereto belonging lying & being in the p'rish feilds pr'cincts & territorys of Milton al's Middleton Malsor aforesaid & Collingtree al's Collingtrough."

The rights of Common were also specified in the Deeds when homesteads were sold. One such homestead, now two cottages situated between the Church cottages and The Grove, was in 1747 occupied by Thomas Tebbutt and had "Commons and Common of Pasture for one Cow and two Sheep to be yearly had and taken within the ffields and Commonable places of Milton otherwise Middleton Malsor aforesaid and Collingtree otherwise Collingtrough."

In these last two instances, the commons were evidently those of "Mantell's Manor," as they are described as being of both Milton and Collingtree.

It must be borne in mind that there were officers of the manor who supervised the pasturing on the commons. Hence, any transgression of the customs in force on that manor, or any abuse of the right of Common, would be punished, usually by a fine, at the Courts of the Lord of the Manor. Any cattle belonging to people who had no right of Common, or any in excess of the rightful number for any commoner, that were found pasturing there, were at once impounded.

The land to which rights of Common were attached could be divided, and those rights would be distributed proportionately amongst the different parts. John Pell, yeoman, of Milton, October 30th, 1676, after bequeathing to his son John his " dwelling house and homestead in Milton aforesaid, with the Close and orchard and all houses and other appurtenance belonging to the same," goes on as follows :

" I do geve devise & bequeath unto my sonne Clement the on moytie or half parte of that half yard land which I did purchase of Richard Brownsword, with half the Com'ons or other appurten'nce belonging to the same—— Item, I do geve devise & bequeath unto my sonne ffrancis the other moytie or half parte of the aforesaid (half ?) yard land with the rest of the Com'ons & other appurten'nce belonging to the same."

MILTON CHURCH, 1924.

Photo, J. L. Hopkins, Esq.

THE PARISH

Another kind of right of pasturing is found in our Milton Wills, and that is the Common of Pasture in Gross. This was a purely personal right. It originated in a grant made by the owner of land possessing the right of Common of Pasture Appendant, and who thus diminished, by the extent of that grant, the right of Common attached to that particular piece of land. This grant was held quite apart from the ownership of land and could afterwards be sold by itself, or otherwise disposed of. We have an instance in the Will of Thomas Garnat, husbandman, of Milton, dated August 24th, 1592.

"Item. I give and bequeath unto my sd. wiffe the comons summeringe and winteringe of 4 sheepe yearlie soe longe as she liveth in and uppon the said messuage at the onely charge of my executor as he sumorethe and wintereth his hone (i.e. his own)."

Here the kind of animal and the number to which the widow's right was limited are distinctly specified. Under this bequest she could not graze horses or cows on the commons, but only sheep, and not more than four.

The right of Common attached to a homestead was apparently regarded as a matter of course, being known to the officers of the manor, and so was not always mentioned in Wills. Stephen Watts, Cottager, September 21st, 1650, briefly summarises his estate :

"In primis, I give and bequeath to my sonne John Watts my cottage, house, and homestead and all ye lands thereto belonginge to enter uppon, possess and enioy immediatly after my decease."

In this bequest it is possible that the phrase " all ye lands thereto belonging " would include the rights of Common attached to them.

Again, " William Payne ye elder of Milton ali's Middleton Maluazor, labourer," under date March 25th, 1648 :

" As ffore other my house, homestead and close, with my goods and chattels moveables and affixed unbequeathed, I give and bequeath to my sonne-in-law Robert Robbins &c."

These homesteads, sometimes called " homestalls " in the Wills, and many others where the commons are not explicitly mentioned, possibly enjoyed such rights. Other labourers beside William Payne possessed their homesteads, as is evident from the Wills, probably by copyhold of the manor, and therefore with a right of Common Appendant. Very poor indeed must that person be who did not possess the right of Common of Pasture for even one cow. This seemed to have been the low-water mark of poverty. We have a hint to that effect in the Will of John Stephenson of Milton, April 10th, 1610.

" Item. I give to ev're widow woman in Milton not having a cowe, ijd. a peece to be paid w'hin one moneth after my buryall."

Not only the tenants of the manor but the Lord of the Manor himself enjoyed rights of Common, for he was really, under the Crown, the owner of the common lands and could do as he pleased with them, as long as he did not interfere with the rights of the commoners. Edmund

Gleed, Lord of the Manor, in his Will dated April 25th, 1679, bequeaths to his son Richard the Manor House with all its " meadows pasture feedings commons Common of pasture woods underwoods trees hedges, ditches fences mounds wayes bushes furzes ponds fishings " &c.

Although the wording is so comprehensive as to be almost indefinite, I understand this portion to mean that the Lord of the Manor is bequeathing all his commons, the Common of pasture, Common of woods and trees and all connected therewith, together with Common of ponds and fishings. If I am right in my reading of this, we have a reference to Common of Estovers and Common of Piscary in Milton.

Common of Estovers was the right to take wood for various necessary purposes ; of timber trees for the repair of dwellings and agricultural implements, suitable wood for the repair of fences, and smaller wood such as lops of branches, underwood and windfalls, for fuel. The cutting of trees could only be done with the sanction of the officers of the manor.

Common of Piscary was the right of fishing, but this was more limited, and it is probable that very few in Milton enjoyed this privilege lawfully. The ponds referred to were the Milton " fishpools " and were situated on the lands of this manor.

All these rights of Common were a survival from early times when provision was made for the support of the villagers engaged in agriculture. They were customs that originated among the old Anglo-Saxon village communities and were continued of necessity under the Normans when the tenants became what can only be described as the subjects of the Lord of the Manor. As years rolled by these customs became acknowledged rights.

It is probable that the arable land attached to the Milton tenements consisted of at least three vast, unenclosed fields, according to the Terrier (page 294). In this are mentioned " the great Southfield," " Cross Field " and " Ladybridge Field." These were divided off by what were locally called " balks," otherwise headlands, which were slightly raised banks about sixteen feet wide, along which carts could pass from one part to another without damaging the growing crops. The fields were really like modern allotments on a huge scale, grain being grown instead of vegetables, and during the time between reaping and sowing there would be rights of Common over this land. Balks were also used to mark the boundary of the parish.

As there were two manors, they each had common lands, side by side, those of one manor comprising commons in Collingtree as well as in Milton. Hence there undoubtedly existed with us, from force of circumstances, a custom usually called Common of Pasture because of vicinage. This originated through the cattle on the commons of one manor straying on to the commons of the adjoining manor owing to the lack of fences, and so was really a recognised trespass which could be terminated at any time by putting up a hedge or fence.

There were of course certain lands and parcels

of ground that had been enclosed before the eighteenth century. These were mainly within or adjacent to the village, and are occasionally referred to as " old enclosures."

The Bill for enclosing the Milton commons was brought before the Houses of Parliament in 1779 and passed. Its title was :

" A Bill for dividing, allotting & inclosing the Open & Common Fields, Common Pastures, Common Meadows and other Commonable Lands & Grounds of & within the Manors & Parishes of Milton, otherwise Middleton Malsor, and Collingtree, otherwise Collingtrough, in the County of Northampton. 1779."

It was stated that " the Open & Common Fields &c in Milton and Collingtree consist of 70 Yard Lands & Three-quarter of a Yard Land (besides odd Lands), about 2,000 acres or thereabouts."

A Yard Land consists of 30 acres.

Three Commissioners were sworn for the partition of the commons, but one refused to act also as a " Quality Man," or assessor of the value of land, so another had to be sworn for that purpose. This was in the summer of 1779. The Commissioners sat at the Angel Inn, Northampton, and signed the award on May 10th, 1780. Altogether, the proceedings cost £1954 9s. 3½d., which included charges for legal aid and the passing of the Act. This was paid by those who received allotments of land.

In the award, the rights of all the commoners were recognised and the commonable lands were divided amongst them in proportion with the extent of their claim. An agreement was arrived at with everyone concerned by which the Rector gave up his right to the ancient tithes in exchange for a proportionate part of each commoner's grant. For these, with his own rights of Common as well as several old enclosures, he was compensated by a grant of land. By this agreement we know there were twelve houses in Milton that had no right of Common, because, as a Terrier of 1798 tells us, they " had not land to exonerate themselves from Tythes at the Inclosure." At least two of them seem to have been larger than cottages, so it must be presumed that the number of poor people in Milton was very small. When the commons were partitioned, several people exchanged their share of the newly enclosed land for old enclosures near their homes, hence certain old enclosures belonging to the Church and Poor's Estate were exchanged for two fields.

Boundaries and fences were determined, and public roads, bridle-ways and footpaths four feet broad were defined by the Commissioners. Several private carriage roads, drift roads and private footways were agreed upon to enable owners to reach their newly allotted lands. By the award, too, the boundary between the Parishes and Manors of Milton and Collingtree was finally settled.

Thus came to an end the old Commons of Milton, with all their benefits and privileges. Although every person having any legal right to the common lands shared in the award, the enclosure was a most unfortunate proceeding for the village, and the dire results were soon seen. The husbandman or small farmer, the cottager and even the labourer possessing his own homestead, had each been able to make a decent living from his bit of land combined with his rights of pasture and the privilege of taking timber and small wood for repairs and fuel. Now, owing perhaps to the fact that the share of the commons allotted to them had so increased the value of their homesteads, they were tempted to sell. By the year 1800, many had sold their little homesteads in Milton. The fields were gradually acquired by the larger landowners, and the little farmhouses, being useless without land, remained untenanted and were eventually divided up to form smaller cottages. In 1800, for instance, the place now known as Barrack Yard was merely the farmyard with a big barn and stables belonging to the little thatched farmhouse, fronted by a garden, that faces the road. No one could afford to rent the large premises without the land, so the barn and stables were, in course of time, converted into small dwellings. Those who, for a time, still managed to keep their small farms going, missed the convenient help of the commons, and they, too, gave up the struggle. This meant the disappearance of a sturdy class of agriculturist, and there arose strong public feeling at the wholesale enclosures of the open fields and common lands of England, as the following lines show :

> " The law locks up the man or woman
> Who steals the goose from off the common,
> But lets the greater villain loose
> Who steals the common from the goose."

The conversion of homesteads into several smaller dwellings caused a great increase in the number of inhabitants. The population was 327 in 1801, 492 in 1821, 541 in 1831 and 607 in 1841.

The passing of the common lands witnessed the passing of the Milton of old, with its numerous small homesteads and few poor.

Not many years after this, the village suffered from a visitation of smallpox. From June to December, 1794, there were ten deaths from this dread disease and three from "fever," whilst in the following January there were no less than six deaths.

In 1805 a beginning was made in the improvement of the village streets, for on June 8th of that year it is recorded in the Churchwardens' Accounts :

" Paid Ed. Johnson for pitching the Church Ways by Mr. Dent's £3.16.0."

This " pitching " was the making of the cobble-stone side-walks.

In December, 1806, Pluck's Lane was pitched, 202 yards, at 4d. per yard. In January, 1807, the " pitching down at Stockwell " was finished, 42 square yards. Other places pitched in the same year are described as " against Mooring's," " Church Lays," " Mr. Dent's Lays," " against Phipps' new house " and " against the blacksmith's." Most of these side-walks may be identified.

At this time there was a workhouse in the village, probably the place known as " Workhouse Yard." In 1815 we find that Thomas

Caswell was Workhouse Master, being paid at the rate of seven shillings per week, and to provide for all the inmates he was to have three shillings and sixpence per head " and to have 3 tons of coal & 1 ton of wood." In 1831 a new site was fixed upon for the workhouse, the houses in Barrack Yard being adapted for the purpose. This, with other property, was in the hands of the Parish Vestry, for which they paid rent to the various owners. In these houses, rented by the parish, and which to all intents and purposes were almshouses, were lodged the aged and infirm poor.

" 1822. Thursday, May 2nd. Sophia A—— to live with Jane Fl——, and the house she occupied Wm Fi—— is to remove to."

Some who occupied houses had their rent paid, as we see from the Vestry Minutes :

" 1822. Aug. 28th. Widow S—— to have half of her Rent paid."

" 1829. Nov. 11th. John B—— being old and infirm, is to have his Rent paid up to Michaelmas last, two Guineas."

By an Act of 1796 poor persons were to receive relief in their homes and they were encouraged to depend upon the parish for a living. Wages were reduced by what was called the "allowance system." Labourers were shared amongst the ratepayers by the " Labour-rate " system, that is, the employer paid part of the wages and the remainder was paid by the parish at the hands of the Overseers for the Poor, the latter payment being described as "out of the book." The ridiculous state of affairs resulted by which it was extremely difficult for any except those in receipt of parish relief to obtain employment. An employer would not engage an independent labourer and pay all his wages when he could have a man in receipt of parish relief and whose wages would be paid partly from the rates. Thus the labourers were pauperised wholesale. We learn all this from the Parish Vestry Minutes of that time.

"1820. December 14th. At a Public Vestry held this day it was agreed that the Labourers out of Employ should be ballotted for, which was done accordingly."

Then follows a list of men who were to go to work under different employers.

"1822. Nov. 14th. The Parish will not find J. H. with work, he having a Pension of 1/- per day."

"1825. Nov. 17th. Thomas W—— having returned from the 3rd Veteran Battn. on a pension of sixpence per day to be employed on the byroad, and have the magistrates allowance, for a short time. To have one pound lent him to purchase some bedding for the children."

"1824. February 5th. John T—— to be employed by Mr. P—— who agrees to give him six shillings per week. The remainder to be paid out of the Book, 5/3."

"1824. Apl. 1st. T. H—— to be employed by Mr. D—— who will pay 7/-. Remainder out of book 4/3."

Relief was also given to the labourer's wife and children. These few cases have been chosen to illustrate the custom and to show the rate of pay then prevalent, 11/3 per week. It was the evil system that was at fault. The employers were compelled, in self-defence, to take advantage of it, because, through heavy levies, they themselves indirectly paid that part of the wages given in Poor Relief. Instances are here given of the annual levies made:

"1821. Recd. by Five Levies at 2/– in the Pound . . £680 6 10½."
"1823. Recd. by four Levies at 2/– & one Levy at 1/– in the pound . . . £612 6 2¼."

Five levies at 2/– each yearly were of course equal to a rate of 10/– in the £.

As may well be imagined, there was an eager desire to assist the migration of those most likely to become a charge on the parish, combined with a strict investigation of a poor man's settlement, i.e. his right to claim that particular parish as his own for the purpose of Poor Relief.

"1823. Jan. 25th. Paid expences at the Record Room for having Wm. D——'s Settlement tried, when it appeared he belonged to this Parish. 3/–
"1824. Feb. 5th. Thomas G—— being distressed is to have Relief & his Settlement tried."
"1825. Nov. 17th. Several persons reside in the Parish who do not belong to it : to be inquired after to know where they do belong."
"1826. Thursday, Oct. 26th. William A—— who has been residing in London for upwards of ten years, applied to the Vestry for money to

pay one quarter's rent for a house, to Michaelmas day last and informed the Gentlemen present that he had three stamped receipts, for the former Quarters, and it was agreed that if he produced them the Overseer was to send him the money for the quarter above named, which would (he said) gain him a settlement.

Qr's Rent . . . . £3 5 0.
Gave him to take him to London   5 0."

It will be seen from this that a period of residence and paying rent would qualify a man for his settlement in a parish. Birth, of course, always conferred that right, but in the case of such birds of passage as tramps it was necessary to take every precaution that the place of birth should be properly recorded, since there were no Registrars of Births in those days except the clergy. Hence we have such an entry as the following in the church register:

"1711. John the son of Tho. Wright & Mary his wife a travelling woman, it was brought to bed in our parish, was baptiz'd Jan. 1."

The parish looked after its own poor, but was by no means charitable to strangers. When a man and his family were destitute, and the magistrates decided they belonged to some other parish, it was ordered that they should be removed thither. Several copies of such orders are preserved in the Parish Chest, some directed to the Constables and Thirdboroughs of Milton, others to the Churchwardens and Overseers. The cost of the removal in those days was, of course, great, as travelling was not accom-

THE PARISH

plished with present-day ease and rapidity. There is an account of the expenses incurred in removing a family from Milton to Halesowen, where they "belonged." It takes up the first page of one of the Overseer's books.

	£	s.	d.
1814. April 25. set off with John M—— & is wife & two Children to Hales Owen			
Expences attending the same Orders		6	0
Surtevicate of the marage		1	0
two Days at the Sessions & Expences	1	0	0
Coach fair & Expences at Northton	3	12	6
Weedon & Dunchurch		1	2
Coventry		1	4
Coachman at Birmingham		5	0
Supper & breakfast at Do.	1	15	6
hackney Coach to Hales Owen	1	0	0
Expence at Hales Owen		4	6
Coach from Birm'g: to Hayford		19	0
Expence at Birmingham Coming back		3	0
Coachman		2	6
banbury Lane		4	6
Pd. John Gleed garding M—— 3 Days & 3 Nights		7	6
Pd. Hill for going with me	1	0	0
M——'s Wife & Children came back & May 7 sent to Gail the Commitment		2	0
Expences at North'ton		2	0
my Time &c. to Hales owen	1	10	0
Pd. Richd Robinson for mending the woman's shoes		1	6
Expences with the Overseer of Hales owen when he came to recind the Order		10	0
Pd. for the Order coming by Post		1	4
Pd. the Overseers Expences coming to Milton & not to appeal against the Order	9	9	0

Pd Nichols expence of M—— & is Wife 2 12 6
August 6. Warant & examination for M——'s Wif 3 0

Total . . £25 14 10

The Act of 1837, which is still the guiding principle of our Poor Law Administration, has brought about a much more satisfactory, though by no means perfect, state of affairs. Families need not now be removed, but the place of settlement is responsible for the relief paid by the parish in which they live.

With regard to its own poor, Milton seems to have done its best, and there is a quaint resolution to obtain medical attendance for two men, but the wording would imply that the Vestry had little faith in the doctor's skill or ability :

" 1827, March 28th. Edward Southam to try to cure B——'s leg, and also to try what he can do with William F——."

Possibly this did not prove satisfactory, for on April 3rd, 1828, it was resolved :

" That application should be made to some professional gentleman to attend the poor of the Parish upon an annual salary."

In one brief entry a lurid light is thrown on prison conditions :

" 1825, March 17th. Thomas I—— expected out of Gaol in a few days, and being almost naked, to have one shirt purchased for him."

Another entry is of a more placid description, being of a pastoral nature :

THE PARISH

"1828, Nov. 13th., John T—— to have a Smock frock given him from the charitable fund."

In 1821 was held the second Census, the returns of which are fully copied out in the Vestry Book for that period, together with a general summary, which is here given:

Number of Males .	227
,, ,, Females .	265
Total .	492

Inhabited Houses .	105
Uninhabited Houses.	3
Occupied by .	108 Families.

Occupations		
	Chiefly Employed in Agriculture . .	82
	Chiefly Employed in Trade &c. . .	19
	Remaining Families .	7
		108

One hundred years later, in 1921, the population of Milton was:

Number of Males .	280
,, Females .	293
Total. .	573

Inhabited Houses .	143
Occupied by . .	145 families.

Milton, even in the early part of last century, was far-seeing and philanthropic. Receipts are preserved showing subscriptions from our parish of two guineas each year from 1814 to 1818 " towards the Establishment and Support of the *General Infirmary*, in the Town of *Northampton*, for the Relief of the Sick and Lame Poor of all Counties." Also, at a Public Vestry, on March 28th, 1825, it was agreed " to subscribe to the Northampton Fire Engine," a wise precautionary step.

This was a time of great distress and unrest throughout the country, and we find the Rector of Milton, Dr. Miller, opening a subscription list for the poor of his parish. Rioting seems to have taken place, and the Vestry Minutes show that another subscription list was opened to pay men who were to keep watch at night in the village :

" 1831. January 6th. It was ordered this Vestry that the men who keep watch in the night shall have two shillings and sixpence each, and that the same be defrayed from the subscription entered into, on the tenth day of December last, in consequence of a threatening letter directed to Mr. J—— D——."

Again, another entry :

" 1831. Feb. 10th., The men who kept watch in the night, to receive 2 shills. each per night and their expences of eating and drinking to be paid for them."

In the year 1827, the present Baptist Chapel was erected in the village. It is a commodious building, with a good-sized vestry, and has seating accommodation in the gallery and below for about 170 worshippers in all. The stone with which it was built is from the local " stone-pit close," and was given by Mr. Joseph Dent of Milton Manor.

This chapel probably replaced an earlier one, registered in 1820 (see below), to which there is a reference in the Parish Vestry Minutes for July 29th, 1824. A meeting of the Vestry was summoned "for the purpose of Awarding the Pews &c lately erected in the Church to the Proper Claimants," and amongst the awards is the following :

" No. 5 Middle Aisle to Mr. Joseph Dent for his House, now occupied by Thomas Tomalin, and Meeting House."

However, the Baptists had begun to make their appearance in the village more than a hundred years before this. The first intimation of this we have from the church register :

" —— the son of Thomas Green, Dissenter & Carpenter, & Anne his wife, was born Feb. 16th. 1701/2 but unbaptised."

From the fact that his four children were unbaptised there is some reason for concluding that Thomas Green was a Baptist, probably the first one in Milton.

Nonconformist Chapels, or Meeting Houses as they were called in those days, were registered and certified as places of worship by the Bishop of the Diocese up to 1852, after which this power was vested by statute in the Registrar-General. The following is a list of the Meeting Houses registered for the Parish of Milton, extracted from the register of the Bishop of Peterborough :

Description of place of meeting.	When certified and registered.
The house of William Collier	16 Janry. 1819.
A Building	13th. July 1820.
(Probably the Baptist Chapel prior to that built in 1827).	
A certain Outhouse the property of William Black and in the occupation of Joseph Hodges	7th. July 1821.
A Building on a plot of ground adjoining the Principal Street	21 July 1827.
(This was the present Baptist Chapel.)	
A House in the occupation of Simon Twistleton	13 Janry. 1836.
A House in the occupation of James Couch	19 Febry. 1838.
A House and premises in the occupation of Joseph Hodge	22nd Octr. 1847

Later on, the Primitive Methodists built a small chapel near Stockwell in 1865, which has seen many ups and downs, and I understand that the Wesleyan Methodists about the same date hired a cottage in which to hold services in Milton.

During the early part of the nineteenth century, the usual conveyance for long journeys was the stage coach, but the tentacles of modern progress were now reaching across the country. Feelers in the direction of means of transport other than by road had been put forth in the latter part of the previous century. William Pitt, who wrote a *Survey of the County of Northampton*, published in 1809, visited the county in

THE PARISH

1797 and found that the Grand Junction Canal had by then been completed from Braunston to Blisworth. It was intended to make a cut from Gayton to Northampton. Nine years later, in 1806, Pitt again visited the county, and found that the new cut had not been made to the town, but that from the canal " the communication with Northampton is by a railway." This was, of course, a tramway for trucks drawn by horses.

Near Mr. W. T. Asplin's brickyard, close to the bridge, the canal widens and a landing-place has been built. At this point was undoubtedly the wharf where goods from Northampton were loaded on to the waiting barges, and near this spot the tramway from the town had its terminus. It must be remembered there was no railway bridge in the way then. From the wharf, the tramway ran along the straight piece of the Milton road, which was levelled, for about a quarter of a mile up to the turn by the next bridge, then it ran along the site of the present canal. Parts of the old tramlines and sleepers were found in position when the canal to Northampton was drained in 1824.

This method of transport did not meet with the approval of the Corporation of Northampton, owing to the extra loading and unloading from tram to barge, so the present canal was eventually cut, joining the other by the " Navigation Inn." Where it joins is locally called the " Arm," owing of course to its branching off. The canal to Northampton was made some time after William Pitt's visit in 1806, and before 1824, when this branch was drained.

A more formidable rival in methods of transport soon appeared in the field. On September 17th, 1838, was opened the London and Birmingham Railway, afterwards the London and North-Western Railway, and now, through amalgamation with others in 1923, the London, Midland and Scottish Railway. This passed through the south-east corner of the parish. The station was at first more conveniently situated for Milton than it is now, the booking office being in the houses south of the bridge spanning the road between Milton and Blisworth, with a covered flight of steps leading up to the platform on the railway embankment. Some few years afterwards the station was moved to its present position, its name being changed to Gayton Station, and afterwards Blisworth Junction.

On June 2nd, 1845, was opened the branch line from Blisworth to Peterborough, through Bridge Street Station, Northampton. A Public Vestry was held on October 9th, 1845, " to consider the propriety of assessing the Northampton and Peterborough branch of the London and Birmingham Railway passing through the parish of Milton." Eventually the assessment for this piece of railway was as follows :

	£	s.	d.
Rateable Value	253	3	7½
Former Annual Value of Land before Railway was formed .	11	1	10½

George Borrow, in his *Wild Wales*, describes his journey from Peterborough to " Blissworth " by this railway in 1854.

THE PARISH

At a Parish Vestry, on December 15th, 1853, it was resolved to build a seven-foot arch over the brook that runs across the road below the churchyard. The work was done in 1854, and the road levelled up for a length of forty yards, the material for filling up being taken from the crown of the Church Hill. In 1855 a culvert was turned between the drain and the brook at Stockwell. About this time, too, the bridge over the stream crossing Gayton Road was built. This was once known as " Croxford's Bridge." The bridge over the stream at the east end of Pluck's Lane was also built. As the road running past Milton House to the top of Pluck's Lane was being lowered, soil was taken thence to level up the road by these two bridges as well as to fill up the three Fishpools. Further measures for the safety and comfort of wayfarers, especially on dark nights, were taken in 1875 when the brook near Stockwell was covered with an arch.

Sanitary conditions were by no means satisfactory, for in 1863 smallpox was again rife in the village, and in the autumn of 1884 typhoid fever raged. The outbreak was evidently traced to the public water supply, for in December the water in the town well was condemned as unfit. The arch of the old well can still be seen in the wall of the garden facing the War Memorial. Eventually, a parish well was sunk in 1887 on the site of the old Pound, a few yards away. Nor had the sanitary state of the village been neglected. Since 1885 it had been continually under discussion, and at last the work of draining was begun in 1890, the drain being taken into "Mr. Manning's second meadow." The drainage system was further extended in 1892. Microbes and bacilli had one more fling in 1893, when several cases of cholera occurred in the village.

Meanwhile the railway was not idle. In 1875 an Act was passed for making a new line from Roade through Northampton to Rugby, called the Bletchley, Northampton and Rugby line. This runs through the parish, east of the church. In 1877, a field on the glebe farm was acquired for a few years by the Railway Company on which to deposit spoil, hence this field has been given the name of "Spoil Bank." As the line approaches the parish, after branching off from the old main line to Blisworth, it quickly dips deeper into the ground, owing to the lower levels to be met. The cutting had to be made not only through the rock but also into the Lias clay beneath. In course of time the clay was so affected after heavy rain that the rock lost its support. A serious slip occurred in November, 1891, and the new line was buried under thousands of tons of fallen rock. To strengthen the enormous walls that were then built, massive iron girders were fixed above the line, stretching from side to side, as a support.

It may here be mentioned that in 1922 the rateable value of the three sections of railway in the parish was £3360, but in 1923 it was reduced to £3057 on appeal.

The Local Government Act of 1894 brought into being the Parish Council, practically putting an end to the old-time Public Vestry, which now only meets once a year at Easter. With its extremely limited powers, the Parish Council is, as it were, but the feeble ghost of the vestries of old, most of whose civil powers are now distributed amongst the County Council, the District Council and the Board of Guardians.

In 1913, Sir W. Ryland D. Adkins generously presented oil lamps, with the posts and brackets necessary, for lighting the village streets at night. The first rate for this purpose was made on December 20th, 1913. However, owing to the abnormal rise in the price of oil and other charges during the War, the lighting of the streets had to be temporarily abandoned. Since then, both the Electric Light and Gas Companies of Northampton have canvassed the village, but so far our hopes of enjoying these benefits have not been realised.

No further event of importance occurred until the outbreak of the Great War in 1914, when the men and lads of the village, with very few exceptions, took their gallant share in the grim task. Nor were the women of Milton without their part to perform, for a Red Cross Working Party was formed and met at the Rectory under the presidency, first of Mrs. A. C. Neely, and from 1917 of Mrs. B. E. Evans who, until her removal to Milton with her husband, had been Managing Secretary of the Great Eastern Railway Rest Room for Sailors and Soldiers at Peterborough. Various articles were knitted and sewn for men on service, and Christmas parcels were despatched to Milton men and lads. The people at home were not to remain in any feeling of security in their Midland village. About 10.30 on Friday night, October 19th, 1917, a Zeppelin airship passed over, dropping four bombs as near to the parish as Hunsbury Hill, much to the surprise of two men who had returned that same night to Milton on leave from the trenches in Flanders. This airship had come from the direction of Northampton, where it had dropped bombs and killed a woman and two children in a house near Castle Station.

For the first time in history since the cessation of the Curfew, no lights were allowed to be seen at night. Windows were shrouded with thick blinds or curtains, and gardeners had to be careful that bonfires were extinguished at dusk.

At last, on Monday, November 11th, 1918, the Armistice was signed. The bells of the old parish church rang out a joyous peal—to some, alas, coming too late—and a united Service of Thanksgiving was held in church on the following Thursday morning. Peace Day was celebrated the next year on the official date, Saturday, July 19th, the festivities consisting of an open-air meat tea on the Green for adults, and a tea for children in the schoolroom, followed by sports and a display of fireworks in the field to the east of the church. A year later, the War Memorial on the Little Green to those Milton men who died on service, was unveiled by General Lord Horne on Saturday, July 17th, 1920. There was a short service, opened with the hymn, " O God, our help in ages past." Prayers were offered by the Rector and by the Rev. W. Wyatt, the local acting Baptist Minister. Afterwards the Rector asked Sir W. Ryland D. Adkins, K.C., M.P., Chairman of the Parish Council, to take charge of the Memorial on behalf of the Parish Council. Sir Ryland accepted the charge in the name of the Council and then asked General Lord Horne to unveil it. When this had been done, the hymn, " How bright those glorious spirits shine," was sung, at the close of which buglers from the Northampton Barracks sounded the " Last Post " and the " Reveille." Amongst those present were the Boy Scouts, of which Milton then possessed a troop, the schoolchildren, the ex-service men, who mustered well to do honour to their fallen comrades, and Brigadier-General H. E. Stockdale, D.S.O., C.B., who had recently taken Milton Manor for a few years.

The Memorial was designed by J. A. Gotch, Esq., F.R.I.B.A. The cost was subscribed by people of the parish, and amounted to £100, with a few extras. The Memorial is a slender stone shaft, terminating in a cross. On each side of the base from which it springs are panels, bearing the following inscriptions :

SOUTH : To keep in mind those who from this place gave their lives in the Great War, 1914–1919.

EAST : James William Collar, Ernest Richard East, Noel Legard Alexander, Frederick Ryland Digby.

NORTH : William Munn, William Frank Hanwell, Harry Cherry, Reuben John Morton.

WEST : William Thomas Clark, Francis James Turner, Frederick George Yates, George Twiselton.

In the above, the points of the compass are given approximately.

During the Great War, so many medical men joined the Army that the number left at home was very small. Unfortunately the winter of 1917–1918 and that of 1918–1919 are to be remembered for the severe epidemics of diphtheria and influenza. With our resident doctor at the Front, and with no nurse, no telegraph, no telephone, we had to do the best we could, but Dr. Ryan, of Roade, who looked after Dr. Jeaffreson's practice, worked untiringly and, one may almost say, unceasingly. The Rectory became something like a Medical Stores, where almost everything could be obtained for sick cases.

After such an experience, the Rector endeavoured to obtain a District Nurse and, although there were a few disappointments, he was able at last to form a District Nursing Committee for Milton and to have one formed at Collingtree. With these the Committee already existing at Blisworth was amalgamated to form one Joint Association affiliated to that of the County. This was inaugurated on March 5th, 1919.

On December 6th, 1923, there were 285 names on the List of Parliamentary Voters for Milton. We may compare this with the " Copies of the Polls taken at Northampton for the Election of

Knights of the Shire, in the years 1702, 1705, 1730, 1748, and 1806." The numbers of Milton people who voted in those years were respectively 11, 13, 22, 20, and 7.

This chapter would not be complete without some reference to the Free Gardeners. One of the oldest of Friendly Societies, it is of Scottish origin, and there is evidence that lodges existed in Scotland about 1680. Among the different federations are the Ancient Order of Free Gardeners, the British Order of Ancient Free Gardeners, the National United Order of Free Gardeners and the Saint Andrew's Order of Free Gardeners.

The "Lord of the Manor Lodge" of Milton, of which the writer is an honorary member, is No. 1138 in the National United Order of Free Gardeners. It was duly opened for the first time in January, 1873, and now, fifty years after, it has a membership of 320 adults and about 100 juveniles. The "Club Parade" is held on Whit-Sunday, when the members make a house-to-house collection for the Northampton Hospital, and in the evening march to church, headed by a band.

It remains to add that Milton is well served with motor-bus facilities, being on the Northampton to Towcester route. First in the field were Messrs. F. and E. Beeden, who ran a bus in 1912. Afterwards came the "Midland Motor Bus Company," which was discontinued in 1922. In January, 1921, Messrs. Nightingale and Son put their first bus on the route. Beside these there are now several smaller motor conveyances that ply on market days between Northampton and the villages beyond Milton.

Since writing the above a " silver " band has been formed in the village, silver-plated instruments having been obtained. This, it is hoped, will prove of benefit to the men and lads of the village.

CHAPTER XII

PLACE-NAMES

Hemp Land

STRANGELY enough, very few of the younger generation seem to have heard of this, though the older inhabitants of the village know it well. The name occurs in the Minute Books of the Parish Vestry :

"1814 Apl 2. Taking 2 loads of stone to the hempland."

"1829. May 29 Repairing the hempland wall 5/."

Earlier than that, it is mentioned in the Enclosure Award and is marked by that name on the map. It also had its place in the Rate Books up to the year 1916, but after that date it appears no more ; for the hempland is that square piece of ground running out from the north-east of the old churchyard, of which it now forms part. Formerly it was a portion of the Rector's glebe, for in a Terrier dated April 21, 1855, signed by the Rev. T. A. Kershaw, in describing two small plots of land the deed runs, " the other being one close or old enclosure called the Hemp Land, containing 24 perches and adjoining Milton Churchyard." In 1912 the Rev. Andrew Cavendish Neely, Rector, conveyed to the Ecclesiastical Commissioners " all that piece of glebe land containing 30 poles or thereabouts " to form an addition to the churchyard.

So the name is passing away, a name with its own historic significance. The " hemp land " carries us back to the days of Henry VIII. To encourage home manufactures the King discountenanced the importation of certain foreign goods,

" amongst the which wares one kind of merchandise in great quantity, which is linen cloth of divers sorts made in divers countries beyond the sea, is daily conveyed into this Realm ; . . . And also the people of this Realm, as well men as women, which should and might be set on work, by exercise of like policy and craft of spinning, weaving and making of cloth, lies now in idleness and otiosity, to the high displeasure of Almighty God, great diminution of the King's people, and extreme ruin, decay, and impoverishment of this Realm. Therefore, for reformation of these things, the King's most Royal Majesty . . . hath, by the advice and consent of his Lords and Commons in Parliament assembled, ordained and enacted that every person occupying land for tillage, shall for every sixty acres which he hath under the plough, sow one quarter of an acre in flax or hemp." (24 Henry VIII).

This piece of legislation, however, did not meet the need, but in many parishes there is still a " flax piece " and in some the " hemplow," and in others, as in Milton, the " hempland," that has survived in name for so many years.

The Village Pound

As was the case with most, if not all, other parishes, Milton possessed its " pound." This was an enclosed space into which cattle might be driven and shut in securely if they had been found straying. The pound at Milton stood in that wide recess that still exists in the garden wall where the pump now stands, close to the Little Green. A fence and a large gate formed the side nearest the road. In this enclosure the straying beasts were " impounded," or in common parlance " pinned," a word derived from the Old English word " pyndam," which meant to " dam up " or to " enclose," and survives in the verb " to pen." From this, animals thus secured were said to have been " penned," or pounded.

There were two kinds of pounds, one called the " pound overt," that was built by the Lord of the Manor for his own use or that of his tenants, or was one that belonged to the parish or village ; the other was the " pound covert," which was owned by one person for his own use, and so was a private pound. That at Milton was a " pound overt," it being a public one, and a man was appointed by the Parish Vestry to take charge of it. In his possession the key remained. To him application was made if animals were to be impounded or taken out of pound. In Milton this official was called the " pinnier " or " pynyerd." Mr. W. W. Clarke informed me that as many as twenty horses could be " pinned " in the Milton pound.

The method of impounding was as follows : A farmer or other occupier of land, finding straying animals damaging his crops, or gardens, would drive them to the pound in the village. The " pinnier " would then unlock the padlock so that the beasts could be driven through the gate. Then in some places he would snap a stick in two pieces, giving one to the aggrieved farmer and retaining the other piece himself. The owner of the straying cattle on finding them " pinned," would demand the name of the impounder, and this being given him he would go and learn what amount of damage his animals had done. On paying the cost of the damage, he would be given in receipt the piece of broken stick which he would take at once to the pinnier. That official would join the broken ends together and, if they matched, it was proof that the cost of the damage had been paid. But then there was another bill to pay. If the animals had been in the pound several days, there was the cost of their keep to be accounted for, and only after this was paid would they at last be delivered to their owner.

Sometimes the amount of costs incurred would be so considerable that the owners of the trespassing animals would in desperation endeavour to commit " pound-breach," that is, break open the gate or otherwise damage the pound and drive off their property without paying anything. This was a misdemeanour and punishable by law.

Pounds fell into disuse through the greater convenience afforded by the County Court for recovering of debt and cost of damage. It is not generally known, however, that under the Public Health Act, 1875, Urban District Councils have the power to provide a pound in their district for straying animals and to impose penalties on the owner. The last pynyerd of Milton was a Mr. Voss.

The earliest reference to the Milton Pound occurs in the Will of Thomas Wells, Yeoman, of Milton, June 8th, 1686 :

" Unto my sone Richard Wells the little close in Milton wch adjoyneth to the Common pound."

The following Parish Vestry minutes may prove of interest :

Nov. 5th, 1827. " That a Pinnier be appointed to the Parish, and that the office be offered to Benjamin Oxley—and that he may demand the sum of four pence for each lot of animals found at large in the public streets or otherwise trespassing."

March 6th, 1852. " That in consequence of the many complaints which have been made respecting stray cattle in the lanes and streets damaging property and crops, a printed notice be posted in the village " that all such cattle will be pounded," and also that a new substantial lock and key be provided for the pound door, the expenses of the same to be inserted in the surveyors' accounts."

March 21st, 1872. " It was agreed that Mr. Fisher should make an offer to Mr. J. P. Roe of the ground on which the old pound was, subject to the Clerk of the Board of Guardians opinion as to the legality of the parish being able to make the offer."

Decr. 12th, 1884. " It shall be suggested to the Hardingstone Local Authority that a well be sunk on the site of the Parish Pound, and if a good and pure water supply be found a parish pump shall be erected."

Anchor Close

In the village is a yard commonly known as " Barrack Yard," but which is also called " Anchor Terrace." On the Enclosure Award Map this piece of ground with the site of the neighbouring nursery gardens is marked Anchor Close and formerly belonged to the Rector. Part of it, at the time of the Enclosure, was exchanged for the tenement and piece of ground known as Pluck's Close, now occupied by the Rectory and grounds in Pluck's Lane. The old Rectory used to stand somewhere near the present Post Office, adjoining Anchor Terrace, and tradition tells us it was burnt down about the end of the eighteenth century.

The term " Anchor " takes us back to mediæval days. It has nothing to do with ships, but with hermits or " anchorites." These men, who lived the solitary life, would seek a spot for their habitation near a church and also, if possible, near the priest's abode. They lived on the food provided for them by the pious villagers, and as it was an easy method of gaining a living if the religious exercises were omitted, it came about that amongst the Anchorites, many of whom were, doubtless, very holy men, there were also unfortunately to be found some impostors.

Thus it came about that the place where the Anchorite of Milton had his little hut in days

gone by, came to be known as " Anchor Close."
As one died, he would in time be succeeded by
another, and let us hope for the credit of Milton
that the Anchorites who lived here were of
blameless reputation.

Fishpools

This is another name that takes us far back
into the past, when the laws of the Church were
strictly observed. During days of abstinence
fish could be eaten when meat was not allowed,
but it is a far cry from Milton to the sea and
there were no fast trains in those days, while ice
in summer would be regarded as a miracle.

In fact, there was a proverb bearing on this :
" The Mayor of Northampton opens oysters with
his dagger." An old work, *A Collection of
English Words not Generally Used*, by John Ray,
F.R.S. (1737), explains this as follows :

" To keep them at a sufficient distance from
his nose. For this Town being eighty miles from
the sea, fish may well be presumed stale therein.
Yet have I heard (saith the Doctor—i.e. Doctor
Fuller, author of *Worthies of England*) that
Oisters put up with care, and carried in the cool,
were weekly brought fresh and good to Althorp,
the house of Lord Spencer at equal distance :
and it is no wonder, for I myself have eaten in
Warwickshire, above eighty miles from London,
Oisters sent from that city, fresh and good, and
they must have been carried some miles before
they came here."

Vegetarianism not being just then a popular
notion, provision had to be made for the lords
of the two manors of Milton and the strangers

within their gates, for the Rectors of Milton and Collingtree, for the old Anchorite if in residence, and for the husbandmen and labourers of the parish. According to what I have been told by men of Milton, who had it from their fathers, there was a chain of three well-stocked fishponds, which was the usual number, behind the field to the south of the east end of Pluck's Lane, fed by the little brook that still runs there. I was told that in the ponds were " carp as big as pigs." The third field on the west side of Barn Lane, about fifteen acres in area, is called Fishpools, and formed part of the glebe before it was sold in 1919. The little cottage called Water Hall was built as a fishing lodge. About seventy years ago, when the road from the Rectory to the cross roads was levelled, the chain of fishpools seemed peculiarly adapted to accommodate part of the surplus earth, which was accordingly tipped therein. Old Terriers mention extensive osier beds near " the Lake," which, I presume, was the largest of the fishpools.

CHAPTER XIII

VANISHED INDUSTRIES

MILLING

By far the most ancient of the vanished industries of Milton is that of the miller's craft. In the extracts from *Domesday Book* on page 31 will be found, relating to the manor held by Goisfrid Alselin:

" There is a mill rendering thirty pence."

Where that mill stood, and whether it was a water-mill or windmill, are things difficult to conjecture.

A mill was once connected with the Church Cottages, the "toft" granted by Thomas Rage to the church of Milton. In 1517, the feoffees granted to Richard Hut of Blisworth a lease of the tenement, "with a horsmylle and a close to the same perteynyng, togedir as they byn sett in the Town of the forseid Middylton." Richard Hut was promised what seems like preferential treatment. He was to grind for three days in every week, "yt is to sey Monday, Wednysday and Friday to serve the seide Town of Middilton. And all the seide Town of Middelton promysith and granntith to grynde at the seide mille before any other as long as they may be as well served there as thei can be in any other place by thise presentes." For the lease see page 248.

Close to Stockwell, where the Church Cottages stand, is a field known as Mill Banks. Its name tells us there was a mill standing here at one time, and Mr. Wm. Clarke informed me he was told one stood there until the time of the Enclosure of the Commons, when it was pulled down. A windmill stood in Mill Close on the Collingtree Road, where there is now an orchard to the east of the railway. This in its turn was demolished about the middle of the last century.

Amongst the manuscript notes about Milton written by Wm. Taylor, the schoolmaster of Heyford, who collected information for Dr. Bridges when compiling his history, is a description of the brooks. Of the " Blysworth Brook " he writes that it " rises from Dykes and small springs in Blisworth field, Drives an Overshott Mill, makes a small Brook on ye west side of this town."

Taylor wrote his notes in 1718–21, so there was a water-mill working in those days, but where?

The following old advertisement, taken from the *Northampton Mercury*, dated Saturday, May 26th, 1798, may be of interest. It refers to the mill that stood in Mill Close.

A Windmill

FOR SALE BY AUCTION

By Benjamin Mason

At the Dolphin Inn, in Northampton on Sat. the 9th. of June, 1798, at Four o'clock in the afternoon, subject to such conditions as will be produced.

A substantial well-built Windmill, standing

and being at Milton, otherwise Middleton Malsor, in the County of Northampton, in the occupation of Mr. William Bray, at the yearly rent of Ten Pounds, clear of all Deductions.

For further particulars, or to treat by private contract, apply to William Bellamy, or Joseph Bennett, both of Hasely, near Warwick, and for a view of the premises apply to the Tenant.

N.B.—Milton is three miles from Northampton.

In the parish registers are references to Wm. Bray, Miller, in 1817 and 1821. Then in 1825 we find that Widow Bray " failed in her business with ye windmill and disposed of the lease for £20 and her horse and cart for £15." So in 1837 we find " Wm. Marks, Miller " and his son " George Marks, Miller " ; but the Bray family seem to have resumed the business, as in 1849 and 1851 John Bray is described in the registers as " Miller."

There seems to have been some dispute as to the ownership of the mill in Mill Close, and for several years it stood idle and tenantless, being used only by tramps as a shelter at night. Bits of it were taken away by stealthy hands for firewood, and at last, about 1864, some half-dozen Milton boys daringly removed one of the four brick piers on which it stood, leaving one brick on end as a temporary support. At this, from a safe distance, they hurled stones until the brick was shattered and the huge structure toppled over with a resounding crash. Some of those boys, old men by this time, are still in Milton. The two millstones are now in the garden at Mortimers.

Weaving

This seems to be one of the earliest recorded of the other industries that once flourished in Milton. We know that in the fifteenth century the weaver's craft flourished in Northampton and, being so near the town, Milton must have possessed its share of woollen weavers. This idea is supported by the existence of St. Catherine's Chapel in Milton Church, because the weavers had their annual festival on St. Catherine's Day. In all probability this was the Guild Chapel for the Weavers' Guild in Milton, but although such a Guild undoubtedly existed, no reference to it has yet been discovered.

In the time of Henry VIII there was perhaps more sheep-farming than agriculture in the country districts, and the cottagers would possess their spinning-wheels both for woollen and linen yarn. It was the woman's work to spin, and the wheels would be handed down from mother to daughter. Thus Alice Gaddesden, widow, of Milton bequeathes by Will dated October 26th, 1599:

" I give and bequeath to Katherine Gadsden my daughter . . . one woollen wheele, one lynnen wheele."

And Mary Hooton, of Milton, November 26th, 1688:

" I give to Ann Hooton my youngest Daughter . . . one woollen whele."

The Will of William Dry, Lord of the Manor,

October 10th, 1677, shows us how Milton ladies passed their time :

"Item. I do geve and bequeath unto my sd. loving wife all the linnen & other goods she brought to me with her & also all the linnen yarne, which is in my house, which she lately span with her own hands."

In his Will dated July 1st, 1676, Richard Dix describes himself as " of Milton, Weaver," which is the first reference we have to the weaving industry in Milton.

The church registers give very meagre details of the persons entered therein until we come to the eighteenth century, and then we find men described by their occupations. Amongst them are the following connected with the weaving industry :

1729. Jonathan Rowlatt, fell-monger.
1734. Edmund Rogers, weaver.
1737. James Bibswell, weaver.
1739. Henry Garriot, Jersey-comber.

The latest entry of a weaver is that of James Bibswell, which occurs again in 1744.

So it is evident that there were some cottages in Milton where the hand-loom was worked, and very many where the whir of the spinning-wheel was heard. The linen that was spun on the wheels of the cottagers was of home production. Flax was cultivated in the neighbourhood up to about fifty years ago and provided employment for many, as an entry in the school Log Book for July 31st, 1865, explains that several children were absent " Gleaning peas and pulling flax."

LACE-MAKING

The art and craft of lace-making is another vanished industry. This art was introduced into the neighbouring county of Buckinghamshire by Henry VIII's first wife, Queen Katharine of Arragon, who lies buried near the High Altar in Peterborough Cathedral. Immigrants from Flanders were the persons principally engaged; but by the seventeenth and eighteenth centuries it had become the chief local industry and had spread to Northamptonshire. During the last century pillow lace was made in almost every cottage in Milton, and there were schools in the village where little girls were taught how to ply the bobbins. One near the Green was kept by Mary Caswell about fifty years ago, and in the school Log Book we find occasionally a note to the effect that some girl had left school " to learn lace-making," e.g. in 1873, May 23rd, " Mary H—— left. Gone to learn lace-making," and in 1874, March 20, " Ann S—— gone to the lace school."

The lace-makers had a very ingenious contrivance by which they could ply their art at night in the light of a home-made rushlight. They had what was called a " candle-stool," something in shape like a three-legged stool, but not quite so high as a table. On this the rushlight would be placed and, to intensify its feeble glimmer, glass globes filled with water were placed in position, one for each lace-maker. These globes had long narrow necks sealed with a cork, and the necks were inserted in wicker holders that were fastened to the table. Thus the globe-shaped part of the bottle was uppermost and the rays from the rushlight, or candle, streaming through became brilliant enough, when focussed on the pillow, to enable the lacemakers to see their delicate task. The work was, of course, done on the ordinary lace pillow, which was placed on a small crescent-shaped table, commonly called a " horse."

A curious inventory of the effects of a poor man, ound pinned in one of the overseers' books, mentions a candle-stool among the rest :

" 1816. May 21st. Lace pillow, meat fork, tinder box, flag basket, candle-stool, boot legs."

From an entry in the register it would seem as if some men employed several lace-makers to work for them.

" 1705. John Bandidge, Lacemaker, died on ye 7th. and was buryed on ye 8th. day of May."

On the other hand, John Bandidge may have been himself a lace-maker. Buyers of lace made periodical visits to the village and the lacemakers took their wares to them, when there would be much chaffering. In the registers, under date 1698/9, January 11th, we find mention of " John Stanton, lacebuyer," and farther on we read that " John Staulton, lacebuyer, was buried April ye 13th. 1699," very likely one and the same person. Probably his successor in the business was " Richard Robinson, a lace buyer, of this parish," who was married " Feb. ye 26th. 1703/4." In the Parish Vestry Books for 1823 mention is made of Wm.

Turland, Milton, Lace Merchant. From 1700 onwards we find lace-makers frequently mentioned in the registers, the last entry being in that for marriages under date February 3rd, 1868.

There was no picture palace or " Palais de Danse " in those days, no parish dances or whist-drives for long winter nights. Bobbins furnished one means of recreation, not only for winter nights but also for summer evenings, as the poet Cowper describes it :

" Yon cottager who weaves at her own door,
Pillows and bobbins all her little store."

About sixty years ago the Milton lace-makers used to bake an ornamented cake, called a " Tander's Cake," for St. Andrew's Day. This day was observed in Milton as the lace-makers' festival, and an old bellringer told me it was customary to ring our church bells on " Tander's Day," i.e. St. Andrew's Day.

Lace-making declined during the last century, when machine-made Nottingham lace flooded the market, so that now it is, if at all, only practised as a pastime in Milton.

Brewing and Malting

These industries are not now carried on in our village. In olden days the aleman brewed his own liquor. The names of some who kept an alehouse here in years gone by are found in the register : 1719, " Sarah Dunckley, widow, who sold ale " ; 1720, " Wil Burman who sold ale," and " John Bull, aleman." In 1739 is mentioned a representative of an allied trade, " James Harris, Cooper," and in 1824 we find " William Marks, Brewer."

The first maltster referred to as being of Milton is James Palmer, who in his Will dated January 3rd, 1683, describes himself as " of Milton alliis Middleton Malzor, Maulster."

At the beginning of the last century a malting business was carried on in Milton by Mr. Thos. Cockerill, who kept the Greyhound Inn, where he sold his own home-brewed ale. In 1806 he began operations on a larger scale and built a brewery close to his inn, called the Hope Brewery. He carried on the business of brewer and maltster for many years, being succeeded about 1825 by William Minards. In 1835 Minards sold the business to James Lilly, who kept the business going until 1866, when it was purchased by the late Mr. Wm. East. His son, the late Mr. Herbert East, became a partner in the business in 1880. Mr. East was a man of some enterprise: the old brewery was considerably enlarged and new plant added, and in 1888 a new brewery was built adjoining the old one. There is a well on the premises, thirty-five feet deep, from which water is pumped to an iron tank in the roof, which holds 3000 gallons. When the well was made, the workmen who were digging at the bottom suddenly came upon the spring. The water poured in so rapidly that they had to be drawn up at once, leaving their working tools behind.

In 1905 the Hope Brewery was sold to the Northampton Brewery Company, who dismantled the premises and possess the "Greyhound" as a tied house.

The maltings connected with the business were considerably older than the brewery, and once belonged to Mr. John Marriott, a Baptist minister. "The Stackyard Malting," as it was called, has since been converted into a row of eight cottages, bearing the name of "Maltings Terrace," situated at the back of the Little Green. A description of it published before the alteration may be of interest :

"This ancient malthouse is 153 feet long, and is, in part, two storeys high. It is built of brick and stone, and, with its old-fashioned outside stairs, has a quaint appearance. It comprises, besides a growing floor, barley stores, malt-bins and a kiln. The basement of the building contains the pale ale cellar, and a large portion of the upper storey has been converted into a hop store."

This malthouse evidently existed long before the time of Mr. Marriott, and from it the farmers and villagers obtained their malt to brew their ale.

Hops for brewing were once successfully grown in Milton, and a field bears to this day the name of "Hop Close." By the courtesy of Thomas Phipps Dorman, Esq., of Northampton, I am able to give the following extract of an Excise statement signed by his grandfather, the late Thomas Phipps, brewer and maltster, under date July 27th, 1852 :

"I, Thomas Phipps, of Bridge Street, Northampton, ... do hereby make an entry of

One Kiln or Oast, marked 2 K, for the purpose of drying Hops, the produce of my hop ground in Milton Field, in the parish of Milton &c."

Pin-making

Curious though it may seem to us nowadays, this industry once flourished at Milton, the factory being situated at the end of a garden next to the Baptist Chapel. Here the Lever family made brass pins, employing a good many workmen in the time of business prosperity. A writer in the *Victoria County History*, Vol. II, page 339, states that the Lever family had a factory at Hardingstone and Stony Stratford as well. At Hardingstone the manufacturers were Edward Lever and his nephew William, and the latter continued making pins there after his uncle Edward's death. Another uncle, John Lever, manufactured pins at Milton and other members of the family at Stony Stratford.

Pins used to be imported into England, but in 1626 the industry was introduced into Stroud, from where it soon spread to London, Bristol and Birmingham. The pins then made were not all of one piece, the heads being formed of coiled fine wire, each head consisting of two complete twists. Thousands of these heads were softened by heat, and the " heading boy " pushed the " shanks " (the lengths of wire forming the pins) into the mass of heads. When the shanks had each a head stuck on, he passed them on to another person who put the finishing touches to the heads. As may well be supposed, these heads were very liable to come off. It was a tedious business, for each pin had to pass through no less than eighteen processes, a man or a boy being responsible for each process. This is instanced by Adam Smith in his *Wealth of Nations* as a remarkable division of labour. In 1817 Seth Hunt patented a machine for making head, shaft and point in one entire piece, and various improvements in the machinery brought it about that by 1840 the machine-made pins had almost entirely driven those made by hand out of the market. So by degrees the smaller pin factories were extinguished.

At Milton, the pins were, of course, manufactured by the old process of sticking on the heads, and there are some records of the factory in existence.

In the Overseers' Book, 1823, J. Houghton is referred to as working at the Pin Manufactory, and there is a Parish Vestry note on September 22nd, 1826, that two Milton men were " to be sent to Thomas Lever to head pins." In the parish registers there are entries concerning " Thomas Lever, Pin Manufacturer," on various dates from 1820 to 1843.

Photo, H. Walter Manser.
ST. CATHERINE'S CHAPEL.

PLAN OF WHEEL WINDOW.

CHAPTER XIV

MISCELLANEA

I. OLD CUSTOMS.

MOST of the old Milton customs have ceased to be, but it is still possible to glean from various sources some account of what used to take place in our village. Elderly people retain vivid memories of what they did as children, and scattered about the pages of the old school Log Book we find references to various happenings.

Plough Monday, for instance, is not now observed by the farm labourers of Milton, but sixty years ago it was recognised to the full. From the Log Book we find that January 9th, 1865, the first Monday after the Epiphany, is entered as " Plough Monday," presumably a holiday, while against January 13th, 1868, is the note : " Plough Monday ; usual visitation of coloured faces."

St. Valentine's Day was well kept by the youths and maidens of the village up to fifty years ago, and the school-children usually had a half-holiday, when they went about singing and collecting money. Again from the school Log Book we find in 1868 : " Feb. 14th. Valentine's Day. Usual half-holiday," and on February 26th : " Distributed the money collected on St. Valentine's Day. Thirty-nine children received 3d. each. Many of them bought slates." In 1871, however, there was no holiday and the observance of the feast of St. Valentine seems to have fallen gradually into disuse. Some elderly people remember going in their young days to the bigger houses for pippins and gingerbread, which were given away every year to the children on that morning.

The Shrove Tuesday bell is dealt with in Chapter VIII.

A custom popular in Milton from ancient times and still observed, is the eating of figs on " Fig Sunday," the name by which Palm Sunday is sometimes called. This custom is based on the incident of the Fig Tree, when Our Lord wished to eat of the fruit.

" Garland Day," as it used to be called at Milton, according to the old Log Book, was kept on Old May Day, the 12th of the month, until 1906, but from that year this link with the past was severed and the day was changed to May 1st. The school-children choose a Queen of the May and go in procession around Milton, singing appropriate songs, afterwards visiting other villages.

" Tander's Day," St. Andrew's Day, was the lace-makers' festival. As is mentioned in Chapter XIII, the lace-makers made an ornamented cake and the bellringers rang peals in the early morning. Besides this, the children used to " go Tandering," as it was called—they would visit a lace-maker's house and be regaled with games and sweets.

The " Ringers' and Singers' Supper " is a very

old institution, and takes place on New Year's Eve, when the choir and bellringers meet. After the supper, games and songs are indulged in, and as midnight approaches the assembled party proceed to the belfry, where the Old Year is rung out and the New Year ushered in with a peal on the bells.

Cricket and football have long been popular at Milton, as may be seen from the Log Book:

"1865, May 23rd. Cricket match kept some away in afternoon," and again on the 30th a note to the same effect.

"1867, Monday, March 18th. Boys gone to see a football match between Milton men & Patchell (11 a side). Patchell won."

II. Quaint Sayings, Dialect, Superstitions, etc.

Many quaint sayings are based upon observations of the weather. One, often quoted by an old inhabitant, runs:

"If there's ice in November that will bear a duck,
The rest of the winter will be slush and muck."

Another Milton saying to the same effect is:

"If the ice will bear a goose in November, it won't bear a duck afterwards."

A Milton variant of a well-known weather proverb is:

"February fill dyke,
Be it either black or white."

Black or white means, of course, rain or snow. One more rhyming forecast tells us:

"If it rains on Easter Day,
Much good grass, but little good hay."

Another saying is: "When Milton Feast comes, you can shut your door." This alludes to the practice of allowing the cottage doors to stand open during the summer. When Milton Feast comes, after September 14th, the weather is appreciably colder, necessitating the doors being closed. The days, too, are shorter, which accounts for the saying: "On Milton Feast, shut your door at six."

"A Sunday moon brings a flood before the month is out." A new moon falling on a Sunday will be followed by heavy rain during the next four weeks.

An expressive phrase is: "As cold as a clat," a clat being one of the bits of manure that are spread over the field.

Another descriptive saying is: "When mice fight rats, the rats get the best of it." A poor person will have little chance of success if he goes to law against a rich and influential person.

When being "Churched" after child-birth, a woman was said to be "given her liberty."

A "hundred-to-one" pudding consists of a hundred pieces of potato to one of meat, covered with pastry and cooked in a basin. It was an excellent stand-by during the Great War.

Almost every county or district in England has some dialect peculiar to itself, that is, the use of words or phrases representing survivals from the older English speech, and not usually found in an ordinary dictionary.

Some peculiarities of Northamptonshire dialect still survive in Milton, but instances of this nature can, of course, only be obtained by patience.

The almost obsolete word " unkid " is occasionally met with, usually in such a combination as " unkid and dreadful." The word " unkid " means " horrid."

" Don't he look herrikin ? " " Herrikin " means wild, unkempt, rough. In Yorkshire this word is " harrygaud."

" I was fair mommered," means " I was quite worried, or flurried." This being a Midland dialect, is frequently heard in Milton, but sometimes the word " moithered " is used, bearing the same meaning.

A " mawkin " is a scarecrow or effigy, a word still in frequent use.

I have heard the junction of the thigh with the body called the " share." The word means " division."

" Mullock " is in general dialect throughout the country, and means any kind of rubbish or weeds.

" Touch " was the name given to the tinder, when flint and steel were generally used instead of matches.

To be " shut of " someone, means to be rid of that person. Met with in other counties.

To " hold " means to borrow.

" Out " is often used for " away." When people have gone away on a visit, they are said to be " out," literally " out of town." Children from other villages who attended Milton School were described in the Log Book as " outtowners."

To " call " is to tattle, gossip, spread reports.

To " call " another person is to speak slanderously of that individual. As one woman philosophically said, " When they call me, they're giving someone else a rest." Also found in Yorkshire.

To " dout " the flame is to " put out." This is commonly met with in the West Country.

" Middling " is to be unwell, practically the same as " indifferent " as applied to health. If a person is " very middling " he is very ill. Found in most counties.

" Dirt " is the term used for loose earth, or mould. It has no reference to a want of cleanliness. This use is found also in Oxfordshire, Hampshire and Somerset. A gardener, when potting, fills his pots with " dirt "—loose earth. On the ridge of a thatched roof the thatcher places " dirt "—again loose earth—to keep the thatch from being blown off.

To " thack " is to " thatch "; so a " thacker " is a " thatcher."

" Jetty " is a term used for a narrow passage between two walls or hedges. The narrow lane between The Manor and Milton House is so named.

" Pap " is a term of endearment for a grandfather.

" Frit " means " frightened." " I was frit to death."

Anything in a dilapidated state, or of flimsy construction, is said to be " tempory," probably from " temporary."

A hen " burks " her chickens when she gathers them under her wings for warmth.

"Whitterish" means poor, bad, very third-rate. A whitterish thing is of little account.

"Muckle" also means something poor or bad. "I'll keep the good apples and sell the muckles."

A naughty child is sometimes referred to as "anointed," possibly from "annoying." "That boy is a most anointed child."

To "run" is to "chase." "The dog ran the cat."

The use of "while" instead of "until" is found throughout the Midlands and the northern counties. "I will stay here while Thursday," means, "I will stay here until Thursday." To the unaccustomed ear this use will sometimes convey a meaning totally different from what was intended. Take, for instance, such a sentence as, "I'll keep my umbrella closed while it rains." This may be understood to mean that the umbrella would be kept closed during the downpour, though the speaker really meant that it would be kept closed until the rain began. However, there is classic authority for this use:

"We will keep ourself
'Till supper time alone; while then, God bless you."
Macbeth III. 1.

The preposition "to" is frequently used for "of" in such a sentence as, "What do you think to it?" that is, "of it."

Some few instances of pronunciation may be noticed. The bell "clapper" is sometimes pronounced with a long "a" as if spelt "claper." The word "any" has a broad "a" as if it were "anny." The double "d" is in some cases soft, for a ladder is frequently called a "lather."

"Against" is often "agin," and "voice" is sometimes "vice." Some of these are survivals of older rules of pronunciation, just as it was considered correct a century ago for "yellow" to be called "yaller."

There are some quaint beliefs and superstitions at Milton, as there are, of course, in other parts of the country.

It is said that if a "hardy mouse," otherwise a harvest mouse or shrew mouse, crosses a footpath in a field, it will die.

When the "pink pink" note of the chaffinch is at its best and can be thought to say "pincher," then rain is near.

If a hare runs through the village, a fire or some other disaster will occur within a month.

On the parchment cover of our oldest register can faintly be discerned an old Latin "square-word," written probably some two or three centuries ago. It can be read upwards, downwards and across, either way. I transcribe it here:

      SATOR
      AREPO
      TENET
      OPERA
      ROTAS.

This was, in olden times, a well-known square-word commonly used throughout England as a charm against rats. Upon a sheet of paper would be written this square-word, together with a note saying there was plenty of corn or other food on some neighbouring farm or other premises, and requesting the rats to go there. The paper was then placed in the rats' run, and when the rodents read the polite note it was believed that they would be so charmed by the Latin words that they would act on the hint and leave the house.

In an agricultural district, omens from which a forecast of the weather could be obtained would be anxiously consulted. Hence we find certain rules laid down to guide us by some of the old weather-wise inhabitants. The moon apparently plays a great part, for we are told that the weather on the third day of the moon will be the prevailing weather during that month. One old inhabitant told me that he always went to the cross-roads at 11.30 p.m. on Old Martinmas Eve, November 23rd, and the weather that prevailed during the half-hour until midnight would indicate the weather for the next three months. Where the wind was then, it would generally be in the same quarter for the next three months, and if it shifted during the time of observation, it would be the last wind during that half-hour.

The weather on January 25th indicates the kind of summer for that year.

One old man told me that weather forecasts were inspired by the Evil One and were only sought by hypocrites. On my inquiring his reason he quoted, to my astonishment, " Ye hypocrites, ye can discern the face of the sky."

Talking of the sky leads our thoughts naturally to the stars. The various shapes of the constellations remind different people of different things. In the Great Bear, for instance, there is a group of seven stars shaped like a saucepan with a curved handle. In one part of England this is called The Plough, in another Charles' Wain, but in Milton it is Dick and the Wagon, and also the Wagon and Horses.

Another constellation, seen only in winter, is Taurus (the Bull). In the side of the Bull is a cluster of six stars known as the Pleiades, but in Milton it is called the Butcher's Hatchet. This is a name suggested by the shape assumed by the grouping of the stars, but it breathes a different spirit from that of Job when he wrote : " Canst thou bind the sweet influences of Pleiades ? "

Death being the common lot and all destined some day to make the great change, we find that Milton is not without its dread portents of this event.

An owl hooting near a house foretells the death of one living there, but the person about to die does not hear it. There is a Welsh superstition to the same effect, except that the doomed person hears the hooting.

If an inhabitant of Milton dies and the body remains unburied over a Sunday, there will be another death within a month. This superstition is also current in Somerset.

If there are two deaths within a short time of each other, there will be a third very soon after.

If a dead body does not " set," or stiffen with *rigor mortis*, before burial, it foretells that the death of someone very near, both in relationship and place of abode, will occur in a very short time.

It is also supposed to be a portent of death when the church clock strikes the hour in an unusually loud and ominous tone.

For some reason, it is also thought that if the clock strikes during the singing of the last hymn in church at Evensong, some disaster, such as a death, will soon occur.

III. CHRONOLOGICAL.

In some parts of this book there occur dates that seem indefinite, e.g. Edward Wigan took his degree of B.A. in 1508/9. That means the event took place before March 25th of 1509. Such double dates may be seen on some of the old gravestones within the church. The reason is that until 1752 the civil, ecclesiastical and legal year did not begin on January 1st, though for a very long period the historical year did so. Up to the end of the thirteenth century, New Year's Day, as used by the Church and in all public documents, began at Christmas. In and after the fourteenth century the year began on March 25th. Strange to say, the rubric after the Collect for St. Stephen's Day in the Prayer Book directs that it shall be said until New Year's Eve, that is, December 31st. This is accounted for by the fact that when the Second Prayer Book was compiled, a Bill had been drafted in Parliament ordering that the New Year should begin on January 1st, and not on March 25th, but it was not passed. For centuries the year began on

January 1st in Scotland, and for a very long time the English had unofficially used the same date, so the difference between the legal and unofficial calculations caused great practical inconvenience. When the New Style of reckoning was adopted in England in 1752, all this was changed and the year considered to begin on January 1st. By the New Style in 1752, eleven days were left out of the calendar for that year, the 3rd of September being reckoned as the 14th of September. This caused great uproar in several places, because people thought they were being robbed of eleven days of life.

IV. Low-Side Windows.

The reason why a Low-Side Window was inserted in churches remains more or less a mystery. This window is found sometimes in the west end of the north, but more usually the south, wall of the chancel, and often below a larger one. In Milton Church it is in the wall of the north aisle, almost in line with the chancel arch. Various theories have been advanced as to its use.

1. As confessionals. In support of this theory it was the practice for a penitent, after a grave sin, not to enter the church before he was shriven, and in several instances such windows had a seat within, as if for the priest. They seem to have been originally unglazed. A letter to Thomas Cromwell from one Thomas Bedyll, clerk to the Council of Henry VIII and one of the commissioners at the visitation made when the religious houses and chantries were sup-

pressed, seems to refer to this use of the window. "We think it best that the place wher thes frires have been wont to hire outtward confessions of al commers at certen tymes of the yere be walled up and that use to be for-doen for ever." The fact that many of these windows in ancient parish churches are now walled up, and that it was apparently done about this time, would seem to support the theory that they had been used as confessionals. Two such windows, north and south, in Blisworth Church are thus closed. However, it must be borne in mind that the passage in the letter was against a certain religious order, and further, as it was an irregular practice, the bishop could direct that these windows should be blocked up. No such mandate has hitherto been discovered, and the windows may quite possibly have been walled up to save the trouble of glazing them.

2. As windows for lepers, during Mass. Against this theory, very few command a view of the altar and very few are splayed. The Milton window is certainly splayed in that direction, but not sufficiently so to see any of the altars. Further, the lepers of the neighbourhood had a chapel for themselves at the hospitals of St. Leonard in Northampton and Towcester.

3. For distribution of alms. The situation of the Milton window is decidedly unsuitable for such a purpose, being behind the church.

4. For the ringing of the Sanctus bell at Mass. I am inclined to this theory, because most low-side windows seem to have been inserted in that side of the church facing the priest's house or

the main part of the village. The ancient Rectory of Milton was slightly north-west of the church, and the main part of the village lies west and north-west. Therefore, since this window at Milton is on the north side of the church and is splayed on the east side, it would be possible to draw a straight line through it to the site of the old Rectory from some point within the church. The window may have been used for some signal, such as the Sanctus bell, for the villagers in general, but, considering its situation here at Milton in connection with the old Rectory, there is greater reason to suppose it was chiefly for the benefit of the Rector when confined to the house through illness.

V. Entries of Interest.

Church Registers.

1610. " John Reeve, Sheepheard, slayne by a tempest of thunder and lightninge was buried the 13 Daie of July."

1620. " Agnes Stanley the daughter of John Stanley a bedlam man was buried the ffifte day of November."

1634. " Maud Dunkley was buryed ye 23rd of Ffebruary. *Anno ætatis suae (ut aiunt) centissimo.*" i.e. " In the hundredth year of her age (so they say)."

1686. " Elizabeth daughter of Stephen Miles & Elizabeth his wife was baptized 23rd May."

" Elizabeth Miles (ye sd Mother) who dyd in Childbirth was buryd ye same day."

" Ann ye daughter of Will : Burnum & Ann his wife was baptizd 24th May."

"Ann Burnum (ye mother) dyd in Childbirth & was buryd ye same day; both w'ch persons yt so dyd was Cousen Germans & was deliverd & sickned of a feavr in ye same manner & dyd just before one another as they were deliverd."

1771. "Willm Robinson, Parish Clark (an Honest Man & favourite of His Master) buried Apl. 14."

1794. "Oct. 6th. Tax ceases on births, burials &c."

This is in Book 4, which seems to be a duplicate of Register No. 3. It begins with Baptisms on September 18th, 1785, and Burials on October 22nd, 1785, each space for entries bearing an embossed Government stamp marked III Pence.

The years 1793, 1813, 1817 and 1824 have names of persons entered who are described as "Cordwainers," the old name for shoemakers.

CHURCHWARDENS' ACCOUNTS.

"1803. April 10. Pd the Blacksmith for Provideing a Grindlestone . . 15 0
(Some of the old people of Milton still use this term for a grindstone.)
Oct : 11. Pd with the Briefs 1 0
Do. Pd the Court Fees . 12 0
(These were the fees paid at the Archdeacon's Court at the Visitation.)

"1804. April 2d. Pd the Clark is Wagers . . . 17 0

	Dec. 24. Pd for new broom & Churry pint of Ale for cleaning the Church ways		6
"1805.	March 6th. Pd for Surplus	2 12	6
	for the Carrage of the Surplus . . .	1	0
	(According to Canon 58 of the Church of England, a surplice has to be provided by the parishioners for the Rector's use.)		
	May 30th. Pd. the Court Fees	11	0
	Do. with the Briefs . .	2	6
	(What these particular Briefs were for is not stated, but the fees varied, as is seen from the two already quoted, and also one on April 14th, 1807, when an entry occurs: "Pd. with the Briefs 4s. 10d.")		
"1806.	April 5. Pd. for 3 Brooms to cleane the Churchways & Churry 3 pints of Ale to do the same .	1	6
"1807.	Janry. 28. Pd for Letter from Manchester Directed to the Church Warden		11
"1815.	March 27. Pd. Richd Robinson is wagers for being Clarke one year to Easter 1815 . .	3 3	0
"1822.	Oct. 3. Paid Mrs. Morris for Ale for the Church .	5	6
"1824.	Demr. 3. pd a Letter fire Engin		3

		£	s.	d.
	Demr. 11. Bell Windars (windows?) . . .		2	0
" 1825.	July 7. paid for Bear .		5	0
" 1828.	April 8th. Recd. by Twopenny Rate . . .	9	8	11½
	July 28. penting the Stov pd Richd Robinson .		2	6
	Septm. 13. paid Crosby for Reparin the Violincela and a scrue . . .		2	6
" 1829.	Jany. 18. one pound of Wax Candls. . .		3	6
" 1831.	March 1. a Letter from London . . .			9
	July 19. a Letter from the Curte (Archdeacon's Court). . . .		3	6
	Nov. 5. a hood faget .		3	0
" 1832.	Jany. 31. a faget of hood			3
	March 9. a hood faget .			3
	(Presumably these are fagots of wood.)			
" 1833.	June 1. Paid Jno Robinson a oke Beam for the Church . . .	4	10	0
	July 4. paid a Letter from London on the Surples (surplice) . . .			10
	Septmr. 14. a Leter from London . . .			10
	Septmr. 18. paid Mr. Miller the Surples .	5	5	0
" 1834.	July 17. Confirmation 21 Dinnars . . .	1	11	6
	for Beear . . .		7	6
" 1838.	Recd. of Mr. Clarke of Collingtree for some old Commandments . .	3	0	0

	A Church Rate Collected, 1s. 4d. in the pound	87	18	4
	Paid Men 4s. for finding Church property		4	0
"1839.	Paid Men for digging up Nettles in Churchyard	2	10	0
	(This shows that our God's Acre had been allowed to fall into a sad state of neglect.)			
"1849.	Feb. 28. Mr. Phipps, Black Gown for Clerk	1	9	0
"1853.	Dec. 26th. Willm Gleed for Playing the Horgin		5	0

Parish Vestry Minutes.

1822. Mar. 27. "John Gleed to have a fence before his window to keep off the cattle."

1827. Nov. 5th. "That the Rector is requested on behalf of the Parish to attend at the Board Room on Thursday next to support if necessary the Publican J. Lilley in the prosecution of certain individuals for making a disturbance on Sunday morning last."

1828. March 26th. "A meeting to be held on Apl 3rd for the purpose of taking into consideration the mode of remunerating the Teachers at the Sunday Schools."

1828. Aug. 7th. "The Rector is requested to state to the magistrates on Saturday next on behalf of the parish the Publicans James Lilley & John Curran having their houses open for tipling during the hours appropriated for Church service on Sunday last."

Public...
during t...
were ope...
would be...
tion, it...
held in a...
ordered...
public-h...
Sunday...
the ever...
In mod...
generall...
evening...
has rem...
opened during ...

for Morning Service. The object of this old law was that people should have no excuse or temptation to be absent from service.

School Log Book.

1863. July 10. "Weather during the week has been unusually hot."
July 13. "Heat very considerably abated from last week, when Thermom. (in Sun) reached 114°."

1865. April 14. "Mem. Good Friday, Sunday School. Men & some boys at work, others playing about especially in afternoon."

1868. July 22. "Hottest day this year. 130° sun. 104° shade."

1875. Decr. 19–24. "Pig-killing week. Preparation for Christmas—many children away."
(The week before Christmas is still kept as "pig-killing week.")

CHAPTER XV

THE CHARITIES OF MILTON

THE oldest of our Milton charities are the two officially known as the "Town and Poor's Estate," which since 1805 have been included in one Trust Deed. The Town Estate, by which is meant the Church Estate, represents two gifts of lands and houses, with various other small bequests, for the use of Milton Church. The Poor's Estate represents bequests of money made at different times, the interest of which was for the use of the poor, which money seems to have been invested eventually in land.

The story of the Town Estate, the two gifts to our church, as presented in the remarkable series of deeds now preserved in the Church Chest, is most interesting and instructive, because it shows us how it was possible for charities to be misapplied both deliberately and unintentionally. Deliberately, as was done in Tudor times by entirely alienating the Church properties; unintentionally, when the deeds were temporarily missing about 1800, so that upon the appointment of new trustees the exact nature of the Trusts could not possibly be known, and a part of the Church property (the Poor's Cottages) was mistakenly assigned to the Poor's Estate.

THE CHARITIES OF MILTON 245

From the early part of last century, when the Town and Poor's Estates were first included in one Trust Deed, there seem to have been but hazy ideas as to the purpose of the church property. Even the " Parliamentary Report concerning Charities," dated January 30th, 1830, I found misleading. Of the Town Estate, otherwise the Church Estate, it says (pages 381–383) : " This estate appears to have been vested in feoffees in the time of King Henry 7th. for the public use and benefit of the parishioners. . . . The Churchwardens receive the rent, and apply it in payment of the general charges incidental to their office, conformably to long usage." All of which is hopelessly incorrect as will be seen from the translations of the deeds printed on pages 251–3.

In dealing with the Town and Poor's Estate, we will begin with that portion called

The Town Estate
(OTHERWISE THE CHURCH ESTATE).

This consists of two separate gifts. The earlier one is commonly called that of Thomas Rage, but from the deed, which I have fully translated, it would seem that it was originally given by one John Smyth. Thomas Rage, in 1507, granted to certain feoffees one toft and seven acres of land in Milton for the use of Milton Church. This " toft " (for the meaning of which see page 173) is now known as the Church Cottages.

The other gift is that of Robert Park, clerk, who when he lived at Coton bought, in 1506, a cottage with a barn, orchard and close in Milton, which he afterwards gave to Milton Church in 1517 when he was Vicar of Duston. This cottage is now divided into two and is known as the Poor's Cottages.

Two of the old deeds that are in English are given in full owing to their interesting description of the place and a hint as to the life of those days. The other deeds, up to the eighteenth century, are in abbreviated Latin, and as they are all couched in the same legal phraseology, one deed, only, of each gift is translated fully ; of the others, only the Latin of the essential portions, with a translation, is given verbatim.

The first of the deeds, written in English and marked No. 1, is the earliest of the series and is the indenture of a bargain and sale to Robert Park of a cottage, etc. (the Poor's Cottages).

Deed No. 1. June 19th, 1506 :

This indenture made the xix day of June the xxj yere of the Reigne of King Henry the vijth betwene John Whalley of Grafton in the County of Norhampton, yeman & Julian his Wyfe one of the doughters & coheres of Willm Hobson of Wotton in the County of Norht. now decessid John ffosbery of the same Town of Woton & Alice his Wyfe A nother of the doughters & coheres of the seid Willm Hobson And Symon Hobson of the forseid Wotton on the one partie And Robt Park of Coton Clerk on that other partie Witnessith that the seide John Whalley & Julian John ffosbery & Alice and Simon Hobson hath graunted Bargeynyd & solde & by thise presentes grauntith bargeynyth & sellyth to the seide Robt. Park A Cottage Wt. A barne An Orchard & A close Callid Shermans

THE CHARITIES OF MILTON 247

place to gedur byn set & lying in the Town of
Milton in the County of Norht. A foreseide
Betwene the londe of the heres of Robt. Tanfeld
on the Est side & the lond of Isabell Ayleward
on the West side And the hie way on the south
side And a lyttyll broke callid Stokwell on the
North side which somtyme have byn Alice
Larons wedow To have & to holde the seide
Cotage W^t barne Orchard & close W^t thappur-
ten'nce to the seide Robt. Park his heres &
Assignes for evyr for the sume of V marks[1]
sterling of the which seid sume of V marks the
seide John Whalley & Julian John ffosbery &
Alice & Simon Hobson knowlegeth them self to
be fully content & paide the day of the makyng
of thise indentures. And the seide Robt his heres
& executours therof to quyte & dischargid by
thise pr'sentes And the seide John Whalley &
Julian John ffosbery & Alice & Simon Hobson
Covenantith & grauntith to the seide Robt.
Park by thise pr'sentes that thei shall make or
cause to be made to the seide Robt. Park or to
such as he shall name a suer and sufficient estate
in the lawe of & in the forseide Cotage & other
the pr'miss's And do & suffre to be don' All
suertees to be made & hadde in the lawe to &
for the use of the seide Robt. Park his heres &
Assign' in the pr'misses As shall be Advised by
the lernyd counsell of the seid Robt. Park by
feoffament fyne relees recou'e[2] Warrantie or
otherwise at such tyme or tymys here aft' As
the seide Robt or his heres shall desire or requere
it of the seide John Whalley & Julian John
ffosbery & Alice & Simon Hobson or of any of
them At the Costis & Chargis of the seide Robt
And the seide John Whalley & Julian John
ffosbery & Alice & Simon Hobson Covenantith &

---

[1] The mark was worth 13s. 4d.   [2] Recovery.

grauntith to the seide Robt. Park by thise pr'sentes that thei shall delyv' or cause to be delyvyrd to the seide Robt. Park or his assignes all man'r of evydence escripts & munimentts that thei or any other to their use hath only concernyng the seide Cotage & other the pr'misses by the ffest of Seynt Jame Thappossall[1] next After the date of thise pr'sentes. In Witnesse wher'of the p'rties Aforesaide to theise Indentures her seallis enterchanngeably have sett youyn[2] the day & yere above wreten.

The other English deed, or, rather, deeds because it is in duplicate, is a lease of Thomas Rage's toft, now the Church Cottages.

Deeds No. 6 and No. 7. July 12th, 1517:

This indenture made the xij day of July the ixth yere of the Reygne of Kyng Henry the viijth Between John Carter, Clark, Thomas Rage of Middilton Malsore in the County of Northt', John Cowper of the same Willm Harbert of the same Richard Stewynson of Mich' Houghton, Nicholas Billyng of the forseid Middilton, Harry Brafelde otherwise called Davy of the same Willm. Meriett otherwise callid Cutt of the same & Larons Rote of the same Coofeffers of certayne londs of Thomas Rage to the use of the same Thomas Rage And to the Church of the forseid Middylton on the one partie And Richard Hut of Blysworth on the other partie Wytnessith that the seide Coofeffers hath dimysid betakyn granntid & to fferme lett to the fforseid Richard Hutt A Tenement w^t a horsmylle & a close to the same perteynyng togedir as they byn sett in the Town of the forseid Middylton, lately in the tenure of Robt.

[1] The Feast of St. James the Apostle, July 25th.
[2] Given.

THE CHARITIES OF MILTON

Wodeford To have & to holde All the seyde Tenement wt the seide mille & close & other thappurtenn'ce of the seide Coofeffers & their successors to the seide Richard Hutt & to his Assignes ffrom the feste of Seynt mighell tharchanngell[1] nexte after the date of thise presentes unto the ende of the terme of xxj yeres then next folowying & fully to be complete yeldyng & paying therfor yerely to the seide Coofeffers or to their Assignes xiis of gode & lawfull money of England At ij termys in the yer that is to say At the ffests of the Ann'nciat'on of our Lady Mary Virgyn & Seynt mighell tharchanngell by evyn porc'ons And yf yt fortune ye seide Rent of xij.s. to be behynde unpaide in parte or in all by the space of a monyth ovyr or after any terme of payment in any yere in the which hit owyth to be paide yf it be askid, then shall hit be lawfull to the seide Coofeffers & to their Assignes in to the seid tenement mille & close and in to eny p'rcell of them to enter & distrayne & the distressis so takyn leefully for to beer lede dryve chase & cary A Way & theym to W'tholde un to the seide Rent w't tharreragis of them to them be fully satisfied & paid And yf it fortune the seide Rent of xij.s. to be behynde unpaide in p'rte or in all by the space of a quarter of a yere on or after any terme of payment in any yere in the which hit owyth to be paide yf it be asked & not paide, Then shall hit be leeful to the seide Coofeffers & to their Assignes in to the seide Tenement mille & close wt. their appurtenn'ces & in to eny p'rte & p'recll of the same hoolly to reentir & hit to have ageyne retayne & possede as in their primer astate & the seide Richard Hut & his Assignes thereof hoolly to put oute & amove

[1] St. Michael the Archangel.

this p'rsent leese than in to the contrary in any wise not wt standyng. And the seide Richard Hutt & his Assignes shall make alman'r of the rep'cons[1] as well of the seide Tenement as of the hors mille as ofte as nede shall requere wt'in the seide terme & at the ende of the seide terme of xxj yere Well & sufficiently repayred shall leve. Which tenement & mille the seide Richard Hut byndith hym by thise pr'sentes truly to observe and kepe by hym & his servantts iij dayes in eny weke yt is to sey monday Wednysday & friday to serve the seide Town of middilton. And All the seide Town of middelton pr'mysith & granntith to grynde at the seide mille before any other as long as they may be as well servyd there as thei can be in any other place by thise pr'sentes ffor the which co'nantts, rentts rep'cons above specified wele & truly to be p'rformyd & kept on the p'rtie of the seide Richard Hutt. The same Richard Hutt Thomas Stacy of Blisworth husbandman and Richard Dowse of the same Byndith them their heires & their Executours in XLs. sterling to the seide Coofeffers above expr'ssid. In Witnesse wherof the p'rties Aforeseide to thise Indenturis their Sealis entirchangeably have sett youyn[2] the day & yere above seide ∵/ which rent the one half therof to remayne to Joh'ne Hykkis of london for terme of her lyfe & after her decesse the seyde rent to remayne to the Church of middilton for ev'r."

The Latin deeds are now taken. Nos. 2 and 3 are connected with the English deed No. 1 and complete the sale. In No. 2, June 19th, 1506, John Whalley and others appoint Thomas Standiland of Northampton their attorney to

---

[1] All manner of reparations = repairs.   [2] Given.

THE CHARITIES OF MILTON

deliver possession of the Cottage, etc., to Robert Park. In No. 3, June 23rd, 1506, John Whalley and others release the same premises to Robert Park.

No. 4A is a beautifully written Latin deed dated September 17th, 1507, by which Thomas Rage gives the toft (the Church Cottages) and land for the use of the Church of Milton, and No. 4B is a Latin deed dated July 2nd, 1517, by which Robert Park gives the cottage (the Poor's Cottages) with orchard, etc., for the use of the same church. These are herewith fully translated. The Latin of No. 4A is given on p. 291.

Deed No. 4A. Know, present and future, that I, Thomas Rage of Middelton near Colyntre in the county of Northampton have given, granted and by this my present deed, confirmed to John Roberds, clerk, parson of the church of Colyntre aforesaid, John Alyson parson of the church of Middelton aforesaid, William Pegge, gentylman, Robert Stephenson, Lawrence Davies, Thomas Basse, John Cowper, Lawrence Rote and Richard Stevenson one Toft & Seven acres of land with appurtenances in Colyntre & Middelton in the county aforesaid, which late I had to me, my heirs & assigns by the gift & feoffment of Richard Cowper & William Lynge, late of Middelton aforesaid & which Toft & land the aforesaid Richard & William Lynge formerly had to them & their heirs by the gift & feoffment of John Smyth, to have & to hold the aforesaid Toft & land with the appurtenances, to the aforesaid John Roberds, John Alyson, William Pegge, Robert, Lawrence Davies, Thomas, John Cowper, Lawrence Rote & Richard Stevynson, their heirs and assigns to the use & intention that the same John Roberts & his co-feoffees aforesaid & their heirs & assigns permit the churchwardens of the parish church of Middelton aforesaid & their successors for the time being yearly for ever to take the issues & profits of the same lands & tenements with the appurtenances so that they may dispose & expend them yearly for the needs & use of the aforesaid church of Middelton (Latin : *circa necessaria & utilitatem pr'd'c'e' Eccl'ie' de Middelton'*) & thereof render a faithful account to the Rector of the same church of Middelton & the parishioners of that church for the time being yearly for ever. Know further that I, the aforesaid Thomas, constitute as my attorney & put in my place my beloved in Christ, John Davy & William Smyth, my true & lawful attorneys together & singly to enter by way & in my name in all the aforesaid lands, tenements & other premises with the appurtenances & seisin & possession thereof by way & in my name to take & after such ingress & seisin & possession thus by way & in my name taken & had to deliver thereof by way & in my name full & peaceful seisin & possession to the aforesaid John Roberds, John Alyson, William Pegge, Robert, Lawrence Davies, Thomas, John Cowper, Lawrence Rote & Richard Stevynson according to the force, form, use & effect of my present deed. In testimony of which thing to this my present deed I have placed my seal. Given the seventeenth day of September in the twenty-second year of the reign of King Henry, after the Conquest the seventh.

Deed 4B. Know, present & future, that I, Robert Park, vicar of the parish church of Duston, give, grant and by this my present deed confirm to John Carter, clerk, Thomas Rage of Middilton Malsor in the County of Northampton, John Cowper of the same, William Harberd of the same, Richard Stevynson of Great Houghton, Nicholas Byllyng of Middilton aforesaid Henry Brafelde alias Henry Davy of the same, William Meriett alias Cutt of the same & Lawrence Rote of the same, all & singular my lands & tenements with meadows, feedings, pastures & their appurtenances in the town and field of Middilton aforesaid. Which late I had by the gift, grant and deed of confirmation of Simon Hobson of Wotton John ffosbery of the same & John Whalley of Grafton, as in his deed of fee simple thereof made to me, more fully appears, to have & to hold all & singular the aforesaid lands & tenements with meadows, feedings, pastures & their appurtenances as was related to the aforesaid John Carter, Thomas Rage, John Cowper, William Harberd, Richard Stevynson, Nicholas Billyng, Henry Brafelde, otherwise called Henry Davy, William Meriett otherwise called William Cutt & Lawrence Rote their heirs & assigns to the use of the church of Middilton aforesaid for ever, of the chief lords of that fee for the services thereof due & of right accustomed. (Latin : *Ad usu' Eccl'ie de Middilton' pr'dict' inp'rp'tu' De capit'lib's D'm's feod' ill' p'r servit' inde debit' & de jur' consuet'*.) And I, indeed, the aforesaid Robert Park & my heirs, all & singular the aforesaid lands & tenements with meadows, feedings, pastures & their appurtenances as is abovesaid to the aforesaid John Carter, Thomas Rage, John Cowper, William Harberd, Richard Stevynson, Nicholas Billyng, Henry Brafelde otherwise called Henry Davy, William Meriett otherwise called William Cutt & Lawrence Rote their heirs & assigns, to the use of the Church of

Middilton aforesaid against all people have warranted & for ever defend. In testimony of which thing to this my present deed I have placed my seal. Given in the Feast of the Visitation[1] of the Blessed Virgin Mary in the eighth year of the reign of King Henry, the eighth after the Conquest, these being witnesses Robert Stevynson of Middilton aforesaid, John Miryett otherwise called Cutt, John Byllyng, John Larons, Lawrence Brafelde otherwise called Davy, Thomas Stevynson, Nicholas Craswell of the same & many others.

Deed No. 5, dated July 10th, 1517, is a completion of 4B. In this Robert Park releases to John Carter, Thomas Rage and the others, and quits claim in the cottage and lands in Milton.

Nos. 6 and 7 have been dealt with above. From now on the deeds of the two properties run in pairs bearing the same date and the same persons being the feoffees or trustees.

No. 8 (Church cottages & land, Thos. Rage's gift) and No. 9 (Poor's cottages with orchard, etc., Robert Park's gift), are dated November 1st, 1547, in the first year of Edward VIth. In No 8, Robert Stephensen and Lawrence Rote, and in No. 9 John Carter, clerk, and Lawrence Rote, grant the respective properties to new trustees, who are: Thomas Houghton, junior, Willm. Leke, Willm. Garnett, Thomas Byllyng son of Willm. Byllyng, Thos. Rote, Thos. Leke, Stephen Gilbards, Richard Stevenson, Willm. Elwards senr., John Smythe junr., Edward Miles son of Lawrence Miles, John Idell and

---

[1] July 2nd.

THE CHARITIES OF MILTON 255

Richard Garnett. It comes as a shock to find that the survivors of the old trustees handed over the two properties to their successors not " for the use of the church of Milton," but, in both deeds, " *circa necessaria et utilitatem ville de Middelton predicte tam pro relevio pauperi ibidem quam pro emendacione viarum regiarum circa eadem aut pro solucione unius quindecim domini Regis aliquo tempore futur' prout eis inclinis videbitur & inde fidelem compotum reddant Rectori &c.*," which means: " for the needs and use of the town of Middelton aforesaid as well for the relief of the poor there as for the mending of the King's highways about the same or for the payment of the one-fifteenth[1] of our lord the King any time in the future as they can see fit and thereof render a faithful account to the Rector &c."

On the principle, I presume, that " the King can do no wrong," these good people of Milton, one of whom I am sorry to see was John Carter, the curate, followed the Royal example and despoiled the church. Two of the objects to which the trust monies were diverted were good, for it was felt to be a pious duty to repair the roads as well as to relieve the poor, but the third object, the paying of the tax, saved their pockets at the expense of the church.

No. 10 (Park's gift, the Poor's cottages) and No. 11 (Rage's gift, the Church cottages, &c), are dated February 1st, 1598, in the 41st year

[1] This was a tax, such as a hearth tax, levied at times by the King. See page 284. Archdeacon Sponne, Rector of Towcester, gave to that town the " Talbot Inn " for the payment of the fifteenths tax, or for paving the streets.

of Elizabeth. The surviving trustees, Thos. Roote, John Smyth and John Idle, grant the properties to Guy Idle, John Roote son of Thos. Roote, Edwd. Smyth son of John Smyth, Steven Southam, James Dunckley senr., John Stevensonne, Richd. Stevenson son of John Stevenson, Thos. Pell junr., Thos. Leeke, George Norman, Gideon Dunckley, Wm. Ecton and John Johnson junr., " for the needs and use of the town of Milton alias Middleton Malsor," for the poor, the repair of the roads and payment of the one-fifteenth tax, as in Nos. 8 and 9.

No. 12 (Rage's gift) and No. 13 (Park's gift) are dated May 26th, 1622, in the 20th year of James I. Richard Stevenson, Thos. Pell and George Norman grant the properties to Wm. Dry, James Palmer, Robt. Johnson, Thos. Johnson, Wm. Wells, Wm. Pell, Robt. Dunckley senr., Robt. Dunckley junr., Peter Langford, Wm. Wright and Thos. Roote "for the needs and use of the parish church of Milton." After being alienated for nearly seventy-five years, both properties were now restored to the church.

No. 14 (Park's gift) and No. 15 (Rage's) are dated April 13th, 1659, during the Commonwealth. Wm. Wells, P. Langford and Thos. Roote grant the properties to Edmund Gleed, Edwd. Dry, Thos. Dunckley, husbandman, John Pell senr., Thos. Palmer, Thos. Billinge, Richd. Brounsurd, Richd. Wright, Valentine Miles, Thos. Wells and John Palmer " for the needs and use of the parish church of Milton."

No. 16 (Park's gift) and No. 17 (Rage's gift)

PRIEST'S DOOR, MILTON CHURCH.

THE CHARITIES OF MILTON

are dated April 10th, 1701, in the reign of William III. Edwd. Dry, John Palmer and Richd. Wright grant the properties to Wm. Samwell, Richd. Gleed, Robt. Dunkley, Stephen Miles, Nicholas Langford, Sampson Palmer, James Caswell, James Palmer, John Pell and Richd. Wells, "for the needs and use of the parish church of Milton."

No. 18 (Rage's gift) is dated June 21st, 1724. The companion deed for Park's gift is missing. Nicholas Langford and James Palmer grant Rage's Toft and land to Richd. Dodwell, Edwd. Price, John Palmer, Valentine Wells, Joseph Gaffield senr., Joseph Gaffield junr., Thos. Langford senr., Thos. Langford junr., John Elliott, James Caswell junr., James Palmer junr., Henry Watts, Richd. Estall, Wm. Wells and Sampson Palmer, "ad utilitatem et commodum"—"for the use and benefit"—of the church of Milton.

The deeds granting the properties to the successors of the feoffees mentioned in No. 18 are missing. Our next document in point of time is the Enclosure Award, which deals with Park's gift and Rage's gift, both of which were included in the Church Estate. It must be borne in mind that there were, of course, other properties belonging to the church besides these two gifts. The Award runs:

"Unto and for the said Edward Montgomery, John Allen, Francis Gibbs, Fisher Clark, Robert Dunkley, Aaron Thomas, William Clarke the younger, Thomas Palmer, John Perrin and Thomas Gibbs, Trustees of a certain estate lying within the parish of Milton otherwise Middleton Malsor aforesaid called Milton Church Lands and their successors Trustees for the Time being All that one Plot or parcel of Land or Ground within the parish of Milton (etc.) containing Seventeen Acres, One Rood and Five Perches. . . . Which said allotment to the said Trustees of Milton Church Lands is in lieu of and adjudged and determined by the said Commissioners to be a just and proportionable Compensation and Satisfaction for their two Cottage Commons and several odd Lands lying in Milton (etc.).

Also allotted 1 Acre 20 perches in exchange for Milton Church Close containing 2 Roods 22 perches.

Also allotted 1 Rood 28 perches in exchange for Town Close containing 1 Rood 5 perches.

Also allotted 16 perches in exchange for part of a certain garden containing 10 perches.

Also allotted 9 perches in exchange for part of Milton Church Close containing 5 perches."

We see from the Award that in 1780 both tenements, now known as the Church Cottages and the Poor's Cottages, were recognised as part of the Church Estate because two cottage commons were allotted. In the above are included the closes and other lands in Park's and Rage's gifts.

At the same time the Commissioners allotted land for the Poor in exchange for several odd plots belonging to the Trustees:

" And the said Commissioners Have set out divided assigned and allotted and by these presents Do set out divide assign allot award and confirm unto and for the Trustees for the

THE CHARITIES OF MILTON 259

Poor of the parish of Milton otherwise Middleton Malzor aforesaid and their Successors Trustees for the Time being All that one plot or parcel of Land or Ground

1 Acre 3 Roods 17 perches

which said allotment to the said Trustees for Milton Poor is in lieu of and adjudged and determined by the said Commissioners to be a just and proportionable compensation and satisfaction for their several odd lands in Milton (etc.) and all the Lands Grounds Interest rights of common and other rights and properties of the said Trustees for Milton Poor within the said Open and Common Fields pastures meadows and other commonable Lands and Grounds of the said Act directed to be divided allotted and inclosed as aforesaid."

The Poor's allotment under the Award had to appear here, because from now on the two gifts of Robert Park and Thomas Rage with the addition of another distinct property, the Poor's Estate, are all included in one deed. This grouping of several trusts held by the same feoffees was bound to lead to confusion, as we shall see, for in course of time the present Poor's Field was regarded as forming part of the same estate as the Poor's Cottages, just as if it had originally been Park's gift. The origin of the Poor's Estate will be dealt with further on.

Our next deed, No. 19, is dated November 18th, 1805, and is in English. In it, Robert Dunkley, one of the trustees mentioned in the Award, recites that he is the surviving trustee of certain lands and tenements. He grants them to Joseph Dent and John Dent, gentlemen:

" all and every the Messauges, Cottages, Closes, Lands, Tenements and Hereditaments whatsoever and wheresoever of which the said Robert Dunkley is the surviving Trustee as aforesaid or which now stand limited to or vested in him for the Use of the poor of the parish of Milton, otherwise Middleton Malsor, aforesaid, or for the Use of the Church of Milton otherwise etc. or any ways relating to the said poor and Church of Milton . . . to the Use of the said John Dent and Joseph Dent their heirs and assigns upon the several Trusts nevertheless and to and for the several Intents and purposes and under and subject to the several provisoes conditions and agreements as and for which the same premises now stand limited or did stand limited before the execution of these presents and to be by them conveyed and assured accordingly."

The above description of the three properties is of the vaguest and too much is left to a personal knowledge of local affairs, but it is probable the original deeds were mislaid as will be seen from the next document.

On May 5th, 1824, Mr. Joseph Dent and Mr. John Dent appoint ten other trustees to act with them: the Rev. —— Miller, Rector of Milton, the Rev. Francis Montgomery, Clerk, Wm. Montgomery, Esq., Joseph Gibbs, Butcher, Wm. Gibbs, Butcher, John Phipps, Baker, Hungerford Vowe, Esq., Hungerford Vowe the younger, of Northampton, gentleman, Thos. Marriott, Baker, and Wm. Marriott, farmer. The deed runs:

" And Whereas the said Robert Dunkley is since dead and the Deeds, Evidences and writings relating to or concerning the said Hereditaments and premises so granted and conveyed as aforesaid to the said Joseph Dent and John Dent their Heirs and Assigns In Trust for the use of the poor and of the Church of Milton otherwise Middleton Malsor aforesaid are by some inadvertent Means either lost or mislaid so that the nature of such Trusts cannot be herein specified and set forth &c."

That section is interesting, as it explains the mistake made in the deed in defining the properties. The tenement now known as the Church Cottages (Rage's gift), with the Church Feld of 18 acres 3 roods and 38 perches, or thereabouts, were set out as forming the Church Estate, while to the Poor's Field of 1 acre 3 roods and 17 perches was added part of Park's gift, now called the Poor's Cottages, to form the Poor's Estate. The Poor's Cottages were long known by that name, not because the tenement belonged to the Trustees for the Poor, but because only poor people were accepted as tenants by the church (see William Taylor's notes, page 160). As the deeds were mislaid, probably amongst the effects of one of the former trustees, since dead, the name Poor's Cottages would lead people to infer that they formed part of the Poor's Estate.

The last deed was executed on February 16th, 1875. Wm. Gibbs and Thos. Marriott vest the various properties in new trustees:

"The Rev. John Brown, Rector, Pickering Phipps, Esq., Brewer, M.P., Geo. Osborn of Pattishall, Steward, Charles Norman Manning, farmer, Wm. Henry Phipps, farmer, James

Asplin, builder, Wm. Dunkley, general dealer, John Garrett the younger, farmer, Thos. Gaunt Marriott, farmer, Robt. Campion Westley, farmer, Thomas Jackman Elliott, Baker, and John Campion of Collingtree, farmer."

It is interesting to note that the Church Cottages are thus described: " All that messuage Cottage or Tenement and premises with the appurtenances . . . sometime since converted into Four Messuages, Cottages or Tenements."

The lost deeds of the two gifts of the Church Estate had come to light by now, but the deeds of the original Poor's Estate were, and are, still missing. I presume therefore that as there were two estates and two separate sets of deeds it was thought that the deeds of Park's gift were those of the Poor's Estate. Hence the mistake made on May 5th, 1824, was not rectified and the Poor's Cottages, Park's gift to the church, were again set forth as forming part of the Poor's Estate. Doubtless the abbreviated Latin of the ancient deeds proved a stumbling block. In the church chest is the following, written in a good legal hand, which purports to be a translation of the clause in Deed No. 9, defining the objects of Park's gift:

" To the use & intent that the sd. Feoffees & their Heirs shd. dispose of the annual Rents arising from the same Lands & Premises—to the Relief of the necessitous Poor of Middleton aforesaid who should be poor and needy and for the amendment of the Highways as the Rector of Middleton for the time being for ever should

THE CHARITIES OF MILTON

direct and to apply the residue to the repair of Middleton Church yearly for ever."

This translation is merely a wild flight of fancy. However, the deeds were evidently sent by Dr. Miller, the Rector, to learned Counsel in London, who returned correct abstracts. The matter seems to have been allowed to remain as it was, for there was the question of the Poor's Estate. There were no deeds for this, and if it was not Park's gift how then did it come into being ? We will now seek an answer to that by tracing the origin of

THE POOR'S ESTATE.

Early Wills of Milton people show us that sums of money were left to be distributed to the poor after the death of the testator, but it is not until the seventeenth century that we find anything given in trust for the poor of Milton. The first bequest of this kind of any permanence occurs in the Will of Thomas Barker, of Milton, husbandman, January 25th, 1619.

" Item. I geve and bequeath to the use of the poore people of Milton aforesd the sume of fortie shillings of lawfull English money for ev'r : To be put forth w'thin one yeare next after my decease to the benefit of the sd poore people at the discretion of the mynister and churchwardens for the tyme then beinge : And the use thereof to be pd in yearly at the accomte in Easter wicke, and divided presently amonge the sd poore at ye discretion of ye a'sd[1] mynister & churchwardens from yeare to yeare, and so to remayne for ev'r : And my will is that everie

[1] Aforesaid.

man, or woman, that shall and will borrowe any part or p'rcell of the sd ffortie shillings before geven & bequeathed shall have & bringe in at the sd Accomte one sufficient inhabitant of the sd towne of Milton, then and there to be bound, or to geve his word to the sd mynister and churchwardens openly for the true payem't of the sd money so borrowed and also for the use thereof. And the same to be recorded in a booke for the same purpose, And to be kept by the sd mynister and churchwardens from yeare to yeare for ev'r. And my will is that a true noate be made of this sd legasie w'ch I have geven for the benefitt of the sd poore people of Milton : And the same to be delyvred fayre written to the sd mynister & churchwardens to be recorded in the begynninge of the sd booke wherein the money so lent forth shall be recorded. And the same noate to be read yearely by the sd mynister at the Accomte that the same maye be the better kept in memorie for ev'r.

Witness : Sapcoates Harrington, Tobie Prestland his mark, & Thomas Maio, Clarke."

This bequest explains an old Bond preserved in the parish chest. By this, Richard Brownsword stood security, to the extent of £4, for the repayment on the following Easter Monday of the £2 lent to some borrower (presumably Richard Walden), and 2s. 4d. interest. The Bond is given herewith :

" Know all men by these pr'sents yt : I Richard Brownsurd of Stoke golden in ye : County of Buckingham, Yeoman, am held & fimly bound, unto ffrancis Atterbury of Milt'n al's Middleto' Maluazor, Clerke, & Thomas

THE CHARITIES OF MILTON

Billinge & John Palmer of ye sayd Milto' Churchwardens for ye: year beinge, in the summe of ffowre pounds of good & lawfull mony of England to be payd to ye sayde ffrancis Atterbury, Thomas Billinge, & John Palmer, or to eyther of them, their Certeine attorny or Assignes; To w'ch payment well and truly to be made, I binde my selfe, myne Executors and Assignes firmely by these pr'sents; Sealed with my Seale dated the 25th: day of Aprill in ye yeere of o'r Lord, one thousand six hundred and sixtye.

The Condition of yis: Obligation is such, yt: if ye: above bound Richard Brounsurd, his heyres, executors, Administrators, or Assignes, or any of them, doe well & truly pay, unto ffrancis Atterbury, Thomas Billinge & John Palmer, or eyther of them, their successors or Assignes, at or in ye: Parish Church of Milton aforesayd, the sum'e of two pounds two shillings, & fowre pence of good, & lawfull mony of England, one munday in Easter weeke, (being the usual County-day[1] for ye: Officers of ye sayd Milt'n) next ensueing ye date above written, without any Couen,[2] or fraud, yt: then this pr'sent Obliga'on to be voide, & of none effecte, or else it to stand, & remaine in full force & vertue.

RICHARD BROWNSWORD.

Signed, Sealed & delivered
in ye pr'sence of   The mark of
MARGERY PALMER.   RICHARD (R) WALDEN."

The next bequest is that of " Stephen Miles of Milton, al's Middleton Maluazor, Yeoman," September 7th, 1649:

[1] The day for rendering the yearly accounts.
[2] *Couen*, from " Covine," intrigue, false pretence. Akin to Cowan, which would therefore mean a masquerader.

"Item. I give to the poore of Milton ffive pounds, wch sayd ffive pounds my will is shall be paid within one yeere after my decease, into ye hands of the minister and churchwardens then being, to be putt out uppon good security, and the consideration thereof, every county day, to be distributed by ye sayd minister, & churchwardens, to those that have most need :

Item. I give to ye poore of Hardingstone three pounds to be payd and disposed of for time and manner as the before mentyoned ffive pounds bequeathed to ye poore of Milton."

This last item gives us part, at least, of the reason why the Trustees for the Hardingstone poor should have had, until lately, a field in Milton. The bequest was to be disposed of and administered in the same manner as that for the Milton poor, that is, I presume, by the Rector and Churchwardens of Milton. Therefore, if they invested it in land, as they probably did eventually, it would naturally be near at hand in Milton.

The term "county day" is explained in Richard Brownsword's Bond, given before.

Our next bequest is that by John Palmer, Yeoman, of Milton, on June 1st, 1704.

"I give ye sume of fortie shillings to ye poore of Milton and for ye minister and ye churchwardens to put it out and improve it, and for ye minister and ye churchwardens of Milton for ye time being to pay ye use of it yearely and every yeare to ye poore of Milton one Easter Tuesday to such poore as may have need."

The last is a bequest by John Pell, Yeoman, of Milton, November 23rd, 1720.

THE CHARITIES OF MILTON

"Item. I give and bequeath to the poor of Milton aforesaid the sum of Ten Pounds of lawfull money of Great Britain to be paid by my Executrix hereinafter named into the hands of the Churchwardens and Overseers of the poore of Milton aforesaid for them to set to use & the Interest that shall arise from the same Shall be divided amongst the poore yearly on Easter Munday."

We may safely conclude that it frequently happened there were no borrowers for these various sums, or, rather, no bondsmen willing to give security. Hence it was probably thought best, in the interests of the Milton poor, to purchase with the money, lying idle, some small enclosures. This, of course, is conjecture, but I am convinced that in these bequests we have the origin of the Milton Poor's Estate, which consisted of "several odd lands" up to 1780 when they were exchanged for the Poor's Field.

DODWELL'S CHARITY.

This was a charge of one shilling per week on a certain "yard land," which was redeemed on March 21st, 1917, by Edward M. Alexander, Esq., £104 Consolidated Stock being purchased instead. The bequest was made by Richard Dodwell, Barrister-at-Law and Lord of the Manor of Milton. Extracts from his Will (P.C.C. Plymouth 142, April 30th, 1726) relating to Milton are here given :

"I desire to be buried in the parish church of Milton if I die near that place.

Item. I give fifty pounds to the Reverend Mr. Benjamin King of Northampton and to Mr.

Fletcher in trust that they shall erect a monument of that price in the parish church of Milton within one year after my decease. Item I give to the Minister and Churchwardens of the parish of Milton for the time being and to their Successors for ever one shilling weekly to be laid out in six two penny Loaves to be distributed every Sunday morning after divine service to such of the poor of the parish of Milton aforesaid as shall then and there attend the publick service of God in the said Church of Milton and for this I charge the yard land which I lately purchased of the Lord Guilford with the weekly payment of the one shilling aforesaid for ever which I will shall be distributed in the Chancell by the Minister and Churchwardens and their successors for ever."

The Parliamentary Report, 1830, states: " There are no documents to be found concerning this donation."

On February 4th, 1898, a new scheme for the regulation of this Charity was issued by the Charity Commissioners, when the following body of Trustees was constituted :

One Ex-officio Trustee, to be the Rector of Milton for the time being.

Two Representative Trustees, to be appointed by the Parish Council of Milton.

One Representative Trustee, to be appointed by the owner for the time being (if of full age) of the land charged with the rent charge belonging to the Charity.

This bread charity is still distributed every week in church, but not in the chancel, the administrators being the Rector and Churchwardens.

Gaffield's Gifts.

Although this charity has long since ceased to exist it cannot be passed over without some reference to it. These gifts were three in number, one under the Will of Elizabeth Gaffield, dated July 4th, 1746, and two under the Will of her brother, Joseph Gaffield, dated July 24th, 1761.

Elizabeth Gaffield charged the half yard land she bequeathed to her brother Joseph, with the sum of 52s. to be paid yearly to the Rector and Churchwardens of Milton.

" And I do hereby will order and desire that the Rector and Churchwardens with the aforesaid yearly sum of two and fifty shillings to sett six poor children to Schoole belonging to the aforesaid Parish of Milton otherwise Middleton Malsor to learne to read and to give two pence a week with each and to pay the Master once a quarter as they shall receive it. And my will further is and do hereby order and desire that so often as the Master of the said poor children shall make complaint of the misbehaviour of either of them or of their neglect not constantly coming to Schoole then my will is that the Rector and Churchwardens upon such complaint shall, in case they shall adjudge the same to be a just complaint, Discharge them from the benefitt of the Charity and put in such other poor children belonging to the Parish of Milton otherwise Middleton Malsor aforesaid as they shall think most proper to keep up the number of six poor children to Schoole."

Joseph Gaffield charged the same land with another sum of 52s. to be paid yearly to the

THE STORY OF MILTON MALZOR

Rector and Churchwardens, also for the purpose of setting six poor children to school. The wording is similar to Elizabeth Gaffield's bequest, but with two reservations:

" Reserving a power for the Owner (of the land) . . . to make choice of two of the poore children which shall be set to Schoole out of this my Charity."

In case of misbehaviour the children could be dismissed by the Rector and Churchwardens, " first having the consent of the owner " (of the land).

The Will continues for the next gift:

" Also I give unto the Poore of Milton aforesaid the sum of Twenty Shillings to be paid them yearly and every year in Easter Week for ever hereafter out of the aforesaid Wright's half yard Land. And I charge the said half yard Land with the payment of the same and order the same to be distributed by the Rector and Churchwardens (etc.) and by the owners of the said Land . . . amongst such poor people as they shall think proper."

According to the Parliamentary Report, 1830, one of the sums of 52s. had not been paid for some time, but a schoolmistress was paid for teaching eight poor children to read. The last payment of the other sums of 52s. and 20s. was made in 1858. The land had been sold by auction at the Greyhound Inn on June 11th, 1818, subject to these conditions. It was afterwards discovered that as the earliest of the Wills was dated 1746, these excellent bequests were rendered null and void by the Mortmain

THE CHARITIES OF MILTON

Act, 9 Geo. III c. 36, previously passed in 1736. By this Act, all gifts by Will for charitable purposes were declared void, unless executed by deed in the presence of two witnesses twelve months before the death of the donor, and enrolled in Chancery.

UNDERWOOD'S CHARITY.

This is the New Year's Bread Charity, and the popular idea is that, according to the bequest, every person in Milton was to have a loaf of bread on New Year's Day " while the sun shone and the rivers ran." However, the following is the extract that affects Milton :

" Will of William Underwood, of Newport Pagnell, Bucks, gentleman ; dated July 5th : 1793. (P.C.C. Walpole 142.)

" Also I give and bequeath unto the said George Cooch (of Newport Pagnell, gent.) and Richard White (of the same place, plumber & glazier) the sum of One hundred pounds of like lawfull money upon Trust and to the Intent that they or either of them do pay the same to the Minister and Churchwardens for the time being of Middleton Malsor otherwise Milton in the County of Northampton within six Months next after my decease upon special Trust and Confidence that they the said Minister and Churchwardens of Middleton Malsor otherwise Milton aforesaid for the time being and their successors do and shall put place out invest and continue at Interest in their joint names in the public funds or on parliamentary security and not on any real or other security whatsoever the said sum of one hundred pounds and do and shall from time to time for ever afterwards receive the yearly interest dividends and produce of the said sum of one hundred pounds as the same shall accrue and lay the same out in the purchase of Bread and do and shall on the first day of January in every year for ever at the Parish Church of Middleton Malsor otherwise Milton aforesaid distribute such Bread unto and amongst such poor Inhabitants of the Parish of Middleton Malsor otherwise Milton aforesaid and in such manner as they the said Minister and Churchwardens for the time being and their successors shall in their discretion think proper."

" Proved in the Prerogative Court of Canterbury, Feb. 28th, 1798, by George Cooch and Richard White, the executors named in the will."

This sum of £100 was laid out in or about the year 1799 in the purchase of £184 15s. three per cent Consols. The original Trustees seem to have been : Richard Froane, John Caswell and Joseph Sharpe. They were succeeded as follows :

1829, March 3rd. Rev. Francis Montgomery, William Montgomery, Rev. George Oakes Miller, John Dent.

1848, April 25th. Thos. A Kershaw, Clerk, Wm. Montgomery, Wm. Dunkley Manning, Farmer, John Phipps Roe, Butcher.

1874, Dec. 8th. Rev. John Brown, Robert Campion Westley, Charles Norman Manning, Thomas Gaunt Marriott.

The Parish Council appoint two Trustees. In 1830 the yearly income was £5 8s. 4d., but since 1904 it has fallen to £4 12s. 4d. From 1875 the bread for this Charity has been distributed in the Schools on New Year's Day. The Administrators are the Rector and Churchwardens.

THE CHARITIES OF MILTON

MISS MONTGOMERY'S CHARITY.

Miss Frances Montgomery of Mortimers, in her Will dated January 7th, 1888, bequeathed " to the Trustee of General Charities the sum of One hundred pounds Upon trust that he invest the same in such way as he the said Trustee may for the time being be authorised to invest moneys for Charitable Trusts. I direct that the said Trustee for the time being shall pay one half part of the dividends to be received from the said sum when the same may be so invested as aforesaid to the Rector or other the Officiating Minister for the time being of the said parish of Milton to be applied annually in such manner as he in his discretion may think proper for the benefit of any School or Schools which may be in the said parish of Milton in connection with the Established Church in that Parish And I direct that my Trustees shall pay the other half of the said dividends to be received from the said sum of One hundred pounds when so invested as aforesaid to the Rector or other the Officiating Minister for the time being of the said parish of Milton to be applied annually by him in the purchase of coal such coal to be distributed at his discretion among such poor inhabitants of that Parish as he shall direct."

The Board of Charity Commissioners purchased two amounts of £51 8s. 1d. Consolidated Stock at £2 15s. per cent which were transferred to the Account of the Official Trustees of Charitable Funds, in Trust for this Charity. These investments bear interest of £1 5s. 8d. each yearly. I presume that if at any time our Church Day School should be superseded by a County School, then according to the terms of the Will the School portion of this Charity would be used solely for the Church Sunday School.

MARK BAILEY'S CHARITY.

Mark Bailey's connection with Milton was through his wife, Mary Palmer, who was born here. Both her parents died, leaving a large family, and Mary Palmer undertook the care of the younger children. She afterwards went to Hinckley, to her uncle, Job Lock, who kept the Blue Boar Inn there and it was from this house that Mark Bailey married her. They lived for some time at Kingsthorpe, Northampton.

Mark Bailey, who died on April 6th, 1888, by his Will dated January 24th, 1888, gave " to the Rector and Churchwardens for the time being of Milton Malzor the sum of £10 to be invested and the proceeds to be given away in bread to the most needy and necessitous poor as to the said Rector and Churchwardens should seem best."

By an Order of the Board, dated December 19th, 1888, the sum of £9 5s. 11d. Consols representing this bequest (being £10 less legacy duty) was transferred to the account of the Official Trustees in trust for this Charity. The administrators are the Rector and Churchwardens of Milton and the annual income is 4s. 8d.

CHURCH SUNDAY SCHOOL GIFT.

The sum of Fifty Pounds was given to the Rector of Milton by the late Miss Mary Montgomery of Mortimers, for the use of the Milton Church Sunday School, which sum was deposited in the Post Office Savings Bank. In December,

THE CHARITIES OF MILTON 275

1918, this was transferred to 5 per cent National War Bonds, the interest being paid to the Sunday School Account in the Post Office Savings Bank.

THE KERSHAW BEQUEST.

The late Thomas Herbert Kershaw, barrister-at-law, of Whitchurch, Shropshire, who died December 9th, 1913, was the elder son of the late Thomas Atherton Kershaw, Rector of Milton. By his Will dated October 15th, 1903, he bequeathed

" to the Rector for the time being of Milton otherwise Middleton Malzor in the County of Northampton, One Hundred Pounds to be distributed at his discretion among such poor inhabitants of that parish as he shall select. And I direct the said charitable legacies to be paid exclusively out of such part of my personal estate as may be lawfully appropriated to such purposes and in preference to any other payment thereout."

" Proved at London, 21 February 1914, by Rev. John Frederick Kershaw, clerk, and Henry Plumb Kershaw, gentleman."

This bequest, less duty, realised £90, which was invested in 1915 by the Board of Charity Commissioners in £4½ per cent War Loan, the interest being paid to the Coal Club Account and for coal for the poor. This War Loan was in 1917 automatically converted into £5 per cent War Loan, the annual income being increased from £4 1s. to £4 14s. 8d. Up to the time of writing this sum is still used for these benefits, but some future Rector may see fit to dispose of it in some other way for the use of those in need.

CHAPTER XVI

WILLS AND OTHER DOCUMENTS

THE Will of Thomas Rage, of Milton, is here given in full because he was a benefactor of his church and parish. His Will is, of course, rather a curiosity to us in these modern days, but it must not be thought, on that account, that it possesses any peculiarity that especially distinguishes it from the usual run of mediæval Wills. Every testator left bequests to his church; the " mother church " of the Diocese, that is, the Cathedral; and to his favourite saints and altars in his own parish church.

THOMAS RAGE (1523): " In dei no'i'e Ame.'[1] The yere of o'r Lord 'cccccxxiij ye xiith Day of March. I Thomas Rage of Medilton Malsor havyng good mynd makyng my Will and testame't yn thys maner or forme. First I bequeathe my soul to God Almyghte and to ow'r Lady Saynt Mary and to all ye Seynts yn heving, my body to be burryed yn ye churche yard of Seynt Elyn yn Medylton afforseyd also I bequeath to the mother[2] yn Lyncoln iiijs. It. I bequeathe to my mortuary yt ryght ys. Also to the churche of Colyntre vjs. viijd., also too torchys of iiijs a pece, a torche to Medylton churche & a nother to Colentre churche. Also to ye hye altr of Medylton iiijd. It. to our lade

---

[1] *In dei nomine, Amen* = In the name of God, Amen.
[2] The mother church, Lincoln Cathedral.

awtr[1] a stryke of barley, also to the hye rod a stryke of barley, also to ye rode yn the north hyle ij powndes of waxe in too torches. It. to Seynt Cateryns awter a quarter of wax. It. to Seynt John the Baptyste and to Seynt John Eva'gelyst a pownde of waxe also to Seynt Nycolas awter a stryke of barley, also to ye sepulcar lyght ijd. It. to Seynt Ellyn/ also a pownde of wax. It. to ye bells of Medylton ij stryke of barley also I bequeath my howse that I bowght of John Gar . . . to the churche of Medylton Malsor after the dysesse of Elsabeth my wyfe as yt was purchasyd holly bothe fylde and towne with all the appurtenance thereto belongyth. Also I bequeathe my owen howse to John Lawford the son of Thomas Lawford and to hys heres lefully begoton after the dysesse of Elsabeth my wyfe and yf the foreseyd John Lawford dye without yssue then hys brother Wyllm Lawford shall have yt, to hys es hys heirs lefully begoten and yff the seyd Wyllm dye without yssue, to the churche foresaid, that the foreseyd howse shall be sold and dysposyd for my soul and for Chrysten souls and that the sale of that howse and the dysposers of them shall be the chefe lord of the same and churche wardens of the said Mydelton to be given to churche and to hye way and to pore people where nede ys as God put them in mynd. The residue of my goods not bequeathed I gyffe and bequeath Elsabeth my wyffe whom I make my executrix this my Wyll and testament well and truly to be executed. *Hiis testib's:*[2] William Brabsto, Rector de Colyntre, Dom John Carter, Curate de Myddleton, John Cowper, Thomas Lawford *et inter aliis.*"[3]

---

[1] Our Lady's altar.   [2] These persons being witnesses.
[3] Amongst others.

In the above, Thomas Rage seems to have remembered every Saint especially honoured in Milton except St. Christopher. Some extracts from Wills of Milton people, curious in the spelling or the bequest itself, will now be given.

THOMAS BASS (1521) : "Item to Henry my son to have a calffe, item to Agnes my daughter to have the cowe calffe. It. Nicholas my sone to have a schyppe.[1] It. Thomas my sone to have a schyppe also to Henry my sone to ynherett my lands when he ys xxiiii yere of age."

ALICE CAMPYAN (1546) : "I bequeath unto Sir John Caswell p'rsone off Colyntree one of my best quosshyns.[2] It. I give unto ye forsayd Sir John in money viijd."

The following is very curious as it makes it appear that a man had two daughters, both living, with the same Christian name :

THOMAS LANGFORD (1558): "Item. To Isbell my yongest daughter iij£ and the brasse panne. Item. To Isbbell my eldest daughter x lb."

LAWRENCE ROTTE (1560) was a well-to-do inhabitant of Milton and was one of the feoffees of the church lands, but the following items are given to show how valuable in those days were ordinary household utensils : "I bequethe to Agnes Rotte my daughter in money v lb, a lattyne basoyne[3] and a great brase potte which was bought of Kyslingberye, a thre galland kettell, a newe pewter platter, a pewter dishe, a sawser, vi boxe, a kimnell,[4] and vii paire of shette, a taboule clothe wt a towell new bought by my wiffe."

[1] Sheep. [2] Cushions.
[3] A basin made of latten, a kind of brass.
[4] A tub for domestic use.

WILLS AND OTHER DOCUMENTS

RICHARD NORMAN (1621): " Item. I give to eight of the poorest people in Milton fourepence a peece."

We now have a bequest that is, to say the least, extraordinary and that must have proved a veritable apple of discord.

ROBERT BURTE (1602): " To the children of Mary Clarke and Ursula my daughter one brasse pann amongst them hyn equall porcons."

Was it broken up and divided amongst them ? What measurings and weighings there must have been to give them equal portions ! Most probably, however, the brass pan was sold and the money divided.

JOHN GOOAD (1610), blacksmith: " Item. I give and bequeath to Richard Gooad my brother tenn ewes and ten lambes, my Anfeld and my great hammer."

There is a reminiscence of a " great sickness " of 1625 (not the Great Plague) in London, in the Will of Thomas Mayo, who was curate of Milton. In this pestilence 35,417 persons perished that year in London alone.

THOMAS MAYO (1625): " And whereas I have two daughters, the one dwelling in London whose name is Sara ffyndinge, the wife of John ffyndinge, the other is dwelling in house with me, Thomas Mayo, whose name is Isabell Palmer, Widdow . . . And if my said daughter (Sara) be deceassed in this great sickness at London," etc.

The next extract reminds us of the right to a third of the estate, and the dower, that was formerly claimed by a widow. English law has changed from the days of Henry I, when a widow was entitled to her dower, her mourning-gift and one-third of any increase in the property. Nowadays, she can by Will be left penniless.

ROBERT DUNKLEY (April 5th, 1627), the elder, husbandman : " Item, I give to Alice my wyfe one Coffer wch shee brought with her and all the lynnen therein, and halfe of all my moveable goods within my dwelling house onely. Item, I will that my executors hereafter named shall fynde provyde & alowe unto the sayd Alice my wife during her naturall lyfe, competent & wholesome meats drinke apparrell & lodgeing and all other things fytt & necessary for her, and shall give & pay to her forty shillings in money yerely during her lyfe. All wch shalbee in leiw of her thirde & tytle of dower of & in all my lands and tenements whatsoever."

GEORGE NORMAN (1638) orders his son Fortunatus to pay to his mother " fforty shillings of lawfull English money at ye ffeaste of Phillip and Jacob, comonly called Mayday, next ensuing the day of my death."

We have an instance of the old form of the plural in the next :

ROGER GAFFIELD (1631) : " My will is yt my Sonne William shall injoye all my land & housen w'thin ye parrish of Milton."

Not " houses " but " housen," just as we still say " oxen " and not " oxes."

In several Wills we can see the high value of money in those days. One instance is given :

JOHN WELLS, Yeoman (1719) : " To my son John Wells and to my son in law Thomas Billing and to Jane Billing his wife Twelve pence a peece to be paid to them three months after my decease by my executor."

NICHOLAS TWIGDEN, Rector of Milton (1736) : " Alsoe I give and bequeath unto the Poor People of Milton, otherwise Middleton Malsor aforesaid, the sum of forty shillings to be distributed amongst them by my Executor hereinafter named as he shall think most proper Immediately after my decease. Alsoe I Give and bequeath to my beloved Town or the Inhabitants of Milton otherwise Middleton Malsor aforesaid the sum of fifty Pounds to be paid the first Winter after I am dead that no time may be lost. To buy Willow setts to plant in their Meadows and to pay the Charges and Expences of setting and fencing them and when these Willow Setts or Trees are Lapped or any part or number of them are Lapped and whatsoever and as often, as they are Lapped I will and order that the Churchwardens and Overseers of the aforesaid parish of Milton otherwise Middleton Malsor do receive the money for which the Lap of the aforesaid Setts, or trees is sold yet notwithstanding they are to be Accountable to the Town or Inhabitants of Milton aforesaid for the disposal of it. And I further will and order that the Churchwardens and Overseers of the aforesaid Town or Parish of Milton do pay with the aforesaid money the Poor People of their Town from time to time who receive Parish Collection or reliefe or pay those poor persons with it whom the aforesaid Parish are obliged and forced by law to maintaine or allow them Money for their necessary support."

There was another kind of document, similar in effect to a Will, by which certain witnesses affirmed that the deceased (who probably had no time to make a Will) disposed of his property verbally in their presence. One such is here given:

MEMORANDUM. "Memorandum that Thomas Basse of Milton in the Countie of Northton & dioce of Peterborough on the Eighth day of July 1626 about eyght of the clock in the morninge being in p'rfect mynde & memorie upon demand made of him whether he had disposed of his estate and made his will, he answered noe, and withall speaking to Willm Wells of the same, being then two there pr's'nte, he (being of p'rfecte mind and memorie) sayd I will give you all to paie my debtes after my decease. Then being putt in mind that he had form'ly sayd that John Hollowayes wife (who then attended on him in his sickness) should have his household stuffe, & the bedding whereon he laie, he answered yt it was his will and meaninge that she should have the same after his death. Then he being further putt in mynde, that he had made a former Will, he (being in p'rfect mynde and memorie) answered and said that yt should be burned before Dyvrs witnesses, but willed twice that yt should be burned. Afterwardes his former Will being brought him & laid on his bedd before him, he the said Basse was demanded what his mynd was should be done therew'th who (continuing still in p'rfecte minde and memorie) answered burn yt. Provyded (quoth he the said Basse speaking to the said Wells) that after my death you pay my debts, and pay for the writings of that will. The said Wells making answere to him that soe farre forth as his estate came to he would discharge his the said Basses debte. The said Basse said again publiquely burne yt, and withall he willed John

Holloway that then attended him to goe and burne yt. There being then pr'snte Willm Drye, Thomas Johnson, Lawrence Seybrooke and Richard Keyoh.
Signum Johannis Holloway, Signum Richardi Keyoh, Signum Agmete Knight."

On page 37 in the chapter on the Manors, the Parwich family makes its appearance, in Dr. Bridge's list, for the first time in the reign of Henry VI. They were connected with Milton some time before then, as the following shows us:

LAY SUBSIDY ROLL 155/52.

Northants—Names of persons who apparently held lands in chief there (temp. 6 Hen. IV).

HUNDR' DE WYM'SLEY.

Will's Perewych h'et in Midelton & Colyntr' xxij li redd'us p'r annu' ult'a repris'.

Which means: " William Perewych has in Midelton and Collingtree £22 rent yearly beyond reprisals."

In the Lay Subsidy Roll on page 163 the Collingtree portion was omitted, but it is given here as some of the persons named therein may have been inhabitants of the village of Milton, although living on " Mantell's Manor," the Manor that included Collingtree within its bounds. One such person, John Carter, most certainly lived in Milton, for he was the curate.

LAY SUBSIDY ROLL 155/125.

Northants—15 Henry VIII.

COLYNGTRE.

Richard Bratt	. v li.	ijs. vjd.
John Mirrell .	. xv li.	vijs. vjd.
John Hall .	. iiij li. xs.	ijs. iijd.

Richard Wotton	xls.	xijd.
Thomas Alye	xls.	xijd.
Nicolas Wattes	xij li.	vjs.
John Elward	v li	ijs. vjd.
Thomas Smythe	xxs.	iiijd.
John Carter	xiiij li	vijs.
Johanna Nutman	xxs.	iiijd.
Thomas Roberts	vij li	iijs. vjd.
John Roberts	iij li	xviijd.
Roger Freeman	iiij li	ijs.
John Smyth	xxs.	iiijd.
Thomas Wattes	xxs.	iiijd.
John Myrrell, Jun.	xxs.	iiijd.
Summa		xxxviijs. vd.

THE ONE-FIFTEENTH TAX.

Mention has been made, in the chapter on the Charities, of a tax referred to in a deed as the payment of "one-fifteenth of our Lord the King." It will doubtless be of interest to give an early list of Milton people who paid this tax. The heading of this particular Roll has perished, so that the name of the Hundred is missing, but there is no doubt it concerns our Milton because Blisworth occurs in the same Roll, which is for Northamptonshire, and also the name of John le Fremant is found in it. The original is in Latin.

LAY SUBSIDY, 155/31

Account of a Tenth and a Fifteenth, temp. Edward III (1327–1377).

MILTONE

From Matilda daughter of Robert Austyn	vs. ijd. qu'.
From Eudone, of the above	vijd. o'.
From Galfridus Draper	iiijs. ixd. qu'.
From Isabella of Milton	iijs. ixd. qu'.

From Henry of Milton . . xxijd.
From Peter Peyteuin . . iijs. o'
From Gwydo Balle . . iiijs. ixd.
From John Le Fremant . iiijs. ixd.
From Richard of Milton . vs. xjd. qu'.
From Galfridus Beney . . vijs. xd. o'.qu'.
From Robert son of Sarre . vs. iiijd.
From Nicholas otherwise Put vijs. iiijd. o'
From Cecilia wife of the above xd. o'qu'.
From William Galeweye . iijs. vjd. o'qu'.
From Johanna Charles . xvijs. iiijd. o'.

Collingtree does not appear on this Roll.

In the church chest of St. Giles', Northampton, are various ancient deeds, several of which relate to Milton families and record the transfer of property. From these we learn that the Le Fremant family lived in Milton though Lords of the Manor of Collingtree, so-called (see page 40). In one deed, Agnes le Freman, daughter of John le Freman, of Middeltone (whose name appears in the above Lay Subsidy list), grants to Henry Malesoueres of Throp all her rights in the lands and tenements which formerly belonged to her sister, Lecia, situated in the town of Middeltone by Colyntre, and in Retheresthrope. Given at Middelton on Saturday, All Souls Day, 16 Edward III (November 2nd, 1342), the witnesses being Philip Malesoueres, Wm. Atte Hall, Henry Child, John Bachiler, Thomas Skynnere and others.

Another deed, dated January 16th, 1517, shows that William Pegge, son and heir of Reginald Pegge, grants to Walter Mantell, Esq., and others, certain lands in Rothersthorpe to carry out the provisions of his Will.

"William Pegge, gentylman," is one of the new feoffees named by Thomas Rage in deed No. 4A of the Milton series (see page 251).

On the Assize Roll, 632, for Northants, dated 3 Edward III (1329) there are two items of local interest beside those on page 143.

"M. 60 D. From the same Sheriff, of the price of a horse and cart, old, which fell upon Peter, son of Osbert of Midilton & crushed him so that he died thereof, iijs."

"From the same Sheriff, of the price of a horse and cart which by accident fell on William le Lord, of Colentre, and killed him, iijs."

The next document is a Charter, preserved in the British Museum, by which Queen Elizabeth makes a grant of lands, at Milton, that formerly belonged to the Abbey of St. James, Northampton. The lands are called "Prior's London," doubtless meant for "londen," or lands, from which at one time the Prior of the Abbey probably derived part of his stipend :

Prior's London

Additional Charter 34946. British Museum.
(Translation.)

Elizabeth by the Grace of God, Queen of England, France & Ireland, Defender of the Faith, &c. to all to whom these present letters shall come, greeting. Whereas we by our letters patent sealed with our great seal of England bearing date at Westminster 13th day of February in the 12th year of our reign have sold, granted, to farm let to our beloved servant John Maye (amongst divers other things) all those our lands, meadows, closes, feedings, pastures and commons called or known by the name of Priors London, lying & being in Midleton Malsor & Colentre in our county of Northampton and all and singular our lands, tenements, meadows, feedings, pastures, commons & hereditaments whatsoever with all & singular their appurtenances in Mydleton Malsor & Colentre aforesaid, formerly or late in the several tenures or occupations of Agnes Carter, widow, Thomas Mydleton & Robert Cockes or their assigns & before that late demised to a certain Anthony Wood & late to the dissolved monastery of St. James by Northampton in our said county of Northampton formerly belonging & appertaining & now annexed to our Honor of Grafton, except nevertheless always reserving to us, our heirs & successors all great trees, woods, underwoods, minerals & quarries of the premises To Have & To hold all & singular the premises before recited with all their appurtenances (except before excepted) to the aforesaid John Maye his executors & assigns from the feast of the Annunciation of the Blessed Virgin Mary then next following after the date of the aforesaid letters patent until the end of the term & for the term of 21 years then next following & fully to be completed, if no demise or grant, demises or grants for term or terms, of life or years then before made after the said feast of the Annunciation shall endure And if any demise or grant, demises or grants for term or terms, life or years before the said time of the premises or any parcel of them after the said feast of the Annunciation shall endure, then To have & to hold all & singular the premises aforesaid with all & singular the appurtenances (except before excepted) to the said John Maye his executors and assigns from the time when such demise or grant, demises or grants of the premises for term or terms, life or years by expiry, surrender or other determination of the said demise or grant or any other way first shall be vacant or determined until the end of the term and for the term of 21 years then next following & to be fully completed, rendering therefor yearly to us, our heirs & successors 25s. 4d. of lawful money of England as by the same letters patent (among other things) more fully appears, the right, state, title, interest & term of years still to come of & in the said premises of which said John Maye our beloved subject & farmer, Thomas Reade, senior of Cottenhall in our said county of Northampton having & enjoying by reason of a lawful debt, he made surrender & freely gave to us with the intention that we should deign to make & grant our letters patent & other our demise of the before recited premises to a certain Thomas Reade, junior, son of the aforesaid Thomas Reade, senior & Edward Reade & Thomas Reade, sons of a certain John Reade, of Roade, in the aforesaid county of Northampton in the form following :—Which surrender we accept by these presents be it known therefore that we, as well in consideration of the said surrender as by fine of £3 16. 0 of lawful money of England paid into the Receipt of our Exchequer to our use by the aforesaid Thomas Reade, junr. & Edward & Thomas Reade, sons of John Reade, by advice of our beloved Councillors William Baron of Burghley, Treasurer of England & Walter Mildmay, Knt, Chancellor of the Court of the Exchequer, have sold, granted & to farm let & by these presents sell, grant & to farm let to the aforesaid Thomas Reade junior & Edward & Thomas Reade, sons of John Reade, successively all those our aforesaid lands, meadows, closes feedings, pastures & commons called or known by the name of Priors London, lying & being in Midleton Malsor & Colentre aforesaid in our aforesaid county of Northampton And all & singular our aforesaid lands, tenements, meadows, feedings, commons & hereditaments whatsoever with all & singular their appurtenances situated lying & being in Mydleton Malsor & Colentre aforesaid formerly in the several tenures or occupations of the aforesaid Agnes Carter widow, Thomas Mydleton & Robert Cockes & now or late in the tenure or occupation of Thomas Reade senior, father of the aforesaid Thomas Reade, junr, or his assigns, by the annual rent in all of 25s. 4d, formerly parcel of the possessions of the late Monastery of St. James by Northampton & now annexed to our Honor of Grafton, excepting however always & reserving to us our heirs & successors all & all kinds of large trees, woods, underwoods & quarries of the premises To have & to hold all & singular the premises before demised with all their appurtenances (except before excepted) to the aforesaid Thomas Reade Junr & his assigns for the term & until the end of his life And after the decease, surrender or forfeiture of the aforesaid Thomas Reade, Junr, then we will & grant all & singular the premises above by these presents demised with their appurtenances (except before excepted) wholly to remain to the aforesaid Edward Reade, son of John Reade & his assigns for the term & to the end of his life And after the decease, surrender or forfeiture of either of the aforesaid Thomas Reade junr or Edward Reade, Then we will & grant that all & singular the premises above by these presents demised with all their appurtenances (except before excepted) shall wholly remain to the aforesaid Thomas Reade, the other son of the aforesaid John Reade & his assigns for the term & to the end of his life, rendering therefor yearly to us, our heirs & successors 25s. 4d. of lawful money of England at the feasts of the Blessed Virgin Mary & St. Michael the Archangel to our Exchequer or to the hands of the bailiffs or receivers of the premises for the time being by equal portions during the several terms aforesaid And after the death of each of the aforesaid Thomas Reade Junr, & of Edward & Thomas Reade, sons of John Reade, discending tenants in possession of the premises Then rendering & paying to us, our heirs & successors 25s. 4d after each such death by name of heriot. And the aforesaid Thomas Reade, Edward & Thomas Reade & their assigns shall well & sufficiently repair, support, sustain, clean, purge & maintain all the houses & edifices & all ditches, ways, inclosures, banks & sea-walls & all necessary repairs of the premises from time to time when necessary at their own costs & expenses during the time aforesaid And the premises demised sufficiently to repair & maintain to the end of the term. And we will & by these presents grant unto the aforesaid Thomas Edward & Thomas & their assigns that they & every of them from time to time may take & have of in & upon the premises growing sufficient housebote, hedgebote, fire bote, ploughbote & cartbote there & not elsewhere, yearly to be expended & occupied during the several terms aforesaid. And that they have timber growing in the woods & lands of the premises for & towards the repairs of the houses & edifices of the premises by the assignment & supervision of the steward or sub-steward or other the official of us our heirs & successors there for the time being during the several terms aforesaid, provided always that if it occurs that the rent be in arrear or not paid in part or in whole for the space of 40 days after such feast or feasts aforesaid when it should be paid that then henceforth this present demise & grant as far as the state and interest of him thus defaulting in payment of rent aforesaid be void & of no account anything in these presents to the contrary notwithstanding & any state, act, ordinance, provision, proclamation or restriction to the contrary thereof before had, published, ordained or provided or any other thing cause or matter whatsoever in anything notwithstanding. In testimony whereof these our letters we have made patent. Witness our beloved & faithful Councillor William Baron of Burghley Treasurer of England at Westminster 30th December, in the 30th year of our reign.

By warrant of the aforesaid Lord Treasurer of England & Chancellor of the Court of Exchequer.

THOMAS RAGE'S GIFT.

(For translation see Deed 4A, page 251.)

Sciant presentes & futuri qd Ego Thomas Rage de Middelton iuxta Colyntro in Com' Northt' dedi concessi & hac present' Carta mea confirmavi Joh'i Roberds cl'ico parsone Eccl'ie de Colyntro predicta' Joh'i Alyson parsone Eccl'ie de Middelton predicta' Will'mo Pegge Gentylman Rob'to Stephensen Laurencio Davies Thome Basse Joh'o Couper Laurencio Rote & Ric'o Stevenson unum Toftum & Septem Acr'terr' cum pertin' in Colyntro & Middelton in Com' predicto que nuper habui michi hered' & assign' meis ex dono & feoffamento Rici' Couper & Willi' Lynge nuper de Middleton predicta & que quid'm Toft' & terr' pred'c'i Ric'us & Will'm's Lynge quondam habuerunt sibi & hered' suis ex dono & feoffamento Joh'is Smyth habend' & tenend' predicta' Toft' & terr' cum pertin' prefat' Joh'i Roberds Joh'i Alyson Will'mo Pegge Rob'to Laurencio Davies Thome Joh'i Couper Laurencio Rote & Ric'o Stevynson hered' & assign' suis ad Usum & intencionem qd isdem Joh'es Roberds & cofeoffati sui predic'i & hered' & assign' sui permittent Gardianos Eccl'ie parochialis de Middelton predic'a & successores suos pro tempore existen' annuatim inperpetuum capere & percipere exit' & proficua eorundem terr' & ten' cum pertin' ut ea disponent & expendent annuatim circa necessaria & utilitatem predic'e Eccl'ie de Middelton & inde fidelem comp'm reddant Rectori eiusd'm eccl'ie de Middelton & parochianis eccl'ie illius pro tempore annuatim inperpetuum Sciatis insuper me prefat' Thomam attornasse posiusse & in loco meo constituisse dil'tos michi in Xr'o Joh'em Davy & Will'm Smyth meos veros & legitti'os attorn' coniunctim & divisim ad intrand' vice & no'i'e meo in om'ia predic'a terr' ten' ac cet'a premissa cum pertin' ac sei'am & possessione' inde vice & no'i'e meo capiend' & post huiusmod' ingressum ac seisinam & possessionem sic inde vice & no'ie meo capt' & habuit' ad deliband' inde vice & no'i'e meo plenam & pacificam sei'am & possessionem prefat' Joh'i Roberds Joh'i Alyson Will'mo Pegge Rob'to Laurencio Davies Thome Joh'i Couper Laurencio Rote & Ric'o Stevynson iuxta vim formam usum & effect' presente carte mee In cuius rei testimon'm hinc present' carte mee Sigillum meum apposui Dat' decimo septimo die Septembr' Anno regni Regis Henrici sept'i post conquestum vicesimo secundo.

WILLS AND OTHER DOCUMENTS 293

M.S. LAMBETH 244. f. 72.

HOSPITALE SANCTI JOHANNIS NOREHAMTONE

In causa appellacionis a diffinitiua sentencia Decani de Arcibus Londonie inter magistrum et fratres Hospitalis sancti Johannis Norehamtone partem appellantem ex parte vna et Johannem de Suthorp Rectorem ecclesie de Blyseworthe Lyncolniensis Diocesis Johannem Rectorem ecclesie de Colentre Nicholaum Bonefaunt et Ricardum de Lobenham partem appellatam ex altera. die dato partibus ad audiendam pronunciacionem finalem prout in retroactis plenius continetur. partibus per procuratores comparentibus Nos commissarius domini Archiepiscopi Cantuariensis et cetera processum coram nobis habitum diligenter pro viribus intuentes et curiosius perserutantes spiritus sancti gracia de iure peritorum consilio nobis assidencium ipsius Decani sentenciam sicut rite lata est sentencialiter confirmamus ratificamus et approbamus ipsam que sentenciam dicti commissaris iuxta moderamen expensarum predictarum execucioni fore decernimus per censuras ecclesiasticas demandandas Juris beneficio in omnibus semper saluo. Lata fuit ista sentencia in ecclesia de Maghefeld. V. Kalendas Maij. Anno domini M° CCC^{mo} quinto per magistros W. de Chadleshunte. R. de Morcestre et R. de Heydone.

[Translation.]

HOSPITAL OF ST. JOHN OF NORTHAMPTON

In the case of appeal from the definitive sentence of the Dean of Arches, London, between the Master and Brethren of the Hospital of St. John, Northampton, the party appealing, on the one side, and John de Suthorp,

Rector of the church of Blisworth, in the Diocese of Lincoln, John, Rector of the church of Collingtree, Nicholas Bonefaunt and Richard de Lobenham, the party appealed against, on the other side, a day having been given to the parties for hearing the final decree as is contained more fully in the above, the parties appearing by proctors We the commissary of the lord Archbishop of Canterbury etc. observing diligently to the best of our ability and with much care investigating the process held before us, having invoked the favour of the Holy Spirit, by the advice of men skilled in the law assisting us, in judgment confirm, ratify and approve the sentence of the Dean himself as it was duly passed, and decree that the actual sentence of the said commissary be put into execution, according to the management of the aforesaid expenses, by ecclesiastical censures having been commended, Saving the benefit of the law in all respects. This sentence was passed in the church of Maghefeld on the 27th of April in the year of Our Lord 1305, by Masters W. de Chadleshunte, R. de Morcestre and R. de Heydon.

This is an isolated document. It refers evidently to an earlier record which gives details of the case, but this has not been discovered.

Copy of Ancient Terrier.

This Terrier of Glebe, Tithes and other dues is given in full as it is of great interest and throws much light on Milton as it was before the Enclosure Award.

A Terrier of the Glebe land & houses belonging to the Parsonage of Milton, alias Middleton Malsor in the County of Northampton, lying in

WILLS AND OTHER DOCUMENTS 295

the fields of Milton & Collingtree, & of the tythes & other dues belonging to the same.

Imprimis in Milton field, or parish, in the great South-field, one acre with Hades above Lake-pond, butting east & west, having the town-balkes on both sides.

Item two acres in East-lake furlong, east & west, the town-balk on the north, & Mr Rogers on the south.

Item one acre more in the same, town-balk north & Sampson Palmer south.

Item one acre in Flawdry furlong, butting east & west, town-balks on both sides.

Item one acre in Long-Shittel furlong, east & west, Ric. Eshtol north, & Daniel Poole south.

Item one Acre in Starchloe furlong, east & west, town-balk north, & Ric. Robins south.

Item one acre in two Head-leys in Muddy-mead, north & south, Fish-pool furlong west, & Muddy-mead furlong east.

In Cross-field

Imprimis one acre with Hades in Muddy-mead furlong, north & south, Mr. John Rogers west, and Henrey Welch east.

Item one land with Hades in Church-mead furlong, east & west, Sampson Palmer north, & John Pell south.

Item one acre, & one land in Middle-hill furlong, north & south, town-balk west, and Sampson Palmer east; 3 Dia's in the tithe-book.

Item one Acre, & one land beyond Quatch-mead, next but one to Collingtree-field, north & south, Milton Church-land west, & Daniel Pool east, 3 Dia's in the tythe-book.

Item one Headley, an half-acre in Church-mead, north & south, Rectory of Collingtree west, & the furlong on the east.

Item five leys in Church-mead furlong, east & west, Mrs. Atterbury south, & Mr. Wil : Plowman, & now Mr Bilson of Cotten end, north.

Item one half acre of leys in the same furlong, Mr. Wil : Plowman north and the common high-way south.

In Lady-bridge Field

Imprimis one acre in upper five acre's furlong, north & south, town piece, viz. Orage balk on the east, & another town balk west.

Item one acre with Hades[1] in Hanging-land furlong, north & south, Tho : Wells east & Sampson Palmer west.

Item two roods in the same, Mr John Roger's west, & Mr. Wil : Plowman, now Mr Bilson, east.

It : one acre with Hades in Clanwell, Mr John Roger's east, & Tho : Wells west.

It : one acre with Hades in Fulwell, north & south, Mr John Roger's east, & town balk west.

It : five leys in Fulwell, north & south, Mr John Roger's west, and Hen : Welch east.

It : one rood ley in the same, Mr John Roger's west, & the piece between Hen : Welch, & Wil : Bunch east.

It : at Lady-bridge next the ford, a piece of meadow, shooting north & south, ston'd out & parted betwixt the Rector of Milton & the Rector of Collingtree, & changing every year, viz. the Rector of Milton having one side one year, & the other the next.

It : in Brook-mead meadow three doles, one year lying betwixt the Rectory of Collingtree & Mr Gleeds, now Mr Dodwells piece, & the

---

[1] Probably land set apart for growing hay.

other year between Mr Gleed, now Mr Dodwell, & John Manning, two of wch are taken out of Mr Gleed's two pieces.

It : in Dinner-mead one year eight doles, & the other year nine, lying one year betwixt the Rectory of Collingtree, & Mr Gleed, & the other year betwixt John Manning, & a piece of ground parted betwixt James Palmer, & others, one year five out of Mr Gleeds five pieces, & the other year six out of his six pieces.

It : four doles in East-meadow, one year lying betwixt ye Rectory of Collingtree, Mr Gleed & Gideon Elliot, now John Elliot, & the other year between John Manning, Mr Gleed, & Gideon Elliot, one of wch four leys lyes in a hook by the brook-side, Mr Gleed on the west, three of wch are taken out of Mr Gleed's three pieces.

It : in Costlydole one hook of meadow ground, lying for one dole, one year between the Rectory of Collingtree, & Horse-pool meadow ground, & the other year betwixt the Rectory of Collingtree & Tho : Wells, where ye piece, the dole is took out of, is shorter one side, than the other, every year the dole shifts sides.

It : besides the Church-yard, a piece of ground, call'd the Hempland, adjoyning to Tho : now Rob : Billing's Church-close & the Church-yard.

It : an ancient cottage in Milton town (Tho : Dunckly formerly tenant, now Wil Harris) & a little close, or nook of ground behind it, with a cows commons, & two sheep's commons.

It : a Parsonage house, & out-houses & garden & orchard together.

It : three Cottages tythe to the Rector of Milton, one of wch is his own, to wch Cottages belong a cow's commons, and two sheep's commons.

It : the meadows are divided into Boons[1] & Berries,[2] & there is a rate tythe of eight pence the yard land paid for the Boons, or for less proportionably, & doles are for ye Berries, viz. for every tenth dole, there is one due to the Rector.

It : tythes of the field, or arable land, viz. of about twenty-four yard land, wch. are tythed by the sheaf & cock.

It : the tythe of several closes, & pieces, leys & Hades in the field wch are tythed by the cock.

It : Tythe apples, pears, plums, cherries &c.

It : tythe milk, viz. the milk of all the cows, that go upon the commons, which tythe to the Rector of Milton, every tenth night, reckoning from the time, the Herds-man takes the cows into the field to keep them, wch is on the third of May, & for a barridge cas they call it, or a barren cow a shilling is paid.

It : tythe calves, pigs, lambs, & wool, nay if there be but seven of each, one is due to the Rector, allowing so many half-pennys, as are wanting of the number, to the owner of them, & for all under seven, there are so many half-pennys due, or to be paid, as the number of them is either more, or less, to the Rector of Milton, & as for wool, whatsoever stock, or number of sheep is on the commons at New-year's-day, there are fleeces due to the Rector proportionably to the number of the sheep then, tho sold before the time of sheering, or unsold, & they live, or else pelts, if they dy, but what is bought in after, a rate is paid, viz. an half-penny for a lamb, & so for a fleece.

---

[1] Boons, land for which service in kind or in labour was paid by a tenant to the Lord of the Manor, either in addition to or in lieu of his rent. Akin to " boundary."

[2] Berries = a rabbit warren, untilled land.

WILLS AND OTHER DOCUMENTS 299

Item for every fole that is foled, belonging to those, whose land tythes to the Rector of Milton, a penny.

It : tythe eggs, payable on Good-fryday, viz. two for an hen, & three for a cock.

It : Easter offerings, as garden-penny, wax-shot-penny, & a penny for all, that are sixteen, or above, (& so fit to receive the Communion) in an house wch tythes to the Rector of Milton.

It : for a Chrysom sixpence, & Mortuaries are due by custom, the quantity of wch, or how much money is to be paid for them, is regulated & ordered by law.

It : for every female person, that is married, who lives in an house, that tythes to the Rector of Milton, a shilling, or more, whether he marries her, or not, & for every certificate of the Banns of marriage being thrice publish'd in the Church according to law, a shilling.

A Terrier of the Glebe land & houses & tythes & other dues in the parish of Collingtree belonging to the Parsonage of Milton.

IN CALLOWBRIDGE FIELDS

Imprimis in Cross furlong on the west side the town, against Wil : Landon's close, now Mr Cockeril's five acres, four of wch lie three to the acre, intermixt with the Glebe of the Rectory of Collingtree, & the other, viz. the remotest from the town, lies only two to the acre, viz. a land & an Head-land, butting north & south, the town closes on the east, & Butts furlong on the west.

It : against Marshal's close two acres with leys, butting east & west, lying two to the acre, & being intermixt with the Glebe of the Rector of Collingtree, the High-way on the north, & leys of grass upon the south.

It : against Starmers close in Hedge-furlong, or Crabtree, three roods, Hoby north, & the Rector of Collingtree south.

It : one land in the same furlong, lying east & west, Mr Daniel Cockeril south & north.

In Wootton-bridge Field

Imprimis in Wootton-bridge furlong one land, butting north & south, Hoby east & Arthur Wright west.

It : in street furlong one land shooting east & west, Wil : Davy north, & John Harris south.

In Beanhill Field

One rood in Shortmeer's furlong, lying north & south, Alexander Manning east, & Rob : Herrick west.

It : there is an ancient cottage, or house (Marshal formerly tenant, now Francis Clerk) with a close adjoyning to it, having a cow's commons with four sheep's commons, that belongs to the Rectory of Milton.

As for Wingrave's tenement, it was built by Mr Atterbury some years ago, to put a poor person in, who could not pay him his rent for another house, & has been since pulled down as a poor, sorry & useless thing.

It : four cottages tythe to the Rector of Milton, as these two, that go by the names of Trotter's & Toscut's, & one that appertains to Widow Manning's estate, & the cottage one Church lives in, besides the Parson Of Milton's own cottage, or house in Collingtree, wch is mentioned before, to each of wch cottage there belong a cow's commons & four sheep's commons.

It : tythes, or tythe of field, or arable land, viz. of eleven yard land & an half, or better, wch are tythed by the sheaf, & cock, & tythe of several closes, pieces, leys & Hades in the field wch are tyth'd by the cock.

It : there are two meadows belonging to Collingtree, one year one of them tythes to the Rector of Milton, & the other to the Rector of Collingtree, & the next year the two Rectors change the tythes of the meadows, the Rector of Collingtree having what the Rector of Milton had the year before, & the Rector of Milton having the meadow tythes wch the Rector of Collingtree had then.

In, or belonging to Callowbridge meadow there is a piece of ground, called the Breach, that joins to the Meadow, but only is parted from it by a large furrow, & this tythes to Milton, or Collingtree, as the meadow itself tythes, to the one, or to the other. When the grass is cut down, the tythe is measur'd or lay'd out next the brook in each meadow, & in the Breach the tythe lies next to the meadow.

It : tythe apples, pears &c. & tythe milk, calves, pigs, lamb & wool.

It : for every fole that is foled, a penny, also tythe eggs payable, as at Milton.

It : Easter offerings, as Garden penny, waxshot penny, & a penny a piece for every Communicant, that lives in an house tything to the Rector of Milton.

It : for a Chrysome sixpence, & as for Mortuaries, they are the same, as at Milton.

It : for every Female person, that is married, who liv'd in an house, just at that time, wch tythes to the Rector of Milton, one shilling.

It : there are the same tythes & dues here, viz. in Collingtree, belonging to each Rector, as in Milton.

Now as for the manner of tything several things, it is as follows, viz. in tything lambs & fleeces, they are layd into tens, or ten of them are put together, & then the Parishioners choose the two first, and the Rector the third, & then they choose seven more to make up ten, & then begin, as at first, if the number will allow of it, & so on, but when these be under seven, so many halfpennys are allowed, or paid to him, as there are lambs, fleeces, or pigs.

It : at New-years day whatsoever stock, or number of sheep are on the commons, the Rector is to have tythe fleeces proportionably to the number of them then, if sold, or they live, or else pelts, if they dy afterwards, but what is bought in afterwards, a certain rate is pay'd for them, viz. an half-penny for every calf, & if there be seven, or above, but under ten, then the Parson pays so many half-pennys, as they want for ten, & so for pigs & fleeces.

It : tythe milk is due from the third of May to the first lamb that falls.

It : for a barridge cow a shilling.

It : if an house tythes to Milton, or Collingtree, accordingly Milton, or Collingtree is serv'd with the small tythes first, as with tythe milk, lambs, & fleeces proportionably to the number of cows & sheep, wch belong to that side, as where an house tythes to Milton, & the land tythes to both Collingtree & Milton, then Milton is serv'd first for the commons, that belong to it, & so is Collingtree, where the house tythes to it, & as for pigs & eggs that Rector has the tythe of them all, to whom the house tythes.

It : if a neighbour has his full stock of sheep at New-years tide & another comes after him, & stocks the same commons, the former must pay fleeces, if they live, or Pelts, if they dy, & the latter is to pay a rate tythe, viz. an half-penny for every sheep to the other.

Witness our hands the 2d. day of August in the year of our Lord 1720.

    Ben : Twigden Rectr.
    Nic : Twigden.   Tho : Langford.
    Will. Plowman.

CHAPTER XVII

LIST OF THOSE WHO SERVED IN THE GREAT WAR

A LIST of Milton men and lads who served in His Majesty's Forces, to whom in part this book is dedicated, with the names of their ships or regiments, the date of their enlistment and the rank they attained. The names of those are also included who were married and domiciled in Milton during the War if not before. As the War was more than half-way through before I came to Milton in 1917, I have had to rely on the kind assistance of willing helpers in compiling this list, but I have tried to make it as complete as possible in order that a record, more or less permanent, may be available not only of those who made the great sacrifice but also of those who (after facing, many of them, the same dangers), by God's providence returned to their homes.

Alexander, Edwd. Montgomery. 2nd Lieut. Joined (Pte.) 8th Sussex Rgt. Sept. 7th, 1914. Gazetted 1914.
Alexander, Noel Legard. 2nd Lieut. 9th Yorks Light Infantry. Joined (Pte.) 8th Sussex Sept. 7th, 1914. Served—France. Killed in action July 1st, 1916.
Anson, Oliver. Pte. 7th Northants. Mobilised 1914. Served—India.

THE WAR MEMORIAL.

THOSE WHO SERVED IN THE WAR

Anson, Thomas. Pte. Royal Naval Div. Joined Jan., 1916. Served—Belgium.

Ashby, Fredk. George. Pte. Royal Fusiliers. Joined 8th Northants Nov., 1915. Served—France.

Ashby, Horace. Pte. 19th Northumberland Fusiliers. Joined Oct. 31st, 1917. Served—France. Gassed.

Asplin, Albert. Sergt. Northants Yeomanry and 4th Lancashire Fusiliers. Rejoined Yeomanry Nov. 11th, 1914. Served—France.

Asplin, Arthur Cecil. Pte. 6th Reserve Regt. Cavalry. Joined May 22nd, 1918.

Asplin, Oliver Frank. Pte. 4th Dragoon Guards. Joined May 22nd, 1918.

Asplin, Fredk. George. Wheeler, Army Service Corps. Joined Oct. 28th, 1914. Served—Salonica.

Asplin, Henry Thos. Gunner, R.H.A. Joined Aug. 14th, 1916. Served—France. Wounded.

Asplin, Herbert. Corpl. Northants Yeomanry and Herts Yeomanry. Joined Nov., 1914. Served—Egypt and Palestine.

Asplin, John Edward. Pte. Coldstream Guards. Joined July 26th, 1916. Served—France. Wounded.

Asplin, Philip Charles. Corpl. Royal Sussex attached Mounted Police. Joined June 24th, 1918. Served—Germany.

Asplin, Wm. James. First Air Mechanic, R.A.F. Joined Army Ordnance Corps Aug. 28th, 1916.

Baldwin, George. Pte. Bedford Yeomanry and 20th Hussars. Joined Feb., 1915. Served—France and Germany.

Baldwin, James Thos. Driver, Royal Field Artillery. Joined Feb., 1916. Served—France and Germany.

Baldwin, Wm. John. Stoker Petty Officer 1st Class R.N. H.M.S. "Boxer," T.B.D. Joined 1904.

Battams, Wm. Geo. Driver, Royal Field Artillery, 20th Div. Joined Jan. 1st, 1917. Served—France.

Billing, Wm. Fred. Pte. 3rd Royal West Kent (The Buffs). Joined May, 1918. Served—France and Belgium.

Blick, Arthur. Qtr.-Mast. Sergt. Army Ordnance Corps. Joined Northants Yeomanry Nov., 1914. Served—Mesopotamia.

Bunn, Alfred Arthur. Corpl. Royal Engineers, 31st Light Railway Comp. Joined Feb., 1916. Served—France.

Butcher, William. Sapper, R.E. Joined 1916.

Craig, Charles Thomas. Honorary Driver, British Red Cross. Joined 1914. Served—France, Newmarket and Northampton.

Cherry, Arthur. Pte. Canadian forces.

Cherry, Harry. Pte. Northants Yeomanry and 4th Battn. Beds. Regt. Joined 1916. Served—France. Missing, presumed killed, April, 1917.

Cherry, James A. Bombardier, 32nd Brigade Heavy Artillery. Joined 1915. Served—France.

Childs, Edward. Pt. R.A.M.C. Hospital Ship Orderly. Joined Nov. 16th, 1914.

Childs, Fredk. Pte. Northants Yeomanry. Joined Nov. 16th, 1914.

Childs, Herbert Reginald. Sergt. Northants Yeomanry & 12th Royal Lancers. Joined Nov. 16th, 1914. Served—France.

Clarke, Thomas. Pte. R.A.M.C. Joined Essex Regt. June 3rd, 1916. Served—France. Wounded.

Clarke, Wm. Thos. Pte. 1st South Staffordshire Regt. Joined Jan., 1917. Served—Western

Front. Reported Missing and presumed killed in action at Ypres, Oct. 26th, 1917.

Cockerill, Wm. Lance-Corpl. 11th Labour Battn. Royal Engineers. Joined Oct. 14th, 1915. Served—France.

Collar, Douglas Arthur. Trooper, Northants Yeomanry. Joined Sept. 5th, 1914. Served—France and Italy.

Collar, James Wm. Pte. 12th Lancers. Mobilised Aug., 1914. Killed at Mons, Aug. 23rd, 1914.

Collar, Frederick. Sapper, Royal Engineers. Joined Aug. 1st, 1917.

COLLAR, THOMAS HENRY. Lance-Corpl. 6th Northants and Military Foot Police. Joined Sept. 7th, 1914. Wounded. Mentioned in Despatches. Military Medal 1916. Served—France and Palestine.

Dawson, John. Pte. Suffolk Regt. Joined March 1st, 1916. Served—France. Prisoner of War from Apl. 23rd, 1917.

Digby, Alfred. Pte. 4th Northants. Mobilised Aug. 4th, 1914. Served—France. Died of Trench Fever after demobilisation.

Digby, Fred. Ryland. Pte. Grenadier Guards. Joined 1914. Killed in action.

Digby, Philip. Pte. Royal Sussex. Joined Dec., 1917.

Digby, Samuel. Pte. 3rd Norfolks. Joined May 1st, 1917.

Eales, John Herbert. Pte. Mechanical Transport A.S.C. Joined March 24th, 1917. Served—Egypt, Palestine, Syria and Cyprus.

East, Albert. Petty Officer, H.M.S. " Glasgow."

East, Frank. Sapper, Royal Engineers, Australian Forces. Joined 1914.

East, Herbert. Stoker, H.M.S. " Venerable."

East, Henry. Petty Officer, H.M.S. " Glory."

East, Ernest Richard. Stoker, H.M.S. "Hampshire." Lost in wreck of ship with Lord Kitchener on board, June 5th, 1916.

Ermen, Hugh Basil. Able Seaman. Royal Naval Volunteer Reserves, Dover Patrol. Joined Sept., 1916.

EVANS, ARTHUR HENRY. Comp. Sergt.-Major R.E. Joined Feb. 1st, 1915. Served—France and Belgium. Wounded. Mentioned in despatches Apl. 19th, 1917. Military Medal.

Fletcher, Walter. Pte. Grenadier Guards. Mobilised Aug., 1914. Served—France.

Fletcher, George. Driver R.F.A. Joined Aug., 1915. Served—France.

Fossey, Wm. Pte. 24th Labour Co. A.S.C. Joined Sept. 24th, 1915. Served—Gallipoli, Egypt, France and Belgium.

Goff, Chas. Thos. Corpl. R.A.F. Joined A.S.C. Forage Dept. Nov. 11th, 1915.

Gomm, Harry. Corpl. 3rd Northants and Middlesex. Re-enlisted N.C.O. May 27th, 1915.

Goodridge, Alfred Geo. Pte. 9th Norfolk Regt. Joined Dec. 22nd, 1917. Served—France and Belgium. Wounded.

Hanwell, Wm. Frank. Killed in action.

Harrison, Frank Chas. Pte. 2/8th Lancs. Fusiliers. Joined 1915. Served—France. Wounded in head.

Harrison, Arthur. Pte. R.A.M.C. 44th Field Ambulance. Joined Nov. 1st, 1915. Served —France and Belgium.

Harrison, Leonard John. Sergt. 20th Tank Corps. Joined Feb., 1917. Served—France. Trench fever and wound. Invalided.

Henshaw, Frank. Pte. 2nd Beds. Regt. Joined Beds. Yeomanry Oct. 28th, 1915. Served— France. Wounded.

THOSE WHO SERVED IN THE WAR 309

Hirst, Thos. Pte. 3rd Beds. Joined June 15th, 1917.

Jeffery, Geo. Anthony. Pte. Northants Yeomanry and Cavalry. Machine Gun Corps. Joined 1915. Served—Italy and Egypt.

Johnson, Alfd. Pte. 17th Royal Scots Lothian and Border Horse. Joined Sept., 1914. Served—France. Wounded and gassed.

Kingston, Thos. Pte. Royal Fusiliers. Joined Feb., 1917. Served—France and Belgium. Wounded.

Lainsbury, Chas. Leonard. Gunner, H.M.S. " Collingwood," " Antrim," " Temeraire " and " George IV."

Leeden, Wm. Henry. Pte. 1st Devon Regt. Served—France. Died of shell-shock July, 1921.

Leigh, Edwd. Leonard. Corpl. Machine Gun Corps. Joined Royal West Kents Nov. 15th, 1915. Served—France. Wounded twice.

Lever, Wm. Trooper, Northants Yeomanry. Joined Nov. 11th, 1914. Served—France and Italy. Gassed.

Liddington, Geo. Pte. 6th Northants. Joined Sept. 7th, 1914. Served—France. Killed in action.

Mallard, Arthur. Pte. Reservist 1st Suffolks. Rejoined 2nd Suffolks Aug. 5th, 1914. Captured at Mons Aug. 26th, 1914. Prisoner of War.

Manning, Joseph. Pte. R.A.M.C. Joined 1916.

Manning, Ralph. Sergt. King's Royal Rifles. Joined Nov., 1917. Served—France. Wounded and gassed.

Manning, Wm. Pte. Royal Engineers. Joined March, 1916. Served—France and Belgium.

Marks, Edward. Pte. 2nd Middlesex. Joined March, 1916. Served—France.

✓Marks, Wm. George. Sapper, 113th Co. R.E. Joined July 31st, 1917. Served—France and Belgium.
Morton, Reuben John. Pte. 7th Suffolks. Joined July 19th, 1916. Served—France. Wounded and missing, presumed killed Apl. 27th, 1917.
Munn, Wm. Pte. R.A.M.C. Killed in action.
Newcomb, George. Lance-Corpl. Essex Yeomanry. Joined June 12th, 1916.
Newcombe, Jacob. Gunner. Guards' Machine Gun Corps. Joined Royal Horse Guards Aug., 1914. Served—France and Belgium.
Oxley, Fredk. James. Gunner, R.G.A. Joined Worcestershire Yeomanry Feb., 1917. Served —Ireland and Mesopotamia.
Oxley, James. Pte. 1st/5th East Kents (the Buffs). Joined Army Ordnance Corps, Feb. 1st, 1917. Served—India.
Oxley, George. Bombardier, Canadian Artillery. Mobilised Aug., 1914. Served—France.
Pearson, Harry Clarke. Lance-Corpl. 6th Northants. Joined Sept. 4th, 1914. Served—France. Wounded twice.
Pell, Oliver Wm. Trooper, Northants Imp. Yeomanry. Joined Nov. 10th, 1914. Served —France and Italy. Gassed.
Pell, Samuel Ernest. Pte. 1st/4th Northants and 17th Royal Sussex. Joined July 19th, 1918. Served—Egypt.
✓Pell, Wm. Goode. Pte. Queen's Royal West Surreys. Joined July, 1918. Served—France. Also—Railway Constructional Corps, 1917. Served—France.
✓Phillips, Wm. Ashall. Pte. 10th East Kents (the Buffs). Joined Apl., 1917. Served— Egypt, Palestine and France.
Plackett, Joseph. Pte. Royal West Surrey

THOSE WHO SERVED IN THE WAR 311

Regt. Joined May 24th, 1918. Served—France and Belgium.

Robinson, Anthony. 2nd Air Mechanic, Royal Air Force. Joined March 26th, 1917.

Robinson, Charles. Driver, Horse Transport, Army Service Corps. Joined January, 1917.

Robinson, Edward Daniel. Pte. 3rd Suffolks. Joined Aug., 1918. Served—France, Belgium and Germany.

Saunders, Wilfred Albert. Pte. Machine Gun Corps (Anti-Aircraft Section). Joined Northants Regt. July 6th, 1916. Served—Egypt and Flanders. Torpedoed on H.M.S. "Ivernia," Jan. 1st, 1917.

Shepherd, Frank. Pte. Canadian Forces.

Shipperley, Albert. Stoker, Royal Fleet Reserve, H.M.S. "Bacchante." Called up July 13th, 1914. Battles of Heligoland, Dardanelles, Zeebrugge and Ostend.

Skerry, Fred. Pte. Royal West Surreys. Joined 3rd Northants Nov., 1915. Served—France and Italy. Wounded.

Spriggs, Saml. Ernest. Pte. Oxford and Bucks Light Infantry. Joined June 27th, 1917. Served—France, Belgium and Germany.

Stevenson, Arthur Henry. Pte. Duke of Wellington's and West Riding Regts., and Army Ordnance Corps. Joined 1918.

Tack, Fredk. Charles. Driver, R.A.S.C. Joined East Anglian Divisional Train May 3rd, 1915. Served—Salonica.

Tack, James Henry. Sergt. Norfolk Yeomanry. Joined 1914. Served—Dardanelles and Palestine.

Tompkins, Walter Chas. Mumford. Pte. Royal West Surreys. Joined 1918. Also Railway Const. Corps, France, 1917.

Townsend, John Alfred. Trooper, Northants Imp. Yeomanry. Joined Apl. 14th, 1915. Served—France and Italy.

<u>Turner</u>, Francis James. Pte. 13th Royal Fusiliers. Joined Feb., 1918. Served—France. Fell in action Aug. 23rd, 1918. Aged 18.

Twiselton, Albert. Sapper, Royal Engineers. Joined Dec., 1916. Served—France.

Twiselton, George. Sergt. R.A.S.C., Motor Transport. Joined June 17th, 1916. Died of influenza at Milton, March 9th, 1919.

Twiselton, Wilfred. Pte. Royal Irish. Joined May, 1916. Served—Egypt.

Walker, Albert. Pte. Royal Irish Fusiliers. Reservist. Mobilised Aug., 1914. Served—France and Belgium. Mons Star.

Walker, Chas. Clarke. Gunner, 50th Brigade R.F.A. Joined Nov. 15th, 1915. Served—France and Belgium.

Ward, Harold. Pte. Army Pay Corps. Joined March 11th, 1917.

<u>Webb</u>, Fred. Able Seaman R.N. Joined Jan. 1917.

Webb, Robert. Driver, 7th Northants. Joined June, 1915. Served—France. Killed in action.

Whiting, Albert Alfred. Petty Officer, R.N. Able Seaman before the War. Battles—Jutland and Dogger Bank.

✓Widdows, Richard. Lance-Corpl. 32nd Middlesex. Joined June, 1918.

Wilkinson, Harry. Pte. Northants Imp. Yeomanry. Joined Oct. 11th, 1914. Served—France and Italy.

✓Wills, George. Pte. 264th Constructional Coy. R.E. Joined April, 1917. Served—France.

✓Wood, Wm. Henry Chester. Pte. 3rd Suffolks. Joined Labour Battn. May 15th, 1917. Served—Germany.

Wooding, Francis Benjamin. Pte. R.A.M.C. Doctor's Orderly. Joined 1915. Gazetted 2nd Lieut. Northants Regt. 1918.

Wyatt, Archibald Harry. Pte. R.A.F. Headquarters Motor Transport, Dunkirk. Joined Nov., 1917.

Yates, Edward John. Sapper, Royal Engineers. Joined 1917. Served—France. Also—Railway Constructional Corps previously in France, 1917.

Yates, Fredk. George. Pte. R.A.S.C. Motor Transport. Joined April, 1915. Died of influenza in France, January, 1919.

Yates, Harry Ivo. Pte. R.A.S.C. Motor Transport. Joined Nov. 25th, 1915. Served—France, Belgium, Italy and Germany.

Yates, Harold Arthur. Pte. Middlesex Regt. Joined Apl., 1917.

Yates, Percy Wm. Sergt. Railway Operating Div. R.E. Joined July 14th, 1915. Served—France and Belgium.

Yates, Reginald Charles. Trooper Bedfordshire Lancers. Joined Oct., 1915. Served—France.

Yates, Walter Ernest. Lieut. R.A.S.C. Motor Transport. Joined Northants Yeomanry 1913. Mobilised Aug. 4th, 1914. Served—France. Wounded.

Yates, Thos. Wm. Bombardier R.F.A. Drafted to Western Front. Served—France. Mons Star.

Red Cross Hospital

Mrs. Mary Ann Leigh, Cook, Red Cross Hospital, Berrywood.

Miss Sissie Collar, Kitchen Maid, Red Cross Hospital, Berrywood.

Miss Olive Gomm, Ward Maid, Red Cross Hospital, Berrywood.

HOME DEFENCE

Anthony, Robert Moodie. Corpl. Volunteer Training Corps. Foundation member of Northampton Citizen Corps, founded Nov. 10th, 1914.

BOY SCOUTS

ON VIGILATING DUTY, EAST COAST

At Anderby, near Mablethorpe: Leonard Clarke, George Lever, Frederick James Oxley, Francis James Turner, Wilfred Twiselton, Frederick George Yates, Harold Arthur Yates.
At Sutton-on-Sea: Horace Ashby, Anthony Robinson.

WAR SERVICE

Evans, Rev. B. Edwd, M.A., Assistant Classical Master, Northampton Town and County School, 1917–18.

INDEX

Abbot Sampson and the Mill, 49
Abjuring the realm, 144
Acts of Parliament, 69, 93, 97, 101, 150, 181, 206, 271
Airship drops bombs, 200
Allowance system in labour, 185
Altars at Milton, 63
— demolished, 92
Alteration of church dedication, 55
Anchor Close, 77, 121, 210
Anchorite, 210
Architectural features, 112, 113
Architecture, styles of, 71–80
Assize Roll, 142, 286
Auction in church, 100
Aumbrie, 77, 113

Bagley brothers, bell-founders, 131
Bailey's Charity, 274
Balks, 180
Band formed, 204
Bell-ringers, 138
Bell-ringing customs, 133–6, 220, 226
Bells, bequests to, 132
— inscriptions on, 130
— recast, 131
Bequests to Lincoln Cathedral, 90
Bequests to Peterborough Cathedral, 90
Bishop Grostete, 74, 120
Bond for borrowing, 264
Boons and Berries, 298
Bordars, 30–1, 33
Breach of Sanctuary 147–8
Bread Charities, 267, 271, 274
Bridges built, 197
Briefs, 98, 239, 240
Burials without coffins, 169
Butcher's Hatchet, the, 234

Cambridge, first Regius Professor, 89, 126

Canal to Northampton, 195
Candle stool, 218–9
Celtic survivals, 51
Census returns, 184, 191
Chancel, 73, 74, 97, 103, 109, 112, 115, 236, 268
Chantry, 64, 92–3
Chapels registered, 193
Charities diverted, 164–5, 244, 255
Charity school, 152
Church Estate, 245
— musicians, 105
— plate, 113
— porch, business in, 100
— property alienated, 164–5, 244, 255
— restored, 110
Churchwardens' Accounts, 104–5–6, 136–7, 184, 239
— and Overseers, 168
— election of, approved, 99
— window, 106
Churchyard extended, 112
— superstition, 107
Cimnell or Kimnell, 166, 278
Clock placed in tower, 109
Coal Charity, 273, 275
Cobirens, 166
Collection for poor Protestants, 98
Collingtree, meaning of, 51
— part of Manor of Milton, 31, 39, 157
— Rectory in Milton, 121
Common herd of the village, 67
Common lands, 29, 180
Common, rights of, 173–83
Constables, 168, 171
Constantine the Great, 56
Copyholders, 33
Cost of removing a family, 189
Cover ordered for font, 74
Cowan and Couen, 265
Cricket, 227
Curates of Milton, 89, 95, 126–8

315

INDEX

Death portents, 234
Decorated Style, 76
Dedication of the church, 54
Deeds, 154, 213, 246–62, 286
Dialect, peculiarities of, 228
Dick and the Wagon, 234
Different names for the Manors, 43
Dispensation granted, 99
Dodwell's Charity, 267
Dodwell's, Richd., Epitaph, 118
Doomsday Book, 30, 31, 35, 39, 48, 71, 124, 157–8, 213
Dovecotes, 43–4
Draining of village, 197
Dry, Epitaph of Wm., 116

Early English Style, 71, 72, 79
Earth removed from church walls, 107
Easter Sepulchre, 66
Edward VI's Commission, 91
Edward Wigan, 86, 89, 126
Enclosure Award, 39, 43, 100, 103, 181, 205, 257–9
Epidemics, 184, 197, 202
Epitaphs, 115–9, 153

Feudal tenants, 33
Fig Sunday, 226
First-fruits, 84, 86
Fishpools, 161, 211
Flax-pulling, 217
Font, 71, 73, 108
Football match, 227
Fossil bone of horse, 24
— tooth found, 23
Fossils, 19, 23
Free Gardeners, 203
Freehold tenure, 34

Gaffield's Gifts, 269
Gallery in church, 104, 106
Garland Day, 226
Geological formations, 18
Gifts to church, 69, 107, 109, 111, 112, 114, 115, 119, 245
Glacial Period, 20
Glebe, 36, 100, 129, 182
Great War, 199

Hades land, 296
Hardingstone Poor's field, 266

Harrington, James, 43, 45, 117
Hayward of Milton, 35, 170
Headborough of Milton, 35, 171
Hempland, 112, 205, 297
Hermit, 210
Highways, bad state of, 148, 164
— bequests to, 164
Holy Cross, 54–8
— water stolen for sorcery, 73
Honor, the, 28
— of Grafton, the, 287, 289
Hope Brewery, the, 221
Hop-growing, 222
Hundred of Collingtree, 157

Images of saints, 58, 65, 92
— destroyed, 92
Inter-glacial period, 23
Inventory of furniture, 165, 219

Kershaw Bequest, the, 275
Kimnell or Cimnell, 166, 278
King Charles I and Harrington, 46
Knight's Fee, a, 28

Lace-making school, 218
Lambeth MS., 82–3, 293
Lay Subsidy Rolls, 162–3, 283–5
Lias clays, 18
Licence for marriage, 96
— to eat meat, 99
Lighting the village, 199
Lights in church, 58, 60, 65, 67, 68, 81
Low-side window, 76, 112, 236

Malesoure family, the, 36, 50, 52, 81, 85, 94, 285
Maltings, the, 222
Manning, Dr. F. N., 116
Manorial Courts, 34
Manors created, 29
Manor, the, 43
— of Alselin's Barony, the, 35, 39–43
— of Peverel's Barony, the, 36–9, 45
Mantell's Manor, 42, 116
Mark of the Anglo-Saxon, the, 28
— (money), 247

INDEX

Marlstone beds, 18, 25
May Day, 226, 280
Mayo, Thos., Curate, 95, 126, 264, 279
Medical attendant for the poor, 190
Memorandum of verbal Will, 282
Mill at Milton, 31, 44, 48, 161, 213–5, 248–50
— destroyed, 49, 214, 215
— importance of, 49
— sold, 214
Miller, Dr., and his grave, 128
Milton and Collingtree Rectories separated, 84
Milton and Collingtree intermixed, 120, 132, 158–9, 176, 283
Milton Feast, 55, 228
Milton House, 172
Milton Malzor, 52
Milton Manor, 43
Milton, meaning of, 52
Milton Rectory of old, 77, 121, 210, 238
Monastic lands in Milton, 81, 85, 87–8, 286
Money bequeathed for loans, 263, 266–7
Montgomery's Charity, Miss, 273
Montgomery epitaphs, 115–6
Montgomery family, 82, 128
Montgomery, Miss, gives stained glass, 111
Montgomery, Wm., restores window, 107
Mortimers, 81, 85
Mortmain Act, 270
Mortuary fee, 101–2, 299, 301
Motor-bus facilities, 203
Musicians in church, 105

New Style of reckoning, 235
New Year's Day, 235, 271
Nonconformist chapels, 192–4
Norman architecture, 71, 73
Norman Conquest, 27
Northampton fire engine, 192,
— Infirmary, 192
North door, 76, 107
Nursing Association, District, 202

Obit of Lawrence Davy, 69
Obits confiscated, 70, 92

One-Fifteenth Tax, 165, 255, 284
Overseers appointed, 167–8
— book, 189, 219, 224
Oysters, 211

Pancake bell, 134
Parish boundaries settled, 158, 182
Parish Council, 198
— levies, 187
Park's Gift, 245, 252
Parliamentary voters, 202
Parson, meaning of, 122
Perpendicular Style, 79, 113
Peterborough Diocese created, 90
Peterborough Monastery, 88
Pillar bases, difference in, 76
Pillars built higher, 74
Pillowbier, 166
Pin factory, 223
Pinnier, 171, 207
Piscina, 62, 78, 113
Place-names, 161, 205–12
Plough Monday, 225
Plural, old form of, 280
Poor-box in church, 93
Poor Law, 184–90
Poor's Estate, 244, 259, 263
Porch, 100, 111
Pound, the, 207
Prehistoric river, 20
Priest's door, 72, 77
Prior's London, 86, 286–91
Procurations, 86
Proverbs, 211, 227
Public well, 197, 210

Queen Anne's Bounty, 84, 86
— Elizabeth's Charter, 86, 286–91
— Katharine of Arragon, 89, 90, 218

Rage's Gift, 245, 251, 291
Rage's Will, 276
Railways, 196, 198
Rateable value of parish, 161
— — of railways, 196, 198
Recusants, 95
Red-Cross Hospital workers, 313
— working party, 199
Registers of Lincoln, 120
— of Peterborough, 96, 99, 123, 194

INDEX

Registers to be kept, 95
Register taken from Rector's charge, 97
— extracts from, 55, 96–7, 101–3, 122, 151–2, 155, 159, 169, 170, 188, 215, 217, 219, 220, 224, 232, 238–9
Ringers and Singers, 226
River of ice at Milton, 22
Road-repairing, 164
Romans in the neighbourhood, 26, 52
Rood restored temporarily, 94
Roods, 59–61, 79, 92
— destroyed, 92

St. Andrew's Day, 220, 226
St. Catherine's Chapel, 62–3, 77–8, 111, 216
St. Christopher's picture, 65
St. Helen, 56–8
St. James' Abbey, 31, 81, 85, 286–91
St. John's Hospital, 53, 81–5, 121, 124
St. Nicholas' Chapel, 64, 80
St. Valentine's Day, 225
Sanctuary cities, 139, 149
— laws, 140–2
— sought in Milton, 84, 142
Sand deposit, 19
Santa Claus, 64
School, 111, 153, 269, 272
— Log Book, 154–6, 218, 225–6–7–9, 243
Schoolmasters, 155–6
School Trust Deed, 154
Seating in church, 80, 104, 193
Serfs, 30, 33
Settlements of the poor, 186–90
Sheep-farming, 216
Shrove Tuesday, 133
Sidewalks pitched, 184
Socmen, 31, 33
Spinning, 217
Square-word charm, 232
Staircase to Roods, 61
Staple fixed in font, 74
Statues in church, 58, 65, 92
Stone seat in church, 80
Strike explained, 67
Subsidy Rolls, 162–3, 283–5
Sunday hours for inns, 243

Sunday School gift, 274
Superstitions, 107–8, 232, 234

Tander's Day, 220, 226
Tax for militia, 169
— of one-fifteenth, 165, 255, 284
Taylor's notes, Wm., 34, 115, 127, 160, 214
Tenths, 84, 86
Terrier, 102, 180, 182, 294
— copy of ancient, 294
Timber-stealing riots, 172
Tithes, 100, 102–3, 182, 294
Toft, 173, 251
Torches for church, 68
Tower, 71, 76, 110, 113
Town and Poor's Estate, 245
Tramway to Northampton, 195
Transitional Style, 71, 73

Underwood's Charity, 271

Valor Ecclesiasticus, 81, 84, 85, 87, 89
Vestry Minutes, 100, 107–8–9, 115, 135, 153, 185–8, 190–3, 196–7, 205, 209, 242
Vestry of old, 77–8
Villeins, 30–1, 33

War Memorial, 201–2
Watch kept at night, 192
Water supply, 19, 25, 197, 210
Weathercock on spire, 104
Weather forecasts, 233
Weavers, 216–7
— patron saint, 77, 216
Wheat, price in 1547, 103
Wheel windows, 62, 77, 78, 106–7, 109, 112
Whitewashing the church, 103, 104
Wigan, Dr. Edward, 86, 89, 126
Willows planted, 281
Wills, extracts from, 54, 59, 60, 62, 64–5–6–7, 68–9, 90, 93–4, 97, 101–2–3, 132, 159, 164, 167, 174–9, 209, 216, 263–281
Workhouse, 184